THE COMPLEAT
GENTLEMAN

Also by Brad Miner

Anno Domini 1982: The New Testament in 365 Daily Readings

The National Review College Guide (with Charles J. Sykes)

Good Order: *Right Answers to Contemporary Questions*

The Concise Conservative Encyclopedia

The Compleat Gentleman: *The Modern Man's Guide to Chivalry* (First Edition)

Smear Tactics

THE COMPLEAT GENTLEMAN

GENTLEMAN

The Modern Man's Guide to Chivalry

REVISED AND UPDATED

B R A D   M I N E R

RICHARD VIGILANTE BOOKS

PUBLISHED BY RICHARD VIGILANTE BOOKS

Copyright © 2009 by Brad Miner

All Rights Reserved

www.richardvigilantebooks.com

RVB with the portrayal of a Labrador retriever in profile is a trademark
of Richard Vigilante Books

Book design by Charles Bork

Applicable BISAC Codes:

SEL021000   SELF-HELP / Motivational & Inspirational

SEL027000   SELF-HELP / Personal Growth / Success

HIS039000   HISTORY / Civilization

ISBN 978-0-9800763-4-9

PRINTED IN THE UNITED STATES OF AMERICA

10 9 8 7 6 5 4 3 2 1

Second Edition

For

Wick Allison,

Roy Doliner,

Jim Golden,

Eric Van Lustbader,

George J. Marlin,

and

Robert Mendelson

My friend, blood shaking my heart
The awful daring of a moment's surrender
Which an age of prudence can never retract
By this, and this only, we have existed
Which is not to be found in our obituaries . . .

T. S. Eliot, "The Waste Land"

CONTENTS

PREFACE TO THE NEW EDITION

A lthough it was not published until 2004, I wrote *The Compleat Gentleman* mostly during 2000 and 2001. I won't say it created a sensation when it first appeared, but it made an impression, and I appeared often on radio and TV to talk about the book. I heard a great deal from hosts and listeners about what's known as the "takeaway"—about those aspects of the subjects of chivalry and gentility that folks found most interesting, if not downright provocative.

What I learned is that there is a longing for civility. One example: Americans are genuinely distressed about the nation's dwindling appreciation of etiquette—at the boorishness of some of our fellow citizens and at the rancor in our public conversations, especially the ones about politics and religion. This was not a surprise to me, but I admit to being disappointed at first that folks wanted to talk about manners and didn't want to talk about history. Not to mention that, in the first edition of this book, I devoted only a couple of paragraphs to etiquette. But the more interviews I did, the more I came to understand that people really do grasp that the traditional rules of behavior are simply the big ideas of civilization writ small.

I was surprised at how many women wanted to talk about their sons. It's a favorite subject of mine because I have two sons and because being their father is both my greatest accomplishment and my most profound joy. The callers with whom I spoke worried that their boys weren't tough enough—that they were being alternately bullied and coddled by teachers and coaches and other authority figures (or, as the favorite phrase today has it, "role models"). Well, I'm neither James Dobson nor Jim Tressel, but I suggested that mothers and fathers must never forget that the crucible of character is neither school nor sports but family, and that toughness is as much a spiritual quality as it is physical.

Ah, but then I always come back to the importance of really knowing how to fight. Chivalry is first and foremost the worldview of fighting men, and I am convinced that the decline of the gentlemanly ideal has happened at least in part because men are flabby—physically and spiritually. This really seemed to anger men with whom I spoke, many of them saying words to this effect:

"I don't know how to fight, but still I consider myself chivalrous."

Well, I am not the Tsar of All Gentlemen (one reviewer, a pale and flabby fellow, I'm sure, wrote: "Mr. Minor [sic] himself may hope that a new cult of the gentleman, and the gentlemen to go with it, may be brought into existence by the book itself, but that seems to me to be most unlikely unless he can also provide them with something more than the conceit of their own gentlemanliness."), but I have to insist that, whereas any man is certainly free to call himself what he wishes, without a sword—so to speak—he can't be chivalrous. Words have meaning and we should respect them.

It's not entirely germane, but here's a personal anecdote. When my older son, Lt. Robert B. Miner II, was in high school, we took my younger son, Jon Miner, paintballing on his sixteenth birthday. After one of the games, I dragged myself back to the "base," a cinder block building with a snack bar, and came upon Bobby, leaning back in a chair, feet up on a table, wearing the olive-drab coveralls provided with the sporting equipment, and holding his paintball gun across his chest. He had recently decided to accept an appointment to the United States Military Academy, and I could see already the soldier he'd become. One of the other boys along for the birthday party said:

"Bobby, tell your dad about your career plan."

And Bobby said, holding up a finger to indicate each step:

"West Point. Special Forces. Ultimate Fighting. Batman."

Now *that's* tough.

I've found that Bobby and Jon and young men like them admire Bruce Wayne rather more than Clark Kent, because Wayne—Batman—isn't so much a superhero as simply a hero. He has no alien or accidental superpowers. He's an ordinary man with extraordinary amounts of skill, passion, determination . . . and, yes, an extraordinary amount of money too.

This book is for ordinary men (and their women) who believe in love and learning but also in fighting—who know that there are things worth fighting for and are willing and able to rise to the challenge.

I re-dedicate this book to my sons and to all young men for whom duty, honor, and country are words to live by.

Brad Miner

Pelham Manor, New York

January 2009

CHAPTER ONE

Massed Against the World

Until the day of his death, no man can be sure of his courage.

–THOMAS À BECKET, IN JEAN ANOUILH'S *BECKET* (1959)

This book is about gentlemen and chivalry, topics rarely discussed as the twenty-first century unfolds before us. This was not always so. The concept of the gentleman has a long (some would say ancient) history. Indeed, there were some Victorian—and earlier—commentators who piously proclaimed Jesus Christ the first gentleman. Of course, if that were so, there would be no others. For the purposes of this book, though, we'll say that the idea emerged in the Middle Ages—in 1100, perhaps, at which time it was nascent in the spirit of chivalry—and reached its pinnacle toward the end of the nineteenth century, just as it began to languish. So to raise these subjects now is, in the phrase of T. S. Eliot, an "act of recovery."

This is a book about an ideal and the importance of aspiring to it. No man who behaves as a compleat gentleman ought to all the time, but the best men never cease yearning to. As G. K. Chesterton wrote at the turn of the last century, it matters not "how often humanity fails to imitate its ideal, for then all its old failures are fruitful. But it does frightfully matter how often humanity changes its ideal; for then all its failures are fruitless."

Edmund Burke's famous statement that "the age of chivalry is gone," succeeded by that of "sophisters, oeconomists, and calculators," was a *cri de coeur* against the rending of the fabric of French life by the rabid enthusiasms of Jacobin terror during the French Revolution. But Burke's point was not reactionary; he was not endorsing the *ancien régime* per se. He simply feared in his bones that what was good about Frenchmen—and not least their tradition of chivalry—was as threatened by their revolution as was Queen Marie Antoinette. She was not yet dead when Burke wrote (1790), but he was certain the French radicals would kill her. (And she was indeed guillotined three years later.) He lamented, reflecting upon her seizure and imprisonment, that he had lived to see "such disasters fallen upon her in a nation of gallant men, in a nation of men of honor and of cavaliers. I thought ten thousand swords must have leaped from their scabbards to avenge even a look that threatened her with insult."

Above all Burke feared the leveling scythe of egalitarianism, which cuts as ferociously today as it did in the eighteenth century. The egalitarianism that is offensive is the notion, whether embodied in an opinion or a law, that every way of behaving is as good as any other, and that the man who stands apart, by reason of his dignity, his restraint, and his discernment, is somehow an enemy of democracy.

William Butler Yeats spoke of the problem as "Whiggery." It was, he wrote in "The Seven Sages":

> A levelling, rancorous, rational sort of mind
> That never looked out of the eye of a saint
> Or out of a drunkard's eye.
> . . . All's whiggery now.
> But we old men are massed against the world.

Knights on a Sinking Ship

Let me tell you exactly when the idea for *The Compleat Gentleman* first began to take shape in my mind.

I was with my older son (then a teenager, now a second lieutenant in the United States Army) at a screening of James Cameron's maudlin and deceptive blockbuster *Titanic*. It was during the climactic scenes of the sinking ship (which, I admit, are breathtaking) that something happened in the theater that brought home to me how far fallen from reverence the idea of the gentleman has become. And it's a good place to begin this book since—thanks to Cameron (and despite his pseudo-Marxist spin on the disaster)—the story of chivalry on board *Titanic* is probably more familiar to readers than any earlier tale of knights and damsels in distress, even of Arthur, Guinevere, Lancelot, and the rest.

Here's what happened in the theater that day.

Up on the screen, the cinematic Benjamin Guggenheim (whose flesh-and-blood equivalent was a real passenger on the doomed liner) has come into the ship's barroom dressed in evening clothes, complete with a top hat and his liveried manservant. When offered a lifejacket, he refuses.

"We are dressed in our best," he says, "and are prepared to go down like gentlemen." Then—with a twinkle in his eye—he adds:

"But we would like a brandy."

Across the aisle and a few rows back from where my son and I were sitting, several twenty-somethings guffawed. They began talking among themselves and their cachinnations became sniggers. A few folks shushed them, but that just turned their sniggering into snorting. I turned around and stared at them. My intent was no different than a bird-watcher's, I suppose, a hobbyist's interest in identifying the specimens whose screeches I'd just heard in the bush. But one of the young men caught my gaze. He raised his eyebrows, an insouciant gesture meant as a challenge. The look of curiosity that, I assume, had been on my face disappeared and was replaced by—well, an expression of ill will, I'm sorry to say. He looked away; I didn't. Then suddenly he said to his companions, "Oh, let's get the hell out of here." He made a dash for the exit, his stunned friends following.

An elderly lady sitting in the row just behind us leaned forward and whispered, "You shamed them." She even patted me on the shoulder.

Let's deconstruct this curious collision of fact and fiction, starting with *Titanic*'s portrayal of Mr. Guggenheim.

But I need first to confess that, as far as I'm concerned, you and I are on *Titanic*. By that I don't mean to postulate some apocalyptic vision of modern culture. What I mean is that we are all sailing through life mostly heedless of tangible peril.* Or, as Stephen King, who knows a thing or two about such matters, puts it in *The Girl Who Loved Tom Gordon*, "The world has teeth and can bite you with them anytime it wants." I'm certain that the sad saga of the great ship appeals to us in large measure because we recognize that their fate is our fate. Something about the *Titanic* story certainly makes it special. After all, nearly as many people were killed when the *Lusitania* was torpedoed in 1915 (three years after *Titanic* hit the iceberg), and that incident helped propel the United States into World War I. Yet it is *Titanic* that haunts the collective memory, probably because there is a great difference between an act of war and an act of fate. This

---

* This was originally written in the month *before* the terrorist attacks of September 11, 2001, which proved the point once and for all: from this the reader may conclude that the author seriously believes it.

and the fact that *Titanic* was hubristically thought "unsinkable." Just like our dreams of greatness and immortality.

God willing, you and I will not face the horror *Titanic*'s passengers and crew did. Still, we cannot help but wonder how we would endure what they endured. Such speculation—a kind of aspiration—is by way of preparing us for such a crisis if and when it does come.

It's fair to say of Guggenheim that choosing black tie and a brandy snifter over some (any!) attempt to survive was hardly the only course open for a gentleman on that horrible night. Guggenheim knew his chances of survival were abysmal—if not absolutely nil—and yet he might at least have tried to come through, by grabbing on to some buoyant bit of the disintegrating ship, for instance. It would not have made him less chivalrous and certainly not less intrepid. Indeed, another gentleman on the ship that night did manage to survive without sacrifice to his honor.

Colonel Archibald Gracie IV—of the family whose New York mansion became the home of the city's mayors—had retired for the night on April 14, 1912, and was awakened by the jolt of *Titanic*'s collision with the iceberg. He dressed and went up top to investigate. He ran into a friend, Clinch Smith, who handed him one of the chunks of ice that now littered the top deck.

"Here you are, Archie," the other man joked. "A souvenir."

The perfect souvenir, literally and figuratively. Freezing cold but melting fast.

The mood of most passengers was lighthearted until a few levelheaded fellows such as Gracie (who in the movie is played by English actor Bernard Fox, with no attempt to hide his British accent) began to note the tilt of the deck. When the colonel realized that the situation was very grave, he set about organizing the women he knew and leading them to the lifeboats. He assisted

Second Officer Charles Lightoller in repelling an attempt by panicked men to seize boat no. 2 and saw to it that the escape craft was not lowered until it was filled to capacity.

At 2:15 in the morning, the bow broke and sank, pulling down with it Gracie and hundreds of others. Nearly all were drowned, but Gracie, tough as nails, managed to kick to the surface. Gasping for air, he looked about at the horrible scene and saw that his friend Lightoller and several other men were clinging to an overturned collapsible lifeboat. The gallant Lightoller eventually filled—covered—the capsized craft with thirty men, organizing them into two balanced rows, and successfully navigated his odd ark to the hoped-for rendezvous with the rescue ship *Carpathia*. So Mr. Gracie went down with the ship, and yet he survived.

So perhaps Guggenheim might have survived had he given himself half a chance.

But he did not. Still, he died like a gentleman. So, presumably, did John Jacob Astor, great-grandson of the first to have that name in America, and at the time of the accident one of the richest men in the world. (An interesting parenthesis to the story of the fate of *Titanic*'s first-class passengers is how close the ship came to carrying three more of the wealthiest men in the world: G. W. Vanderbilt, Henry Clay Frick, and the richest of them all, J. P. Morgan. Vanderbilt canceled at the last moment, and his luggage went down with the ship, as did the servant charged with transporting the bags back to New York. Frick's wife sprained an ankle in Madeira, causing the couple to miss *Titanic*'s departure. And Morgan, who gladly took the Fricks' tickets when offered, ended up missing the ship because he could not resist closing one more deal before leaving the Continent.)

We'll never know what was on either Guggenheim's or Astor's mind that night, because no one survived with whom either may have discussed his motives (not that the situation allowed much time for philosophizing). But my guess—and it's only a guess—is that, being men of the world (knowing, perhaps, about the suction of sinking ships and the force of hypothermia), each believed with utter certainty that this was the last night of his life and was able to accept that fact and what the code of conduct to which he aspired accordingly demanded of him.

Mr. Astor was a decorated veteran of the Spanish-American War, so clearly he was a man who did not simply coast on the fortune bequeathed to him. Only forty-eight on the evening of his death, he had a new young wife and much to live for. It's tempting to think of him as a man inured to having whatever he wanted and as the sort of privileged character who might well have decided simply to seize a seat in one of the lifeboats, as does the fictional Cal Hockley in the movie, who unctuously asks of the stewards filling up one of the lifeboats, "Any room for a gentleman, gentlemen?"

Although he is denied a place at first, Cal later finagles a seat, which is in keeping with the instrumentalist philosophy he declares:

"I make my own luck."

The real Astor and the real Guggenheim were powerful enough that had they demanded to board a lifeboat they might not have been stopped. Bruce Ismay, one of the White Star Line's directors, did just that. But neither Astor nor Guggenheim did. Astor asked at first if he might be allowed to accompany his pregnant wife onto the lifeboat (it was one of those that Lightoller and Gracie were loading), but when he was informed that only women and children were being permitted to board, he nodded courteously and stepped away. Astor then organized a number of men into recruitment parties of a sort, seeking out women and children from all of the ship's classes and helping them into the lifeboats.

Ismay never lived down his act of "cowardice." (I put the word *cowardice* in quotation marks because there is some debate about the actual moral content of Ismay's decision. This is not the place to go into the intriguing arguments one way or the other, but I encourage the interested reader to get hold of *The Titanic Story* by Stephen Cox, a stunning book that controverts much conventional wisdom about *Titanic*.) The others' names, especially Astor's, entered the pantheon of heroes. This is history's way.

Photographing the Past

What is *history*, by the way? In the beginning—in English, anyway—the word itself meant simply an account of events, akin to its shortened form, *story*. Some overly enthusiastic feminists have suggested a fundamental bias in the word—and also in the process it represents—and have enjoyed proclaiming their account of women in the past as *herstory*. But *history* comes from Middle English (*histoire*, which is exactly the modern French word for both *history* and *story*) and before that from Latin and Greek, languages in which *his* is not the masculine personal pronoun. But of course wordplay, especially among contemporary theorists, works whether or not it's true.

A few years back, when political correctness was the rage in our universities, all the social sciences found themselves under assault by those determined to employ these academic disciplines as means to various political ends. It wasn't just that professors in the thrall of feminism, Marxism, and especially deconstructivism[†] sought subjectively to redress the grievances of the past but that

---

[†] This is a term borrowed by the literary theorists from architecture. For the guys who design buildings, it means the freedom to construct spaces that ignore function—to make things uncomfortable for residents if the architect likes the way things look.

they asserted that the disciplines themselves were bereft of objectivity. By their reasoning, all the "facts" we know about history are political declarations, since whoever records a fact—both first and subsequently—does so through the screen of his or her own ideological assumptions. Since, therefore, all facts are political, all interpretations are political, and since both fact and interpretation are political, it is not only permissible but also appropriate to "use" history politically. Thus a feminist historian properly appraises "sexist" knighthood with rage. This is hailed as demystification, which only the avant garde will comprehend, since the rest of us suffer from false consciousness, the urmystification arising from a belief in objectivity.

As David Lehman summed up in his *Signs of the Times*: "The right-minded assistant professor of the post-Vietnam era imposes his or her own politically correct attitudes upon the literature of the past—at the cost of eliminating the sense of the past. In a fit of historical superiority, the critic proves himself or herself guiltless of the sexism, racism, and assorted other isms that damn the benighted denizens of earlier eras."

Which means that the knight on horseback and the gentleman aboard *Titanic* have become contemptible because they fail—and how could they not?—to conform to current notions about enlightened thought and behavior.

My interest is not with current notions. I do confess—and who wouldn't—that I bring to a study of history prejudices born of my experience and imagination, but I will not admit that this disqualifies me from seeing some bit of the truth about the past, even if only a bit. To me it is axiomatic that, when we look back, our task—to the extent possible—is to see the subjects of study as they saw themselves. A hurdle is before us, of course, but a leap of faith is not required to surmount it, any more than some profound spiritual transformation is necessary in order to know a friend.

The editor of *Reader's Digest* once asked me with whom of all people from history I'd most like to have lunch.

"Well," I said after a moment's thought, "I won't say Jesus, because you said lunch. I'll say G. K. Chesterton."

My reason was simple. Having read so much of G. K. C., I believe I would actually have a lot to discuss with him. I like him—his anti-Semitism notwithstanding. Can I say the same for Benjamin Guggenheim or William Marshal, the "flower of chivalry," whom we will meet in the next chapter? Not so easily, perhaps, but yes. All I'm trying to do here is catch a glimpse of the real men—to see them as if in snapshots. But snapshots are different from the literary and graphic portraits of these men made in their own time. Those images were rather static, flat, and emotionless, often lacking perspective.[‡] In pictures from the year 1900 BC to the year AD 1900 nobody grins. Neither are there scowls nor tears. But living, they laughed and they wept.

Above all, I don't judge—in the moral sense. I do not feel superior to nineteenth-century gentlemen or twelfth-century knights. Far from it. As Chesterton put it in *Lunacy and Letters*:

> You cannot be just in history. Have enthusiasm, have pity, have quietude and observation, but do not imagine that you will have what you call truth. Applaud, admire, reverence, denounce, execrate. But judge not, that ye be not judged.

A Philosophical Quandary

The young people in the theater watching *Titanic* and laughing at what they took to be Guggenheim's stuffy stupidity were

---

‡ This is generally as true of literary work as of the plastic arts.

reacting in a way that, I guess, we've come to expect from many people. I believe it was the word *gentleman* that ignited their ridicule, not Guggenheim's peculiar choice of attire. (They did not laugh at the sight of him, only after he had spoken.) They probably assumed that his courage was a sham; that his true feelings were repressed; that only embarrassment prevented him from weeping like a baby or from trampling men, women, and children in a mad scramble to survive. Interesting, if true, since one would expect imminent death to overcome such scruples in an upper-class cad, which is pretty much how all the wealthy are portrayed by Mr. Cameron.

Yet there's a part of the Guggenheim story the director doesn't tell. When Guggenheim first came on deck after the collision, he was dressed appropriately in a warm sweater and a lifejacket. He was among the men recruited by Astor to help find women and children and to assist in their evacuation. But when that work was done—and knowing that there would be and should be no place for him in a lifeboat—Mr. Guggenheim returned to his stateroom and put on his finery, as did his secretary, Mr. Victor Giglio. As Stephen Cox describes the moment: "We may not honor, or even understand, the code of moral dignity, of responsibility to oneself, that Guggenheim thought was embodied in his evening clothes. But we can respect his decision to live up to it."

As for me that day in the theater, well, I simply should have ignored the hecklers. I'm probably lucky the bunch of them weren't waiting outside for me when the movie let out. (They'd have been in for it if they had decided to make trouble. My son is a black belt.) The truth is I felt the need to defend Guggenheim. But don't ask me to further deconstruct the confusion of reality, fantasy, and history that's bound up in the incident, except to say that the elderly woman who thought I'd mortified the hecklers knew why I'd reacted as I had, and no doubt she was pleased to think that the virtues of the gentleman were not entirely lost on at least one person born since the big ship sank. She might even have been alive when the wife of the president of the United States dedicated a monument to *Titanic*'s heroes. "I do this," Nellie Taft said, "in gratitude to the chivalry of American manhood."

When I tell this story, I find that many women are particularly troubled by the clearly chivalric assumption that their sex should be evacuated ahead of mine. I know no one who would not say "children first," but "women and children first" gives pause these days. Which raises the fascinating question—given the actual circumstances faced on the sinking ship—of who ought to have been saved. It's a compelling philosophical quandary.

Given that there was not sufficient time to organize any adequate evacuation plan (there were only 160 minutes from impact with the iceberg to sinking), and given that fewer than half of those on board might have been saved if all the available escape craft were filled to capacity (poor planning by White Star), what approach might reasonable people have taken to determine who would live and who would die? The first thing to say is that there would have been no need to identify a class of "doomed." Without a place in a lifeboat one's chances for survival were slim (hypothermia sets in very quickly in the bitter North Atlantic waters, especially in the vicinity of a huge iceberg), but nobody's fate needed to be a result of his having been chosen to die.

The "women-and-children-first" rule had one great virtue: it was efficient. It provided a design and a method on *Titanic*, as it would in a similar emergency today. The circumstances on *Titanic* were too chaotic, and her crew was too poorly trained to use the rule to full effect. There was space on the lifeboats sufficient to save every one of the ship's women and children, yet more than half of those from third class were lost. Still, the precept did provide such order as there was that night.

Would judicious people today decide that these classes of individuals, the female and the juvenile, should *ipso facto* be the ones to enter the boats? In the case of children: certainly, we instinctively protect them. In the case of women: possibly, they may reproduce, to which capability instinct also dictates an allegiance. In 1912, of course, there was also the assumption and the probability that regardless of age most women were less likely than most men to survive the extreme conditions that awaited those who would sink and swim. But in the year 2009, women are as fit as men: they neither feel helpless nor are helpless. We would expect some women to decide to give up their places in the boats, and I'm afraid there may be more men today who would be only too happy to take those places.

Old Ideas and New Rules

What does all this have to do with the definition of chivalry or of a compleat gentleman? Without undertaking here to catalog gentlemanly virtues, it is nonetheless obvious that conditions have changed, that the chivalric ideal is no longer as cherished, either by women or by men, as it was in 1912, and that a gentleman today—however we may characterize him—may find his environment less congenial to his temperament. He may even encounter hostility, not necessarily when he decides to give up his life so a woman may be saved, but very likely when he steps aside to allow a woman to precede him through a door.

What follows is an examination of the histories of chivalry, the civility that grew out of it, and an inquiry into the extent to which the compleat gentleman has a role to play in our democratic age. Mostly for purposes of discussion, I propose three models—archetypes if you like—that comprise the dimensions of a chivalrous gentleman's character: the warrior, the lover, and the monk. Each will be dealt with in due time, but I will say here that, few as there may be these days, gentlemen are nonetheless rich in their diversity.

Finally, it seems essential to consider the reasons why this small circle of men must become masters of the art of *sprezzatura*—a term coined by Baldassare Castiglione, one of the Renaissance popularizers of chivalry, which by then was already an exercise in nostalgia. His term has found its way into trendy literary usage as a description of a writing style that seems accessible but is loaded with symbolic content. But what Castiglione intended was a way of life typified by discretion and decorum, nonchalance and gracefulness. Think of it as the gentleman's art of concealment, an essential survival tool. We even have a modern equivalent: *cool*. But it's a poor equivalent.

In that same section of his *Reflections on the Revolution in France* in which he bemoans the fate of Queen Marie, Edmund Burke speaks of chivalry as the "unbought grace of life" and says that it once felt the slightest nick to honor as though it were a mortal wound, that it "inspired courage whilst it mitigated ferocity" and ennobled whatever it touched. Burke makes the rather sweeping declaration that "all the good things which are connected with manners and with civilization" depend upon two things: the spirit of religion and the spirit of a gentleman.

Burke was right, especially in fearing the consequences that would befall a society that abandons chivalry. "If it should ever be totally extinguished," he wrote, "the loss I fear will be great." The gravest risk is the banishment of subtlety and singularity, the things that make a man both lovable and useful.

The most self-satisfied of our forbears would cringe to witness the twenty-first-century version of illiberal individualism. A gentleman, I hope it will become clear, is not simply a man who stands apart. He is a man who stands up for others—sometimes even for his enemies—often when those others have no clue that he is there for them.

I'll say plainly that the American Republic—and this is true, I should think, of all free societies—was founded by gentlemen and depends upon their gentlemanly ideals for both its prosperity and its posterity. Our Republic, in fact, is the gentleman writ large. Societal civility is the extension and expansion of individual gallantry; it's all about—or ought to be about—balance and restraint.

Which brings me to Superman. I don't mean some neo-Nietzschean *Übermensch*; I mean the guy from Smallville with the red cape. Most of the time a gentleman is just a mild-mannered fellow whom folks may take for granted. But when the job of saving the world comes up, there's a change in the man. Few will know the gentleman's secret identity, but that's as it should be. If ever there was a fellow with *sprezzatura*, it was Clark Kent. I'm sure that somewhere in the pages of his comic book adventures, Clark's latter-day Guinevere, Lois Lane, has one of those text bubbles where we read her thoughts: *He's my knight in shining armor.* Of course, she'd probably be looking at Superman, not at Clark, and the question is: *Would Lois really admire one of the real knights whose histories inspired her comic book hero?*

What was chivalry really like when it was as gleaming fresh as a polished cuirass?

Read on.

CHAPTER TWO

The Knight

A Short History of Men on Horseback

Miniver sighed for what was not,
And dreamed, and rested from his labors;
He dreamed of Thebes and Camelot,
And Priam's neighbors.

Miniver mourned the ripe renown
That made so many a name so fragrant;
He mourned Romance, now on the town,
And Art, a vagrant.

–EDWARD ARLINGTON ROBINSON, "MINIVER CHEEVY" (1910)

What follows is a series of snapshots of the medieval knight, as he was then and as we see him now. For those of us who live in the West, images of the chivalrous knight are vividly fixed by the arts—by novels and movies and painting—and it is probably the case that the impressions of most people about knights are sentimental, romantic, and even nostalgic. Strictly speaking, it isn't possible for twenty-first-century people to be nostalgic for the twelfth century, since nostalgia properly means severe homesickness, a yearning for familiar conditions from a prior period in our own lives. There is, however, a secondary meaning of the word that comes close: *a wistful longing for a lost dominion.* Without getting

too far ahead of the discussion, we are idealistically attracted—
as perhaps we should be—to the qualities of the knight, such as
honor and bravery, and we incautiously suppose—as no doubt
we should not—that these qualities arose at a time and in places
congenial to virtue.

Sir Walter Scott, whose *Ivanhoe* (1819) has exerted a tremendous influence on modern impressions about chivalry, wrote that
the knight "was not called upon simply to practise these virtues
when opportunity offered, but to be sedulous and unwearied in
searching for the means of exercising them, and to push them
without hesitation to the brink of extravagance, or even beyond
it." This sounds like Lancelot, doesn't it? The vigilant man of
nearly spotless character and colossal strength. It sounds also like
his son, Galahad, and the other Grail knights selflessly pushing
themselves to exhaustion in their noble quest for the Eucharistic
cup that Christ used at the Last Supper. This is what we want in
a knight, a man commended by duty to seek fearlessly and
achieve decorously the highest ideals. These thoughts of Scott
appear in his article about chivalry for an early edition of *Encyclopedia Britannica*; so far so good. But just a bit further on, he breaks
down into a sorrowful lament. The "devotion of knights," he
writes, "often degenerated into superstition—their love into licentiousness—their spirit of loyalty or of freedom into tyranny
and turmoil—their generosity and gallantry into harebrained
madness and absurdity." Given the age in which we live—an age
of gaudy skepticism—this does not surprise us. Indeed most people would be shocked to discover that there actually were noble
knights—noble in the sense of being truly high-minded.

My own view is that there were chivalrous men all right, just
not very many and not one of them a saint. Needless to say, there
was no census of virtue taken in the year 1100, any more than
such a survey is done (or could be done) in our own time. But if

there had been, sanguine opinion probably would not have tallied with the mundane truth; the promise would not have squared with, as Scott said, the *practise*. Chivalry was more an ambition than an accomplishment, but—and this is the important thing—*it was the common ambition of increasing numbers of men*, and it had the effect of elevating and concretizing their sense of civil righteousness. Religion also did this, of course, and you can say of chivalry what G. K. Chesterton said about the Christian ideal: "It has not been tried and found wanting. It has been found difficult and left untried." Still, taking the good with the bad, chivalry—like Christianity—had a healthy effect upon Western man.

It was not possible—and never will be possible—to purge man of his propensity to violence and haughtiness; man will never be completely tamed. But chivalry was a mechanism whereby men were allowed—as men—to rise toward what Abraham Lincoln would call "the better angels of our nature." Indeed, for seven centuries beginning in about 1100, the idea that a man could be both fearsome and gallant took firm purchase upon the Western imagination, culminating in the attempt by the American Founders to make a chivalrous republic—one that was a counterweight between wretched realities and intrepid aspirations.

If the actuality of chivalry in the Middle Ages turns out to disappoint the more starry-eyed among us, we may do well to recall Benjamin Disraeli's comment that in the face of baseness we need to nurture great thoughts. "To believe in the heroic," Disraeli said, "makes heroes." We worry too much about hypocrisy, about our failures throughout history to achieve honorable goals. Knights were imperfect men. So what? "Every society invents for itself a type, a model, an exemplar of what the perfect member of that society ought to be," wrote English author-statesman Harold Nicolson. "These heroes and heroines are much more than the products of existing social and economic conditions: they are myths which repeat the legends of the past and enhance the dreams of the future. In a materialistic age it is salutary to remind ourselves of such fictions."

The idea of the compleat gentleman arose from the principles and the traditions of knighthood, and—more important still—any definition of a modern compleat gentleman must also be constructed upon this ancient bedrock.

We Band of (Younger) Brothers

Chivalry was first and foremost the worldview of fighting men. Early in its development, it became allied with Catholicism and a primitive version of feminism known as "courtly love." It's illuminating to think of it as a call to men to be both manly and mannerly.

It is remarkable, no matter how actual or chimerical it was in its day, that chivalry appeared when it did—in fact, that it appeared at all! The early medieval period was a time of instability and violence, seemingly at odds with notions of honor and restraint.

To make a very long story short, after the Roman Empire withdrew from its colonial outposts in Britain and on the Continent, a classic historical power vacuum was created. Into this condition, which is abhorred by nature, galloped so-called barbarians. They came from the Muslim south, the Viking north, and the Mongol east. There seemed to be endless swarms of them. For protection, troops of men—on horseback and on foot—began to organize for the defense of the lands that would eventually become France, Germany, England, and so on.

There was not much to recommend the cure over the affliction. Once the stirrup made its appearance in the West, sometime in the eighth century—courtesy of the Eastern invaders—armed horsemen became for several centuries the dominant military force, and when the barbarians either put down roots and assimilated or headed back from whence they had come, the indigenous *chevaleries*, as they were called, remained—all dressed up (you might say) with no place to go. Here's a brash reduction of the predicament: what the Europeans faced then was what some urban dwellers face today—gangs of armed youth, dropouts from settled society who had no education to speak of except in the ways of war, and who needed to brawl in order to put bread in their mouths and steel in their hearts.

Because of the feudal system of primogeniture, by which inheritance passed only to the first-born male heir, many of these menacing youths were younger brothers. Some younger brothers might go into the church, and some might make good strategic marriages—often arranged by their older brothers—but some others learned the arts of war and roamed the countryside spoiling for a riot. A lucky few won employment from feudal lords, and they were called "knights-bachelor." If they were very fortunate and were rewarded with land of their own (called a *benefice*, which was a practice borrowed from the Romans), they would ride under their own heraldry, and they were called "knights-banneret." The brawlers were called "knights-errant" (or *iuvenes*, youths), and it was especially for them and from them that the rules of chivalry and the practice of tournaments first emerged.

Chivalry combined military, religious, and social concepts into a unified way of life. That much we can safely say by way of beginning a definition; then it gets dicey. As the finest writer on the subject, Maurice Keen, puts it, chivalry is "a word that was used in the Middle Ages with different meanings and shades of meaning by different writers and in different contexts." A thousand years of history hasn't changed the situation, and a definition of chivalry remains elusive, its meaning, as Keen concludes, "tonal rather than precise in its implications."

This is not to say that some have not attempted to be precise. Writing at the end of the nineteenth century, Léon Gautier came up with the Ten Commandments of Chivalry:

I. Thou shalt believe all that the Church teaches and shalt observe all its directions.

II. Thou shalt defend the Church.

III. Thou shalt respect all weaknesses and shalt constitute thyself the defender of them.

IV Thou shalt love the country in which thou wast born.

V. Thou shalt not recoil before thine enemy.

VI. Thou shalt make war against the Infidel without cessation and without mercy.

VII. Thou shalt perform scrupulously thy feudal duties, if they be not contrary to the laws of God.

VIII. Thou shalt never lie and shalt remain faithful to thy pledged word.

IX. Thou shalt be generous and give largesse to everyone.

X. Thou shalt be everywhere and always the champion of the Right and the Good against Injustice and Evil.

You can't get much more precise than that. Gautier's is an especially pious and martial list, short on chivalry's social aspect, but that's because Gautier was among those austere fellows for whom courtly love, which we will consider at length in chapter five, was slightly distasteful. Referring to the Lancelot-Guinevere-Arthur triangle—and really to the whole cycle of Round Table tales—Gautier complained that they "civilized us no doubt, but effeminated us" as well. Perhaps. It's probably the case that no milquetoast is properly capable of waging merciless war against heretics and unbelievers, although there's not much call for that these days.

But even Gautier, much like Scott, was not unaware of the gap between the confession of chivalric charity and the actualization of knightly prowess. "The majority of these heroes had no other shibboleth than 'I am going to separate the head from the trunk.'" The *majority*, he says, and he may not be far off the mark.

Knights Real and Imagined

Arthurian literature (and, as we'll see, King Arthur is the lightning rod of the chivalric imagination) is especially optimistic about the knight's character, although the emphasis is always on the "true" knight. The tales of Arthur, Lancelot, Gawain, and the rest were the era's fiction—indeed they were the very first "romances" and gave that genre its name. The nonfiction writing of the day, which is rare and often as fanciful as the fables, tells a rather grittier story of the knight.

This look back is not an exercise in nostalgia. Part of the truth about the "Age of Chivalry" that emerges from some study is that it was most often bestial and nearly always sanctimonious. (In this latter regard, of course, it resembles every age, ours especially.) It would be foolish to look back with longing for the lost glory of the medieval period. One story will suffice to illustrate why such mawkishness is brazenly vulgar.

There is a *chanson de geste* (one of just under two hundred such "French" ballads of the period written by *trouvères*, or troubadours, about the *paladins*, or knights, of the eleventh, twelfth, and earlier centuries) concerning a great hero, one Raoul de Cambrai. Raoul is a Christian, which means a Catholic, and a loyal son of the church, although possibly a recent convert from one paganism or another. The assumption of his faith makes it rather shocking to read how he razes a convent during one of his campaigns in Normandy. Later on in his tent, shaking the dust and ashes from his clothes, washing the blood from his hands, he tells his seneschal—a combination steward and lieutenant: "Prepare me food and you will do me a great boon." (Murdering and raping nuns must have given men a powerful appetite.) Raoul is very specific about what he wants—"roasted peacocks and deviled swans and venison in abundance"—and he means to see that every one of his men is filled since he "would not be thought mean by my barons for all the gold of a city."

For his part, the seneschal is slack-jawed. At the risk of life and limb he excoriates his liege lord: "In the name of Our Lady," he cries, "what are you thinking of? You are denying holy Christianity and your baptism and the God of majesty! It is Lent, when everyone ought to fast; it is the holy Friday of the Passion on which sinners have always honored the cross."

Here, no doubt, his voice begins to shake with shame and rage. "And we miserable men who have come here, we have burned nuns and violated the church, and we shall never be reconciled to God unless his pity be greater than our wickedness."

Now it is Raoul's turn to be aghast. He shows the seneschal a powerful fist. "You son of a slave," he begins—we can only imagine the look of loathing on the knight's face—and proceeds to shriek at his trembling steward: "Those damned nuns had the audacity to insult two of my squires! They had to pay—and pay dearly. And, by God, they did pay." He is astonished at his aide's impudence and naiveté. The seneschal of so great a lord ought to understand the ways of the world.

But then Raoul sighs and the threatening fist drops to his side. "Still," he shrugs, "you are right. I had forgotten that it is Lent."

As the seneschal backs out of the tent, Raoul, his meal meatless now, sits down to play chess with one of his barons. As one commentator of the *chanson* sums up: "Thus are Christ's forty days in the wilderness piously commemorated."

Since the very inception of chivalry, men have been sorrowfully mindful of the gap between the notion and the fact, have been aware of the tension between bright sanguinity and dark chagrin. But the early knights—who swore to protect the weak even as they trampled them underfoot—weren't exactly hypocrites, if only because they believed in both hierarchy and human frailty in a way we no longer do. They knew the difference between good and evil at least as clearly as we, but they lacked our optimism about the character and the primacy of what is good. And they felt that societal status was ordained by fate, which is to say, by God.

It's *very* complicated historically. As chivalry was emerging, the rule of law was still imperfectly realized. There was a legacy of Roman law (especially in the Theodosian and Justinian codes of the Byzantine Empire and the Salic laws of early—i.e., sixth-century—Europe), and there was a slowly evolving common law that served to adjudicate some conflicts. Yet what we confidently understand as justice today was in the Age of Chivalry confounded by the absence of constitutions, concepts of civil rights, and professional law enforcement. Justice was ad hoc and highly subjective; to most there seemed to be no alternative in society to the oppressive hierarchy of privilege, as for example, in the *droit du seigneur*, the rule by which a feudal lord had the right to engage in sexual intercourse with the bride of a vassal on their wedding night. Although such a claim was honored more in the breach than in the observance, it did loom as an icy reminder of the *seigneur*'s power. But during the eleventh and twelfth centuries, there was also a gradual loosening of feudal bonds. Many serfs—indentured servants—became peasants and began to have some ownership rights. Increased income led to mobility, and European cities expanded; artisans and merchants began to thrive. Various constraints—legal, ethical, and religious—began to temper the knight's reckless sense of empowerment.

It is interesting that some of the earliest recorded references to chivalry proclaim either its demise or its resurrection. But none of the incipient testimonials come from works about chivalry itself, because the oldest manuals of knighthood date from the middle of the thirteenth century and include *The Book of the Order of Chivalry* (*Libre qui es de l'ordre de cavalleria*) by Ramon Llull (1232–1315) and the poem "Ordene de Chevalerie," whose author is anonymous. Llull, a Majorcan Franciscan priest, states with medieval sincerity—which was often disingenuous—that chivalry was instituted shortly after the Fall. No cavaliers were needed in Eden, but thereafter a few have been chosen in every age. And Llull believed that those conscripted to knighthood were very specifically one in a thousand (*ex mille electus*) and were called out of the herd by reason of their loyalty, prowess, and courage. Llull's list of attributes deserves immediate consideration.

The language of chivalry is usually French, and the words used to describe the knight were *loyauté* and *prouesse*, which are the attributes cited by Llull (*loyauté* meaning loyalty or fidelity; *prouesse*, prowess, standing for both strength and bravery); then *largesse*; *courtoisie*; and finally *franchise*. By *largesse* was meant generosity, both of spirit and of purse, and is perhaps best expressed by the English word liberality. By *courtoisie* was meant kindness and manners but also the grander notion of gallantry. *Franchise* is the hardest to define precisely, although it's also the most important. It is honesty—in our English-language sense of frankness—but it is also the much more elevated conception of honor, or "nobility of mind." Llull also stressed that a knight needed to be of a noble family, and perhaps as a consequence of that, wealthy.

Being a knight took money, and plenty of it, because the costs of horses and weapons and armor and—well before Llull's time—tournament entry fees were substantial.

The Training of a Knight

To become a knight in the year of our Lord 1100, a lad from a well-to-do family would leave his home for the castle of a great knight—or so he would hope—to be educated there in the ways of combat and courtesy. There were no military colleges such as America's West Point or Britain's Sandhurst (but then there were no nations either), and without a patron a boy could not hope to receive the years of training required to win his spurs. The whole of his education could take up to a decade or more, and it began at age seven when he entered the knight's service as a page.

The page (or, in French, *damoiseau*, "little master") was a seen-but-not-heard servant who was expected to learn the ways of the knight by observing, not by doing. His tasks were almost certainly domestic, although in the home of some fine lords he probably received a rudimentary education as well—an education that often included lessons in chess and, with the local priest, religion. Practically from the very institution of chivalry, a knight was expected to be a man of culture and poise, honor and prowess. In this regard the page was often at the call of the lady of the house as well as the lord, and she would attend to the page's early education in the refinements of courtly love. Rarely would this have involved anything remotely carnal.

At fourteen, the page would have spent years watching his knight—or knights, in a larger household—dressing and eating and laughing and lying and doing everything that was appropriate, and much that was not, in the life of a gentleman warrior. As he reached the end of this period of apprenticeship, he might begin to learn the finer points of hunting and falconry that would spearhead his schooling in the arts of war, and, in particular, guarantee that he knew how to "horse." He was probably a fair-to-excellent rider even before he became a page, just as modern boys master bike riding at a very early age. The horse was the knight's indispensable companion and as familiar to a twelfth-century lad as a racing bike is to a twenty-first-century kid.

Now a teenager, the page would become a squire (in French sometimes *valet**). In this new status he began to handle his knight's weapons and to watch closely how a proper soldier fought and rode. It is likely that he received advanced lessons in combat horsemanship and in the uses of each type of weapon as well as being party to the conversation of his knight in a way he hadn't been as a page. Now he could ask questions and express opinions. He was likely to accompany his lord into battle or a tournament and, in extremis, to take up a sword himself if an enemy broke through and threatened his side.

There remained a lot of drudgery: polishing and repairing armor; cleaning and storing weapons; grooming and training horses. But it was all beneficial to his education as a knight. There was no set rule for determining when a squire was ready to become a knight. In times of relative peace, he might be seven years a page and seven years a squire before his knighting ceremony. If he had been steadfast at the side of his knight in combat, he might be knighted earlier—in some cases much earlier, especially if a battle were imminent and his knight believed the looming danger made imperative the ceremony of dubbing, a reward for the lad's loyal service on the eve of his early death. But

---

* In Britain, the words *valet* and *squire* were never synonymous. *Valet* is a common English word, but it has a meaning equivalent to *groom*.

this was rare, since the range of skills required of a knight was not easily acquired in less than a dozen years.

As the era of chivalry began its decline and knights were needed less and less for fighting, more and more squires decided that this intermediate stage was sufficient, especially given the cost of horses and equipment. In England, especially, the title of squire, or "esquire," became an end in itself, eventually applying to a class of men below noble and above peasant who never in their lives rode a charger or swung a sword—or knew anyone who had.

A Real King for the Ages

Besides the books, songs, and poems mentioned earlier, there are other medieval sources from which we know about the lives and the honor code of knights. They come in three types: romances such as *The Art of Courtly Love* by Andreas Capellanus and the Arthurian stories of Chrétien de Troyes, both written between 1170 and 1174 for Countess Marie of Champagne, the daughter of Eleanor of Aquitaine; ecclesiastical treatises such as *Policraticus* by John of Salisbury, who was a student of Peter Abelard and later the secretary of Thomas à Becket; and manuals of chivalry such as Llull's, the poem "Ordene," and Geoffroy de Charnay's *Book of Chivalry* (*Livre de Chevalerie*), written in the fourteenth century. (De Charnay is also recognized as the first known possessor, in 1357, of what we now call the Shroud of Turin. This connection to the shroud is only one of many that give many stories of knights and chivalry a spooky aura.) As different as these sources are in their depiction of knights and of chivalry, they tend to agree on five attributes: fidelity, prowess, generosity, courtesy, and honor. If fidelity approached chauvinism, if prowess was menacingly close to brutality, if generosity degraded into profligacy, if courtesy became hypocrisy, and if honor slipped over into arrogance, then we have reason to doubt the authenticity of medieval chivalry. And we should—so long, that is, as we are willing to acknowledge our own ethical failures.

In any event, these are the knightly qualities that appeared in those romantic *chansons de geste*, the "songs of great deeds," that entertained and educated people of all classes from the eleventh century on. Indeed, to inspire the Norman forces under William the Conqueror as they invaded England in 1066, a famous troubadour named Taillefer sang the most famous of the *chansons*, *The Song of Roland*. Roland is the exemplar of the chivalric ideal—devout, loyal, and courageous, though he is also a bit of a naïf. His character is based upon Hruodland of Brittany, who, like Roland, may (or may not) have been the nephew of Charlemagne (Charles the Great), the "Frankish" king who became Holy Roman Emperor in the year 800. Roland is the doomed defender of Charlemagne's rear guard during the emperor's retreat from the Spanish city of Saragossa. He loses his life, as do most of his soldiers, at the battle of Roncesvalles (or Roncevaux) in 778. In the romance, Roland is hacked to pieces by Saracens (as most Muslims, regardless of tribe or locality, were known in the West until after the Renaissance, similar to the way Americans would later refer to the tribes living in North America before European settlement by the ludicrously reductive misnomer *Indians*.) In actual fact, Charlemagne's retreating force was decimated by Basques, but there is at least some historical basis for the story of Roland.

There had been trouble in Saragossa, which indeed had a Muslim governor, but Charlemagne had given up trying to compel its allegiance after previous attempts to negotiate a cessation of hostilities had been met with creative resistance by that governor,

Marsile. He had sent home two successive Carolingian ambassadors chopped up and stuffed into wicker baskets.

What matters in the tale of Roland, of course, are his honor and bravery (though how honorable his actions are is questionable—he's about as chivalrous as Achilles in the *Iliad*), as well as the celebration of the wisdom and beneficence of Charlemagne, whose memory was glorified because Western Europe degenerated into chaos after his death. (Here then is another example of nostalgia.) The old joke that the Holy Roman Empire was neither holy nor Roman nor an empire is false. Presumably it was as holy as any other political enterprise, which is to say not very, although unlike many later governments its sanctimony was very explicit. It was Roman, if not in kin—Charlemagne was German and his seat of power was French—then in kind, since Charlemagne did for Europe what the Romans had done hundreds of years before: he provided security and unity. And it was certainly an empire, given that Charlemagne was ruler over many states. That his government of conquered territories was often rapacious—he forcibly relocated peasants in order to pacify conquered regions—is true, but he also exerted lasting influence on the development of educational institutions and sound political administration. One of the troubadours he welcomed at his court dubbed him *rex pater Europae*, the king-father of Europe.

What matters with regard to Le Grand Charles is the effect of his apotheosis on the imagination of not only those Norman invaders but also of the knights who built the institutions of law and order from which modern nations and modern men have arisen. We would not much admire Charlemagne today. He would feel asphyxiated in our republican democracies, but we owe him. His influence on the ideals of chivalry, by virtue of the troubadours' celebration of his and his knights' deeds of derring-do, is second only to King Arthur's.

Once and Future King

Charlemagne was every inch a real man—and there were a lot of inches. Some say he was seven feet tall. King Arthur, on the other hand, is yard after colorful yard of pure fabrication.

This is not to say that the legend of Arthur has no antecedent in history or that there is no edification in his legend. There was a chieftain in Britannia some time after the Roman evacuation and during the early incursions of the Angles and Saxons, between AD 400 and 500, who may have inspired the first Arthurian legends. That being said—with a bit more to come—it remains the case that almost everything we "know" about King Arthur, Camelot, and the Round Table is the product of dynamic woolgathering.

A fair comparison could be made between Arthur and George Washington. Washington has always been surrounded by legend. Great leaders usually are. In 1800, Mason Locke ("Parson") Weems wrote his *History of the Life, Death, Virtues and Exploits of George Washington*, in which he tells the story of our future president chopping down a cherry tree and then honestly confessing the deed to his angry father. It was applesauce, of course. But so beloved an image did the apocryphal tale become (and so educationally alluring is the "I-cannot-tell-a-lie" chestnut) that even today, more than a century after it was discredited, Weems's account persists in the popular imagination. American schoolchildren believe the story until well into their elementary school years, just as many of them persevere in credulity regarding Santa Claus. With Washington, though, we have so much accurate historical information that a few fantasies never detract from our vast factual knowledge of him.

In the case of King Arthur, the problem is rather reversed. The preponderance of fantasy detracts from the negligible reality. But scanty as the evidence for a historical Arthur may be, there is some evidence. Still, what little fact there was in the tradition, and it was probably never reliable, began in the Middle Ages to be swallowed up by artistic license. If we look at the sources upon which our knowledge of Arthur is based, there's not one that was written (at least in the form that has survived) less than five hundred years after he died, assuming that he ever really lived. And these portrayals suffer from the accretions common in medieval art, from the practice of presenting historical settings in a contemporary milieu. To tell a story as much as to paint a picture is to provide details, and those could only come from what the writer or artist saw around him, there being in 1100 no organized historical or archaeological record. There would not begin to be such a record until the eighteenth century. In Arthur's time there were but a handful of literate men, and—with only rare exceptions—they were not writing about anything except the Christian faith. (One of these anomalies is none other than Saint Patrick, an Arthurian near-contemporary, who left behind an autobiography, religious without being didactic, modeled on Saint Augustine's *Confessions*.)

As a consequence, from the inception of their romantic glorification Arthur and his knights have always been arrayed in the trappings of the High Middle Ages—the period in which the stories about them were first popularized—and the timeline of events in later novels and films, such as it is, usually reflects the fifteenth century more than the fifth. (For one thing, Arthur and his knights are always competing in tournaments—an impossibility without stirrups that in the fifth century had yet to be introduced into Europe.) By now we've come far enough in our knowledge of these periods that no credible account ought to ignore the matter of a five hundred- or thousand-year difference. The trouble is that Hollywood, and the literary genre it has spawned, is the source for most of what most people "know" about Arthur, and with regard to Arthurian narrative Hollywood hasn't a shred of credibility. Or am I too harsh? Perhaps, since the point of tales of the Knights of the Round Table—then and now—isn't dull history, but shining myth.

To say that the myth persists is an understatement. If you were to log on to the Internet and begin a search for "King Arthur" or "Holy Grail" or "knighthood" or "chivalry," you would discover sites devoted to both the fact and the fancy about these subjects. The Web sites of departments of history and literature at top universities are showcases for the work of scholars who have devoted careers to the study of Arthuriana. And there are, of course, Web sites aplenty dedicated to Arthurian fantasy, including many put up by members of the Society for Creative Anachronism (SCA), whose members dress up in medieval garb and spend their weekends wielding swords in city parks and town squares.

They have a whole feudalesque system of orders and titles and much sound knowledge of the period they love, just as Civil War re-enactors do. Still, for all their seriousness, theirs is also an exercise in adult dress-up play. There are scadian (es-KAY-dee-an)-driven sites devoted to the provision of full suits of armor—provided that you have $3,500—and other accoutrements of medieval role-playing. You can buy tallow soap, leather jerkins, authentic ceramic plates, and spoons made of cow horn. You can purchase wonderful handmade boots with pointed toes, exactly the kind they wore in 1200. At MackenzieSmith.com and albionarmorers.com, you can find dazzling steel suits that, honestly, take your breath away. And the swords!

In the sword are the Middle Ages manifest—heavenly beauty and hellish savagery.[†]

But there are also numerous and very solemn Web sites established by contemporary orders of chivalry (some religious and some secular), devotees of heraldry, and believers in conspiracy. One finds that the notion of *ex mille electus* is very much with us at the dawn of the third millennium.

The conspiracy theories are precious and infatuated with an air of spiritual enchantment of the sort that fails Karl Popper's test of falsifiability, by which negating evidence is as important as positive "proof." All the documentation piled up by those who believe themselves the remnant of the Knights Templar, as well as those who would expose the latter-day Templars' insidious influence on world events, ignores the contrary and overwhelming evidence that the modern "knights" and their inquisitors are mostly people with too many illusions and too much leisure. Still, it would be fascinating to know just how many people believe that Joseph of Arimathea brought the Grail to Britain—specifically to Glastonbury—and accept the whole fabulous genealogy that comes with it. (In one recent news report, a British fellow claimed to have found the Grail in the rubbish gathering dust in his mother-in-law's attic.)

But Joseph of Arimathea?

Imagine! The Gospel accounts—he is mentioned in all four—make plain that there was such a man and that he was a respected member of the community in Jerusalem. Indeed he was a member of the Sanhedrin, the ruling council of Israel.

[†] I considered buying a sword for home defense. How remarkable it would be, I thought, to confront a burglar with a medieval longsword or even a cavalry saber. Imagine the look on the felon's face as the hall light glints on the sword's edge, falling swiftly to behead him. Upon further reflection, I realized that even a sword with a four-foot-long blade puts you in too-close proximity to the felon. So I bought a shotgun instead.

Joseph was "a good and a just man," we know from Luke, and from Mark that he "was also himself looking for the kingdom of God." John tells us that Joseph kept his admiration for the Nazarene to himself "for fear of the Jews," but then (and Matthew tells the story too) had a change of heart; we learn how he went "boldly" to Governor Pilate and asked for the crucified man's body, and then prepared the corpse for burial and placed it in a tomb he owned—presumably the one he'd purchased for the occasion of his own death. (Not surprisingly, Joseph is the patron saint of undertakers.) With his friend (possibly his son) Nicodemus, Joseph rolls a stone slab across the opening to seal the tomb and leaves—literally; this is the last we hear of him in the Bible. But it's only the beginning of his legend.

They say he traveled to France (Gaul, as it was known then), which is entirely plausible, given that he was a man at home in the ambit of Rome. They further say that he left the Continent and went to Britannia, arriving there at some indeterminate time. With him were—take your pick—Pilate, Mary Magdalene, Salome (who had danced for Herod Antipas and won John the Baptist's head), and, of course, the Holy Grail, which some say was his to begin with, the Upper Room of that first Eucharist being the upstairs of Joseph's own Jerusalem house and the Grail part of the family's drinkware.

They even say of Joseph that he had been many times to Britannia, because he was a tin merchant (the area around Wales and Cornwall being ancient tin-mining sites), and further that on at least one occasion he'd brought with him his nephew, a boy called Jesus, thus accounting for at least one Lost Year. William Blake wrote of this in his poem "Jerusalem," which became the hymn made famous in the 1981 film *Chariots of Fire*:

And did those feet in ancient time
Walk upon England's mountains green?
And was the holy Lamb of God
On England's pleasant pastures seen?

And did the Countenance Divine
Shine forth upon our clouded hills?
And was Jerusalem builded here
Among these dark Satanic mills?

Bring me my bow of burning gold!
Bring me my arrows of desire:
Bring me my spear! O clouds unfold!
Bring me my chariot of fire!

I will not cease from mental fight,
Nor shall my sword sleep in my hand
Till we have built Jerusalem
In England's green and pleasant land.

And this is what men have been trying to do for a thousand years—find Jerusalem in Glastonbury, if not also heaven in their hearts.

Of course, tracing the old tin merchant's path to England takes some effort of imagination, and the resulting genealogies are fantastic indeed. According to the so-called *Prose Vulgate* version of the legend, which includes *La Queste del Saint Graal* (*The Quest for the Holy Grail*), the descent of Galahad, one of the finders of the Grail, actually begins with the biblical King David, runs through Solomon, of course, and then through the Blessed Virgin (of the House of David, recall), and eventually reaches King Ban of Benwick, the father of Lancelot, who was in turn the father of Galahad.

Galahad's mother, the Lady Elaine, is the daughter of Pelles, the Fisher King, guardian of the Grail. What makes this genealogy perfectly circular is the one name that is not given but would have been assumed once Mary, the mother of Jesus, appears— her *uncle*, Joseph of Arimathea. Thus when Galahad puts hands on the Grail, he is reclaiming a family heirloom—on both sides!

But who can believe all this, then or now? The answer for today is simple: *believers*, who by definition . . . believe. In the medieval period, belief was a bit more complex, however, and the explosion of Arthuriana then had as much to do with politics as with faith . . . which brings us to Henry II of England.

The Angevin Dispensation

Henry, famously played on film by the Irish actor Peter O'Toole in both *Becket* (1964) and *The Lion in Winter* (1968), ruled England within a century of the Norman Conquest and was very concerned about the legitimacy of his reign in the eyes of England's older inhabitants, most notably the Saxons and those whom they had displaced, the Britons. He had his own very considerable iron hand, of course, and also a superb ability for administration, but while those assets might secure power, they could not win hearts. To accomplish the conversion of Britain's people to his charismatic self, he and his wife, Eleanor of Aquitaine, undertook to evoke a glorious past, one even grander than the descent from Charlemagne claimed by the kings of France. Henry and Eleanor asserted themselves as the guardians of Arthur's legacy.

Now, during the actual Arthurian period, which was more or less during the fifth and sixth centuries, Britain was a land in which the "native" populations—mostly Celts (who were Iron Age interlopers themselves)—were besieged by invaders. The Romans (whose invasion had begun under Julius Caesar in 50

BC) were in the process of withdrawing—after AD 410 troops were needed elsewhere in the crumbling empire—and warriors and colonizers from the Continent were attempting to fill the void there as other "barbarians" were throughout Europe. Most immediately, there were Angles and Saxons, both coming from what is now northern Germany (Vikings would come later), from whom we derive the familiar "Anglo-Saxon" modifier. These groups pushed the Celts, or Britons (a term inclusive enough to encompass the prehistoric inhabitants such as those who built Stonehenge—who were not, as is often thought, Celtic Druids), into Wales and Cornwall, and legend has it that it was from there that the "Arthurian" insurgency against the Anglo-Saxons arose.

There is evidence that some aspects of the Arthurian legend may have their genesis in myths brought to Britain by Sarmatian mercenaries in the employ of Rome. (Sarmatians lived on the territory of modern-day Poland.) But the substance of the claims about a historical Arthur relate to a two-decade period in the late 400s. It was in this window of time that the earliest texts position a leader who succeeded—albeit temporarily—in halting the advance of the Saxons and the Angles. It's notable that this chieftain, Arthur, we assume, was Christian, while the Anglo-Saxons were not—not yet, anyway.

The earliest probable reference to the "Arthur" figure is in a nearly contemporary book (circa 550) by the monk Gildas, later Saint Gildas. He gives credit to a Christian king for unifying the Britons and defeating the advance of the invaders, but he also chastises this Arthurian figure, whom he does not name, for being too secular. The theme of his book, which is titled *On the Ruin of Britain* (*De excidio Britanniae*), is the perennial message that spiritual failure leads to political ruin. As a result of his Christian "prejudices," experts often dismiss Gildas. Yet just about everything he presents as fact has subsequently been confirmed as such by historians and archaeologists.

The first actual mention of the name "Arthur" was in a Latin document called the *Life of Saint Columbanus*, by one Jonas of Bobbio, an Italian monk writing in the 640s. But it was the Welsh *Annales Cambriae*, written nearly 500 years after Arthur's death, which gives the fullest account of his career prior to those given by the scribes of Henry and Eleanor. In the *Annales*, Arthur remains the victorious champion of the Britons, but his godly character is unchallenged. At the remove of a half-millennium, he is less crudely human than he would have been to Saint Gildas, some of whose information probably came from first-hand sources now lost.

But none of these early references were in their time more than a reflection of what was doubtless a rich folkloric tradition, oral, of course, and philologists can only conjecture about the content of the songs and tales we will never hear.

Then enter the Angevins.

Angevin (from Anjou, a duchy in northern France) refers to the dynastic line that begins with Henry II. He was Count of Anjou before becoming King of England. It was under his and Eleanor's influence that the story of Arthur catapulted from mere myth—from being a fuzzy tale akin to America's Johnny Appleseed—to national (even international) ethos. This was done in careful stages as part of a plan to secure legitimacy for the new rulers of Britain. Like all such movements, it had unintended consequences, some of which were welcomed in the glorification of chivalry, while others were less pleasant for the Angevins, as with the barons' demand for rights: Runnymede and Magna Carta. The causal relationship between tales of Camelot and rules of gallantry is not absolute, but the nexus is more than tenable.

What Henry and Eleanor did was similar to what modern politicians often do when they pose for photos with movie stars or athletes or soldiers: they achieved heroism by association. The

Angevins saw in the promotion of Arthur a force for nation building, a dynamic myth in which they played the role of executors of Arthur's legacy. The greatest beneficiary of this effort was neither Henry nor Eleanor but their son Richard the Lionheart, who in his time (and since) was second only to Arthur in utter Englishness—this despite the fact that he was French. The Angevins commissioned nearly every work of consequence written about Arthur—by William of Malmesbury, Geoffrey of Monmouth, Robert Wace, Chrétien de Troyes, Marie de France, Walter Map, and Robert de Boron—until we leap forward three hundred years to Sir Thomas Malory, whose *Le Morte d'Arthur* is the definitive redaction of the legend (based largely on Chrétien). Henry even conspired with the monks of Glastonbury Abbey to "discover" the graves of Arthur and Guinevere—after nearly seven hundred years, the queen's skull still had lovely blonde locks; Eleanor succeeded as no one else could have in making indissoluble the marriage of chivalry and courtly love.

To be a knight had become nearly the secular equivalent of sainthood, except that the apotheosis, the glory, came during one's own lifetime.

The Glory of Templar Knighthood

For a very long time—no one knows for sure how long—a knight might receive his "accolade" from another knight. The accolade was the familiar dubbing with the flat of a sword blade. While we now associate the accolade with kings and queens, it was once the right of any knight, just as the granting of a black belt in the martial arts is the right of anyone with the rank of sensei. Prior to the Crusades there was little religious content to the ceremony. Kings and popes, princes and priests were not required in the making of a knight, which may explain in part why the Knights Templar, despite their fervid religiosity, kept their ceremonial functions hidden from both secular and religious authorities. Their secrecy was certainly a major cause of their downfall.

We know something about the ancient rite of the investiture of knights from a description in the "Ordene de Chevalerie" (circa 1250), which recounts how during the Third Crusade (1189–1192) an imprisoned knight, a Christian count called Hugh of Tiberias, takes his captor—no less than the great Saladin himself, bane of all crusaders—through the entire knighting process. Apparently it was not enough for Saladin simply to hear about it; he had to experience it.

First Saladin's hair is dressed, if not actually tonsured (trimmed), as a religious postulant's would have been. Next he receives a ritual bath, a kind of second baptism for the knight to be—or, in Saladin's case, a pretended first. He is then led to a bed, signifying the "repose of paradise," and after some period of rest is dressed in a white robe (for purity) topped with a red cloak (for sacrifice). His brown stockings remind him of the earth in which he will lie after death.

The red cloak is bound at the waist by a cord that hangs down between his legs, a reminder of the importance of chastity. Maurice Keen relates that gold spurs fastened to the candidate's boots "show that the knight must be as swift to follow God's commandments as the pricked charger." (The ritual of placing spurs on a new knight gave us the still popular reference to "winning one's spurs.") Last but not least, Saladin is presented with a sword, the sharp edges of which signify justice and loyalty to the oppressed. Hugh wisely decides to omit the *collée*, a ritual slap that must have seemed both inappropriate and perilous when initiating one's captor, especially so since he was the Sultan of Egypt. Instead Hugh gives Saladin the four binding rules of a knight's life: He must not consent to any false judgment or be party in any way to treason; he must honor all women and damsels and be ready to aid them to the limit of his power; he must hear, when possible, Mass every day; and he must fast every Friday in remembrance of Christ's passion.

As Keen points out, the story of Saladin's knighting reflects the assumption that, notwithstanding a very strong theological subtext, knighting was not a religious ritual and no priest was required. Literary critic H. B. Parkes agrees: "Despite the [usual] vigil and Mass in church, no clergyman took part in the actual ceremony, which was derived from pagan rituals. When in 1213 the son of a high French nobleman, Simon de Montfort, was dubbed by two bishops, there was much comment on this break with tradition."

Throughout the centuries, the content of the ceremony varied greatly. Once exclusively military, soon it was largely religious, but even among the Templars a knight was at least as much a man of the world as he was a servant of the Lord.

For the next eight or nine hundred years, men saw in Arthur and the knights of his Round Table the models of chivalrous behavior. Here were men of fidelity, prowess, generosity, courtesy, and honor.

But there was yet another great quality of knights we have not mentioned—their ardor for glory. It was not enough for knights simply to love and fight well; they needed to sacrifice everything for the highest ideals, such as a Grail quest. For most men this was a pipe dream—a gnawing emptiness in the pit of the stomach after too many romantic stories told over too many flagons of ale; however, there were a few knights whose extremity of virtue was remarkable. As a group, the Knights Templar were such men, and one of their number, William Marshal, was the most remarkable of all, even if he was a somewhat reluctant Templar.

The Templars, whose name is an abbreviation of "Poor Knights of Christ and the Temple of Solomon," were founded in 1118 by Hughes de Payens. They were a military and monastic force dedicated, first, to defending the sacred places wrested from Muslim control during the Crusades, and, second, to protecting the pilgrims who now flocked to these shrines through dangerous territory. Indeed, the Crusades—there were ten of them over the course of nearly two hundred years (1095–1271)—were probably the most important force in the development of chivalry as a doctrine, which was at least a part of the intention of Pope Urban II when he initiated the Crusades. "Instead of trying to curb the belligerent western knights," Stephen Howarth has written, "[Urban] could actively encourage them—and get rid of them. Instead of tearing the West apart they could fight—in the East—for the West; for the unity of Christendom; for the salvation of their souls; and with every chance of material gain." The rule of the Templars would be among the first systemizations of chivalry, and it demonstrates the extent to which the church had embraced—and sought to define—knighthood.

Originally the Templars were just Payens and seven comrades. They lived on alms, which they begged from pilgrims and crusaders traveling to and from the Holy Land. But what they lacked in funds they more than compensated for in zeal. With the aid of the era's most powerful man, Bernard of Clairvaux (a future saint), they began an ascent that seems in retrospect rather like that of Microsoft today—especially given their evolution into the era's most powerful financial force, really Europe's first bankers, and their later breakup by the powers-that-were. They adopted and adapted the rule of the recently formed Cistercian order—a more severe version of the Rule of Saint Benedict— which meant extreme austerity and a white habit, although the Templars wore the famous red cross on theirs, which thanks to them, we imagine today as the garb of all crusaders. From a vow of poverty—and an actual condition of pauperism—they became within a century the wealthiest and most powerful institution in Europe, save for the Vatican itself.

In Bernard of Clairvaux (Clairvaux being the site of a monastery he founded) the Templars had the best possible ally. He has been called the "Second Pope" and "the greatest moral force of his day"—and a lot of other things less flattering. But whatever one thought of him, the force of his energy and the power of his intellect were undeniable. When, in his thirties, he took over leadership of the Cistercians, the order possessed just a handful of monasteries. By the time he died, just prior to his sixty-fourth birthday, he had personally established 163 chapter houses, and from those had come another 179. It's no wonder that the Templar spirit appealed to him and that the Templars responded to his brand of enterprising piety.

The Templars were exactly, perhaps perfectly, suited to their times. Piety and prowess were a powerful combination, and the Templars began to receive benefices from both temporal and ecclesiastical authorities, including exemption from all taxes, with the result that they became fabulously wealthy and almost immediately began to alienate local church officials and lesser political leaders. With Bernard and successive popes on their side, they were immune from attack for the better part of two centuries, during which time they stood as exemplars of the religious version of chivalry. Whereas it was the style for knights at court to wear finery and keep their hair long, the Templars dressed plainly and cut their hair short. Courtly knights—who were hardly sissified—developed personal habits more akin to our own, but Templars were prohibited from bathing, trimming their beards, or even cleaning their teeth. Some knights back in France and England interpreted the rules of courtly love as justifying adultery and fornication, but the Templars swore never to marry, never to lust, never to be anything but chaste.

This might all have been a cultish sham were it not for the fact that in war they were the first into battle and the last to retreat. In business they were both scrupulous and honorable. The heroism of the Templars in battle (they refused to be ransomed when captured, and they never apostatized) fulfilled Bernard's exhortation to them in *De Laude Novae Militiae,* or *In Praise of the New Knighthood*, as warriors battling for Christ (*militia Christi*) against the infidel Saracens, to remember how "blessed [it is] to die there as a martyr! Rejoice, brave athlete, if you live and conquer in the Lord; but glory and exult even more if you die and join your Lord. Life indeed is a fruitful thing and victory is glorious, but a holy death is more important than either. If they are blessed who die in the Lord, how much more are they who die for the Lord!"

This sounds a little like Mabel sending forth the local policemen to destroy the Pirates of Penzance, except that those Victorian constables are horrified when she calls for them "to go ye forth and die!" The Templars, however, were blissful, knowing—as Bernard had also told them—that a "Christian glories in the death of the pagan," and that the Christian soldier is guaranteed a place in heaven.

According to Desmond Seward, the Templar synthesis of monk and knight wedded ancient traditions with the New Dispensation: "Christ for Woden, Paradise for Valhalla." He goes on: "Again the syncretic genius of Catholicism harnessed a pagan hero cult—just as once it had metamorphosised gods into saints and converted temples into churches—transforming the ideal into a spiritual calling whose followers sacrificed their lives for Christ not only in the monastery but on the battlefield with a startling mixture of humility and ferocity." This may make them appear to have affinity with Al Qaeda, but they were not so narrowly fixated on dying for the cause—and not at all on the murder of innocents. But war was war and innocents did die.

The Templars emerged in the decades after the great success of the First Crusade—the "liberation" of Jerusalem in 1099. The report of this "triumph" had electrified European public opinion and was hailed as a great event: the sure hand of God in history. But many a veteran of the battle found it hard to discern a divine influence. The city and its inhabitants, whether Muslim or Jew, had been torched and butchered—seventy thousand had died, and the streets had literally become streams of blood. In the moment it may have seemed almost right—they were Christians reclaiming the city of Christ, but reflection and conscience haunted the warriors. The screams of dying women and children echoed in memory, even as they watched the new European "kings" of Jerusalem, Antioch, and the other crusader states "going native," dressing in burnoose and slippers with turned-up toes, reveling to the songs of Arab musicians and the dancing of Saracen maidens. The Templars—those, that is, who would become the first of that order—could see that things had gone terribly, terribly wrong. Their response was twofold. First was religious chivalry, by which they limited their ferocity strictly to the armed enemy, applying the church's doctrine of the Truce of God, under which non-combatants were protected, to infidels as well as to believers. Second, the Templars were diligent in their defense of Christian institutions. It wasn't enough to protect the shrines and the pilgrims; they would also be a bulwark for the church and their order. As fate would have it, this would be their downfall. Everybody admired their heroism, but eventually too many came either to fear or to covet their power, their wealth, their mystery.

The Templars believed they had important things to protect, and their zeal in protecting them led to measures of secrecy that to this day fire the imaginations of both scholars and kooks. Toward the end of the thirteenth century, when the jealousies of the order's enemies reached the level of popes and kings, charges were brought against them that were almost entirely specious but which the Templars could not refute because to do so would have been to violate their vows of secrecy. They became victims of a legal system that was the mirror image of our own, meaning that everything was in reverse. They were accused of sodomy, blasphemy, apostasy, and thievery, and instead of the presumption of innocence, they were assumed culpable, most especially because, initially, they were silent in the face of the charges. The silence did not last, though, because the Templar prisoners were tortured without mercy. Torture was justified under the law since it was the only way the accused could be made to give evidence. This all came after the entire Templar order resident in France was seized on a single day, Friday, October 13, 1307, and some think it was the beginning of the association between the sixth day and triskaidekaphobia.

There were "confessions" and there were recantations, and the process of trials and retrials dragged on for several years, until fifty-four Knights Templar were burned at the stake on May 12, 1310. All Templar wealth and property were seized and divided up among princes, priests, and other "military" orders (most notably the Hospitalers). But this was not quite the end.

Among those who had recanted was the last grand master of the order, Jacques de Molay. (His name may sound familiar. If you come from an area where the Masonic order is popular, you'll recall that its youth organization is called DeMolay.) Along with Geoffroy de Charnay—of shroud fame and the author of one of those manuals on chivalry—de Molay was burned, in March of 1314; as the flames consumed him he famously cursed his persecutors, Philip the Fair of France and Pope Clement V, both of whom died within the year. But this is still not the end.

They say that on the eve of the arrests (or on the eve of the executions) a wagon loaded with Templar treasure left France; that the treasure was not worldly, but was in fact the Holy Grail, or the Ark of the Covenant, or both; that the Templar remnant took this mysterious treasure by ship to Canada (nearly two centuries before other European explorers); and that the Templars walk among us today (rather like the Grail guardians in Steven Spielberg's *Indiana Jones and the Last Crusade*), still protecting their secrets and awaiting a final vindication in God's good time.

However apocryphal their tales or apocalyptic their destiny, the Templars have a way of taking hold of the imagination. And it was always so. They attracted the best men to their cause, although not all those good fellows were comfortable actually living as Templars. William Marshal was a Templar, but he did not reveal his membership in the order until the final moments of his life, when he asked on his deathbed to be dressed in the Templar uniform he'd never worn until then.

The Flower of Chivalry

Although the great William Marshal will be part of the focus of this book's fourth chapter, we need to consider him here as an example of how the prowess of a knight was tested and refined in the great medieval sport—the tournament.

In the various cinematic versions of Camelot, or even of the days of Richard the Lionheart, tournaments are depicted as rather jolly sporting events. In *Knights of the Round Table* (1953), Lancelot and the other knights have spirited jousts, and their mêlée is a hilarious pillow fight. In the later Middle Ages this might have been accurate, but in Arthur's time there were no tourneys nor were there jousts. As we've noted, horsemen of the fifth century rode without stirrups, an essential element in jousting, since you cannot receive a lance blow and stay horsed without stirrups. Even the self-consciously gritty and portentously "realistic" *Excalibur* (1981) has its jousting knights in spurs and stirrups, its castle at Camelot decked out as though set up for a children's book (*The Medieval Castle Pop-Up Book*, perhaps), and its gleaming Round Table the envy of any modern multinational's boardroom. The mêlées of the first tournaments that did occur, nearly six hundred years after Arthur, were far from the tame affairs shown in most movies. One historian of the period half jokingly referred to *Monty Python and the Holy Grail* (1975) as the most accurate depiction of the Middle Ages to date, but that is simply a lamentation, given the sorry state of celluloid historicity. After all, the Pythons begin their wacky tale with the caption: "England, 932 AD." It's a totally incongruous date for Arthur, but meant, perhaps, to indicate that the events parodied are from before the Norman Conquest. What makes the Python movie "realistic" is all the mud and tooth decay.

But, really, you have to give Hollywood a pass on this one, since the earliest writers of Arthurian romances (the sources for Malory's *Le Morte d'Arthur*, Hollywood's Arthurian Bible), such as Chrétien deTroyes, also depict tourneys at Camelot. But no film has ever shown the tournament as it really was, perhaps until the fabulously silly and anachronistic *A Knight's Tale* (2000)—a low standard of accuracy indeed.

The tournament began as a medium for training and taming knights-errant. It had, in other words, the dual virtues of providing a means both of testing a knight's prowess and of expiating his violent energies. Tournaments were wildly popular in their day, but they were also controversial and precipitated an international debate then much as Ultimate Fighting has today. A number of American governors, legislatures, and mayors have banned from their jurisdictions this "new" no-holds-barred style of fighting, because the danger to the participants is thought to be too great. Boxing, full-contact karate, tae kwon do, and even tackle football can and do lead to injuries, some of them quite serious. But Ultimate or Tough Man or Cage Fighting, call it what you will, is, its critics assert, so violent and predatory that nobody wants it to happen in their state or city or town, except the audiences.[‡] In fact, although Ultimate matches are full out and often bloody, they usually end quickly, thus saving participants the brain damage that boxers can receive over the course of many rounds of tactical pummeling.

Henry II banned tournaments from England—as had all of his predecessors since 1066—for similar reasons. So right away you know the original mêlée was no pillow fight. Pope Innocent III denounced the tourney, and the ecclesiastical ban was not lifted until 1316, by which time, you might say, the Battle of the Little Big Horn had become Buffalo Bill's Wild West Show. But during Henry's time the tournament thrived elsewhere, and there was even a pro tour of sorts. Henry may have refused to allow tourneys in England, but he had no objection to—or, anyway, did not prohibit—his eldest son, Young King Henry, jousting on the Continent with his friend and mentor, William Marshal. Two of Henry's other sons, Richard and Geoffrey, also competed in tourneys, and Geoffrey was killed in one.

Young Henry was probably a force for transforming the tournament from a rather limited military maneuver into a larger-scale engagement. He had the wealth to do it. He recruited and paid

---

[‡] Since this book's first edition, the CBS television network has begun broadcasting mixed martial arts bouts on a regular basis. The most common word employed by the media to describe these programs is "barbaric."

handsomely the best knights he could find, and they fought for real. The victors could claim spoils in this mock war, including horses, weapons, money (in the form of ransom for captured knights), and even the most precious commodity of all, land.

This was no medieval version of paintball.

At a tournament in 1175, one French count led a "team" of nearly two hundred knights and more than a thousand foot soldiers. Not for nothing did some knights-errant despair that the big-money guys were destroying the integrity of the sport.

William Marshal was the star of the twelfth-century tourney tour; he was a kind of Michael Jordan and Tiger Woods rolled into one. At one point in his career, which included politics as well as combat, he fielded offers from numerous counts and kings all bidding outrageous sums for his services. (There was money, of course, but one bidder also threw in a daughter to sweeten the pot.) We have the details of some of the tourneys William fought in, thanks to a biography of him written shortly after his death—a rare document indeed for its day, and, for us, one of inestimable value.

William Marshal (the Anglicized version of Guillaume le Maréchal—remember that at this time the "Normans" in Britain were more French than English) has been called the "Flower of Chivalry." Certainly no other knight cut quite the same figure during chivalry's formative period, and his career gives the impression of a modern-day athlete turned politician, a phenomenon even more common then than it is today. Historian Richard Barber notes that the "pattern of early training and tournaments leading to real warfare, and retirement from the battlefield to politics, is typical."

Marshal was a knight-errant who made his name as the most formidable of "tourneyers," taking the field against many of the most renowned men—knights and kings—of his era. From most of them he won land and property as well as the fame and honor that came from his victories, and he rose from being one of those lack-land younger brothers, who as we know were knighthood's wellspring, to being Regent of England. Along the way he married into a wealthy family and became counselor to half-a-dozen crowned heads—royals who were often warring with one another. Despite divided loyalties and constant dangers, he managed to come through it all safely and to die in his own bed "full of years and honour."

At one point he spent nearly two years "on tour," traveling from one tournament to another, capturing more than a hundred knights (in partnership with his friend Roger de Gaugi), and becoming a wealthy and celebrated idol of the masses.

If we were to believe Hollywood, you might think eleventh-century tournaments were fairly civilized affairs in which a handful of armored knights rode in the lists—the football-field-long tracks cleaved by dividers, on either side of which the mounted combatants charged one another, lances lowered. In the later Middle Ages, yes; however, in Marshal's time, the main activity was the mêlée. (Jousting went on, but as a kind of under-card to the main event.) These mass brawls might involve scores, hundreds, even thousands of knights in pitched battles with real weapons. Reforms eventually led to the use of dulled swords and blunted lances and then even pillows. But every time William Marshal rode into a mêlée, he did so at serious risk to life and limb. It wasn't until the thirteenth century that jousting and other forms of individual combat became the norm.

The mêlée itself would be held in the hills and fields outside of town and would rage on for a whole day. Then the battered and bloody warriors would repair to local taverns for food and especially drink—tournaments were good for business—and then, exhausted, they would sleep. In the morning they'd rise and do it all over again, all three thousand of them. Men were often badly wounded and some died. How else could it be when real weapons were used and any flesh wound was liable to get septic? But it's important to stress that death and dismemberment were not the point of tourneying. Far from it, since you couldn't collect ransom from or for a corpse. But these guys loved to fight. They thrived on the physical stresses and emotional highs of combat, and there was probably as much laughing in the mêlée as screaming and cursing.

Today someone of Marshal's multifarious talents would certainly have an agent to negotiate among the many offers he received from the great lords who sought his service. But in 1180 (some say 1182) he surprised them all by taking a kind of early retirement (he was in his mid-thirties) and going on a pilgrimage. He was fed up with the high life. For a decade prior he had been advisor to Young King Henry, and that job had ended badly. The prince had a young wife, Margaret, who was the daughter of the French king, Louis VI. (Medieval royals were often closely, oh-so-closely, related. Young Henry's mother, Eleanor of Aquitaine, had been Louis' first wife. Her granddaughter, Blanche, would eventually marry Louis' great-grandson, Louis VIII.) A rumor began circulating around Normandy that Margaret and Marshal were having an affair. The Young King wasn't sure what to believe and that made William livid. In the presence of the prince, he challenged all comers to a trial by combat, and when none took up the challenge—why would they?—he was vindicated. But he was also sick of the whole business and went into his short-lived retirement, a sort of hybrid of an undefeated heavy-weight boxer and a highly respected elder statesman.

His great years were ahead of him, but never again would he be so crowned with glory. With his death, knighthood and chivalry would begin a slow slide into parody and satire. In retrospect, the Age of Chivalry seems to have ended just as it was beginning.

· · ·

By the end of the fourteenth century, the knights' importance in civil society had declined to the point that their chivalric code was the only thing of substance about them that survived, rather like the Cheshire Cat's smile. However, in the scheme of things, it was a long decline: tournaments went on for centuries, in fits of decay and revival. Nostalgia for the Age of Chivalry became a powerful romantic enchantment of the European imagination—so much so that by 1615 Miguel de Cervantes Saavedra's *Don Quixote* became a sensation precisely because it mocked the popular romances. Yet even Cervantes, who certainly did take a derisive tone toward much of seventeenth-century institutional life, felt the magnetism of the knight's calling. Yes, poor old Alonso Quijano, the man of La Mancha, is a comical figure. But he's a tragic figure as well, not because he tilts at windmills, but because his quest for fidelity, prowess, generosity, courtesy, and honor is undertaken in a materialistic world that has grown indifferent to knightly virtue. As Marshal might have quipped with a sigh:

"*Plus ça change.*"

CHAPTER THREE

The Gentleman

A Singular Sanity

*Somebody has said, that a king may make a
nobleman, but he cannot make a gentleman.*

–EDMUND BURKE, "LETTER TO WILLIAM SMITH" (1795)

There is much that could be written about the history
of the idea of the gentleman, but a single sentence
says most of what needs to be said. There have always
been two senses of the word itself—*the fine man of high birth and
the fine man of good character*—and the latter sense has always been
the more important.

According to Philip Mason, the notion of the gentleman in
England was assumed by most to be the natural province of the
wealthy. But there was always more. To nearly everyone it also
meant "a standard of conduct, a standard to which the best born
did not always rise, and which even the humblest might sometimes
display." Shirley Robin Letwin went even further. She argued that
"the definition of a gentleman as a 'man of ancestry' was always rejected by some and never completely accepted by anyone." This is
not a matter to be simplified by claiming that because there was
near universal recognition of this moral component, the gentleman

has always been defined without regard to social or economic status. No, history clearly shows a persistent assumption—call it a benefit of the doubt—that a man "to the manor born" was *ipso facto* a gentleman. Still, Mrs. Letwin was on the mark, I think. Two distinguished antecedents support her view: Richard Steele, writing in the *Tatler* in 1710, claimed that the "Appellation of Gentleman is never to be affixed to a Man's Circumstances, but to his Behaviour in them." And Oliver Goldsmith, writing in 1762 (*The Citizen of the World*), insisted that the "great error lies in imagining that every fellow in a laced coat is a gentleman." *Quod erat demonstrandum.* But the eighteenth century is already far ahead in our story.

There were gentlemen, although not known by that name, in ancient Greece and Rome. (One scholar has even asserted that the Egyptian Ptah-Hotep's *Instructions*, presumably history's oldest book, contains counsel about "gentlemanly" decorum.) Authors such as Plato and Aristotle, Cicero and Marcus Aurelius conjectured that the best citizens are vivacious, athletic men ready and able to fight to preserve the state and to uphold the true and the beautiful. As Juvenal so famously put it in the tenth of his *Satires*: "*Orandum est ut sit mens sana in corpore sano.*" After we *pray for a sound mind in a sound body*, the Roman poet goes on, we must beseech the gods to give us "a heart that fears not death, deems morality one of nature's gifts, can endure any kind of hard work, knows no anger and covets naught, and thinks the labors and hardships of Heracles better than lovemaking, feasting, or relaxing."

As we shall see, such sentiments—although clearly not the practical inclinations of most gentlemen—were remarkably influential ideals beginning in the sixteenth century and culminating in the nineteenth. As noted at the end of the previous chapter, by 1500 the institutions of chivalry had mostly faded away, but the aspirations of the sort of men who once sought knighthood did not disappear. The model of the true knight was gradually supplanted by the *beau ideal* of the complete gentleman, which—arguably—reached its zenith during the long reign of England's Queen Victoria. She was queen for sixty-four years and died in 1901, but the end of her era probably came at some point in the fateful years between 1914 and 1918, when chivalry seemed to so many to be yet another casualty of the Great War.

This is a short history—of telegrams and snapshots. Still, I acknowledge that it is a far leap from the Age of Chivalry to the Victorian Era. There were strides in between. At the very start of the Renaissance, for example, we find the gentleman vividly described—from several points of view—in Chaucer's *Canterbury Tales* (circa 1400). Chaucer's friend John Gower (who died in 1408) wrote that the best man "schal desire joie and merthe, Gentil, courteis and debonaire / To speke his wordes softe and faire."

As early as the late thirteenth or early fourteenth centuries, "gentleman" was probably in common use in both its senses; we know this in part because Chaucer expends so much effort debating the two meanings. He describes the teller of the very first of his tales as "a verray, parfit gentil knight," a lover of chivalry, truth, honor, and courtesy, but his clearest definition of the word comes through the mouth of the very opinionated Wife of Bath. She was married five times, so her knowledge of men is keen:

> But, for ye speken of swich gentillesse
> As is descended out of old richesse,
> That therfore sholden ye be gentil men,
> Swich arrogance is nat worth an hen.
> Looke who that is moost vertuous alway,
> Pryvee and apert, and moost entendeth ay
> To do the gentil dedes that he kan;
> Taak hym for the grettest gentil man.
> Crist wole we clayme of hym oure gentillesse,

Nat of oure eldres for hire old richesse.
For thogh they yeve us al hir heritage,
For which we clayme to been of heigh parage,
Yet may they nat biquethe, for no thyng,
To noon of us hir vertuous lyvyng,
That made hem gentil men ycalled be,
And bad us folwen hem in swich degree.

It's not easy these days to plumb the depths of Middle English, but the Wife's intent is clear enough: the man who does "gentil dedes"—gentlemanly (or lofty, elevated) deeds—is more possessed of *gentilesse* than is the man descended out of "old richesse." That this is an established theme in Chaucer surely reflects a cultural conviction of long standing, and anybody who asserts that an implication of virtuous behavior in the word's usage is a recent veneer is clearly mistaken. Still, as Edwin Harrison Cady wrote more than fifty years ago, "failure to distinguish clearly between objective class [the nobleman] and ideal concept [the noble man] has often bewildered theorists of the gentleman."

At the same time, it's fair to say that Chaucer's views of chivalry and courtly love are somewhat jaundiced. He, no less than the writers of medieval manuals of chivalry and courtly love, was aware of the leaden hypocrisy oppressing everyday life.

Uomo Universale

At least until the nineteenth century, the term "gentleman" had a quasi-legal status. In France, for instance, the Estates-General regularly reported to the king on the number and privileges of the various types of *gentilhommes*, according to the *Code de la noblesse*.

As a rule, the traditional English gentleman was highborn. This follows from the fact that the word *gentle* originally meant to raise to a high position, to ennoble. *The Shorter Oxford* definition runs thus: "**1** A man of gentle (orig. noble) birth. In later use, a man of good birth (according to heraldic interpretations, one entitled to bear arms) who is not a nobleman. . . . **2** A man who demonstrates his gentle birth by appropriate behaviour or moral qualities, e.g., chivalrous conduct, consideration for others, sense of honor, etc.; *gen.* A man (of whatever rank) who displays such qualities."

This last sentence is the theme of this book, of course, but for centuries, a gentleman was legally a man who had won, either by birth or by service, the right to bear arms on behalf of the king and who had the right, consequently, to have his family name memorialized in a coat of arms. "Gentle" was a verb. A king or a baron could "gentle" a vassal—raise him up to a special status, making him refined, no longer base.

The word itself inheres a fundamental sense of moral worth: to be a gentle person was to have achieved social status, to be sure, but that status derived from the qualities of courtesy, charm, grace, and even beauty. This last is nowhere more familiar than in the ancient story of "Beauty and the Beast" in which the Beast's nobility (his ironic beauty) is entirely a hidden—which is to say an *essential*—thing. He is courteous, a fine gentleman in many ways, but becomes complete—*compleat*—only when he loves Beauty, at which point he becomes beautiful too.

Now jump ahead to the Age of Shakespeare, to the Bard himself and the courtier-poet Sir Philip Sidney. What were the elements of the Elizabethan view of the gentleman? According to Cady, they were "virtue and learning and wealth—wealth for leisure and the display of liberality." These qualities were hammered home, often without subtlety, through a veritable barrage of what are called "courtesy books."

A bane of our own time is the plethora of self-help books, themselves the mass-culture manifestation of a therapeutic worldview. But in the sixteenth century a surfeit of "courtesy books" appealed to the heroic and practical ambitions of men. One such book stands out above them all: *The Courtier* by Baldassare Castiglione. Its influence was powerful, international, and enduring.

Castiglione's *Courtier* (*Il Cortegiano*), written in the first decades of the 1500s, was influential throughout Europe and the British Isles. Presented as a dialogue among friends at the court of the duke of Urbino, the book attempts to define the ideal courtier or gentleman. To begin with, there is some dispute among the conversationalists about the ideal gentleman's birth—some arguing that he must be noble, others that he could be base-born. But in the end they decide that his virtues are what count, not his birth, although they agree it is easier for one nobly born to be exemplary.

Our hero must be a warrior, which is essentially the same belief as the chivalric ideal of *prousse*, although he will probably not be a professional soldier.

In the final chapter of the present book, we will encounter one of Castiglione's most interesting ideas: *sprezzatura*. I mentioned the word in chapter one and defined it in passing as "the art of concealment." That's fine as far as it goes, but it must be further explicated. We need to understand that from the Renaissance forward the gentleman's grace, his ability to deport himself with a kind of effortlessness has been considered fundamental. A man's character must be—or seem to be—organic, if you will. There must be no artless pretension. The gentleman must consume his arts, digest them, and then possess them under his skin and sinew, deep in the marrow of his being. This requires dedication and long practice. Author Philip Mason puts it this way: "Perfection lies in achieving such a degree of mastery that everything seems easy and natural."

It is not difficult to apply this to the courtier's prowess in battle, but it pertains to his command of ideas as well. Castiglione's book is the play-by-play of a great verbal joust and reflects a substantial change in the vision of the best man. He remains something of a warrior, but he has become more intellectually serious and possesses an almost monkish commitment to learning. For Castiglione's courtiers, this new erudition must also include artistic knowledge and an ability to paint and make music.

Sir Thomas Hoby translated Castiglione's book into English in 1561. Castiglione himself had visited England and was already known in the Elizabethan court. It was an era that loved all things Italian. (Just think of the number of Shakespeare's plays that have Italian settings.) That *The Courtier* was widely read and imitated is not in doubt. It may even have been the age's most influential book, except for the Bible.

The New Man of Castiglione's *Courtier* is in fact the Renaissance Man, the *uomo universale*, a phrase first used by Leon Battista Alberti who died in 1472 and insisted that "a man can do all things if he will."

He was wrong, of course. Put aside the case of his later contemporary, Leonardo da Vinci—who came about as close as anybody ever has to being a master of all trades—the truth is that Renaissance Men, then and now, are mostly dilettantes; they and we are lucky if they're really good at just one of the things they profess to know how to do. But this is not to denigrate the idea of a solid liberal-arts approach to life.

Such an approach leads to the kind of man, who, if not exactly universal, is nonetheless a "man of the world." He has urbanity, a word that first began to be used in the sixteenth century and was the goal of education and the embodiment of the gentleman's attitude all the way through until the nineteenth century. It is the goal of a remnant of gentlemen even today. Toward the end of the sixteenth century—in 1586 to be exact—Angel Daye characterized urbanity (which, he noted, was not a word in common usage) as being "ciuile [civil], courteous, gentle, modest, or well ruled, as men commonly are in the cities and places of good gouernment," and such a view is really the same as saying an urbane man has civility.

Civility, civilization, civic, civil—each word has its root in the Latin *civicus*, citizen. The grandest of these, civilization, which stands for the collective refinements of a society, means in essence "life in the city," the assumption being that, from ancient times on, it was in the city that one found the best and most refined ideas, institutions, and individuals. Civilization and urbanity—which itself has the original meaning of city dwelling—are signal words of refinement, suggesting not only the sum of cultural knowledge but also of knowledge integrated: of refinement, sophistication, elegance, courtesy. To be urbane is to have these qualities plus suavity, which is the added dimension of *sprezzatura*. What's marvelous about *Il Cortegiano* is its attempt to get at the hardwood beneath the veneer of manners.

One of Castiglione's talking heads (Count Ludovico de Canossa) argues that "the principal and true profession of the Courtier ought to be that of arms," but his is a minor and fading voice. As one thinks about it, sadness creeps in. The chivalrous man was once respected—that we'll agree—but part of that respect was based on fear, and about this we may disagree—not that it once was so, but that it was a good thing.

Count Ludovico goes into one of those dissertations that Shakespeare so enjoyed presenting in parody—for instance, in the "To thine own self be true" speech of Polonius in *Hamlet*. Ludovico says the ideal courtier is neither too tall nor too short since either excites a "certain contemptuous surprise." Indeed, he says, a tree of a man and a stump of a man are equally considered monstrous. Better to be tall, though. Still—as we all know—very tall fellows are often dimwits.

Still, the man Count Ludovico is conjuring is comparable in our time to, at best, a special operations soldier—a Green Beret or a SEAL—or, at worst, a criminal. More likely he'd strike us today as the latter. From 1500 until 1900, the gentleman definitely had a mean streak. He was familiar with weapons and ready to use them, which more than a few gentlemen did in that tradition which is now blessedly behind us: dueling. We can understand why in Ludovico's day it was important for a man to keep in fighting trim: if a dispute was to be settled with swordplay, the fencers had better be able to thrust and parry without sucking wind after a minute or two. And that is possible only if one is sufficiently practiced to be able to remain calm and confident, which in any case were gentlemanly qualities secondary only to martial skill.

Ludovico also recommends tennis, which was literally part of his cross-training regimen. Fencing is excellent, and tennis is excellent, and equestrian sports are excellent, but a man can get bored doing just one of them all the time. He must, Ludovico insists, "always diversify . . . life with various occupations." He ought to live hard and play hard, but—and it is a big *but*—always appear "genial and discreet," so that "everything he may do or say shall be stamped with grace."

This is actually an epochal moment in *The Courtier*, if not also in the grand history of the gentleman. Next to speak, albeit briefly, is Cesare Gonzaga, and Castiglione gives him the best line of all: maybe these really were Cesare's own words, who knows? *You know*, Gonzaga says, *grace is the thing*, and:

> I find one universal rule concerning it, which seems to me worth more in this matter than any other in all things human that are done or said: and that is to avoid affectation to the uttermost and as if it were a very sharp and dangerous rock; and to use possibly a new word, to practice in everything a certain nonchalance [*una certa sprezzatura*] that

shall conceal design and show that what is done and said is done without effort and almost without thought.

Count Ludovico then picks up where he left off. But it's Gonzaga's words that echo, because he has done the count one better. "Grace" was a word they knew, but *sprezzatura* was a fresh idea. It is not certain if he or Castiglione came up with the coinage (Castiglione is usually given credit), but in one way or another the word has come to summarize the chivalrous man's game face: this quality of *sprezzatura* is close to what we now call *cool*, although the modern term hardly does justice to the antique.

And an antique it is, because Castiglione was really creating a (then) modern rendering of Cicero's *neglentia diligens*, or "studied negligence." Because this book's final chapter is devoted to a discussion of "The Art of *Sprezzatura*," I will not belabor its richness and importance here.

If Ralph Roeder is to be believed, Castiglione found a "deceptively simple" truth at the court of Elisabetta and Guidobaldo, the Duke and Duchess Gonzaga in Urbino:

> It was the expression of an urbane, mellow, and balanced spirit, of an exquisite mean which only a ripe culture could produce. A singular sanity was the achievement of that society; and in the evenings, when the company met for conversation, Castiglione listening for its common spirit through the rapid variations of an impromptu symposium, heard something far from commonplace—something familiar yet elusive—the fundamental undertone of the Normal.

Could this be what the proper courtier, the gentleman from 1500 to 1900, turns out to be: a *normal* man? In a way, although it matters what one considers normative. As Roeder says, the "circumstances which begot so normal a life were exceptional . . . a carefree and charmed life in the lee of the world." Castiglione's courtier was a man of the world, familiar with what was best in his world, with what made his world good. If he developed his body, his mind, and his character as reason and tradition dictated, then he could become a proper man.

And the lady a proper lady. Castiglione was something of a feminist. He saw the lady, complement to the gentleman, as a woman of culture and accomplishment. The third book in *The Courtier* is devoted to a comparison of virtues and abilities in which women are clearly the equals of men.

Character was the most important aspect of the whole man, and character is revealed in proper behavior, by manners, which after all are "but the convivial form of morals," Roeder writes, "the minor modulations of a major principle, modified by custom and social practice." Despite the slanders of his later critics, Castiglione's manners were the embrace of self-discipline and selflessness, not slick superficiality.

Not Passion's Slave

Of course this bifurcation of the social (outer) and the moral (inner) man was always a matter for concern and fun. It provided the tension at the heart of some of the West's great literary art, from *Canterbury Tales* and *Don Quixote* to so many of the works of Shakespeare. Shakespeare himself was educated, formally or informally, in classical works and probably read and appreciated Castiglione. Hoby's English translation of *The Courtier* was brought out three years before the Bard was born, in the year Philip Sidney turned seven.

When he was an adult and had received knighthood, Sir

Philip Sidney became a courtier to Elizabeth I, a poet of renown (although his work was circulated only in manuscript during his lifetime), and the very embodiment of chivalry—especially in his death. His friend, Fulke Greville, described Sidney's last moments during a battle in the Netherlands against the Spanish in 1586. Shot through the leg and drawn away from battle by his "rather furiously choleric than bravely proud" horse, the dying poet calls for water, which is brought to him: "But as he was putting the bottle to his mouth, he saw a poor soldier carried along, who had eaten his last at the same Feast, ghastly casting up his eyes at the bottle. Which Sir Philip perceiving, took it from his head, before he drank, and delivered it to the poor man, with these words, *Thy necessity is greater than mine.*"

The story galvanized Sidney's reputation as successor to the chivalrous French knight, Bayard, who had died two generations earlier under similar circumstances, and who was known as "*le chevalier sans peur et sans reproche.*" Each in his time was "the knight without fear and without fault."

Understand this: Sidney was considered the finest poet of his day. Shakespeare even cadged a phrase or two from the master, whose work, of course, he far surpassed. Sidney's poetry is middling, but it has power, especially in its spooky anticipation of his early death:

> Let tears for him therefore be all our treasure,
> And in our wailful naming him our pleasure.
> Let hating of ourselves be our affection.
> And unto death bend still our thoughts' direction.
> Let us against our selves employ our might,
> And putting out our eyes seek we our light.

That is the penultimate stanza of "Farewell, O Sun."

William Andrew Ringer Jr. writes that when Sidney died "the universities of Oxford and Cambridge and scholars throughout Europe issued memorial volumes in his honour, while almost every English poet composed verses in his praise. He won this adulation even though he had accomplished no action of consequence. . . . It is not what he did but what he was that made him so widely admired: the embodiment of the Elizabethan ideal of gentlemanly virtue."

Sidney personified *sprezzatura*, honor, scholarship, and a score of other chivalric qualities; he also represented a new element, one the earlier knights, whose society was more tribal, never did—service. A proper gentleman of the Renaissance was a courtier, one dedicated to king—or queen—and country; he was civic-minded.

In ancient Rome, a soldier who showed great courage in battle, especially if he had saved the life of a comrade, would receive a garland of oak leaves and acorns, called the *corona civica*. On the surface this meant simply the "city-dweller's crown," but the association with the award led, more or less, to the modern sense of *civic*, which suggests a citizen's altruistic actions on behalf of his community.

Many—if not most—of the authors of courtesy books were dispensing advice rather as Castiglione's contemporary Machiavelli had in *The Prince*. Their wisdom, such as it was, was intended to show young men how they might influence those above them, and so the books were partly advice on deportment and performance and partly counsels about politics and diplomacy.

In Sir Thomas Elyot's *The Governor* (1531)—actually *The Boke Named the Gouernour*—there is much advice in the manner of Castiglione, but with a much greater emphasis on the education of youth. *The Governor* is notable as one of the earliest works of what is known as vernacular humanism. Elyot's goal was the gentleman characterized by maturity, a word he brought into English: "Maturitie is a meane betwene two extremities, wherin nothing lacketh or excedeth: and is in suche astate, that it may neither encrease nor minisshe without losinge the denomination of Maturitie. The grekes in a prouerbe do expresse it proprely in two wordes, whiche I can none other wyse interprete in englisshe, but speede thee slowly."

"Speed thee slowly" is a fine motto in any age.

The raising up of men capable of understanding and fulfilling their duties to society was the theme of *Toxophilus* (1545) by Roger Ascham, a book superficially about longbow archery.

In *The Compleat Gentleman* (1622), Henry Peacham created a "modern" version of Cicero's *De Officiis* (*On Duties*), which, then as now, was a standard beginning Latin text. As Geoffrey Beard has written, the idea of a "Compleat Gentleman" was Greek in origin but found its apotheosis in the Renaissance: "It is said that the Emperor Charles V kept three books at his bedside: the Bible, Niccolò Machiavelli's *The Prince* . . . and Baldassare Castiglione's *Il Cortegiano*. . . . Castiglione's treatise, which had great influence, stressed the human values consistent with the attitude of any gentleman: of not hurting the feelings of others, of not making them feel inferior, of behaving with ease and grace, and of experiencing proper joy in the wonders of true love and service, one to the other."

Beard stresses what any student of the subject comes to understand: even in 1500 a man's interest in chivalry was at least partly nostalgic. But this should not lead us to conclude that the gentleman's dreams of virtue lacked seriousness. Like the code of chivalry before it, the emerging methodologies of gentlemanly behavior fairly defined the age.

Peacham's book, the title of which has been used often by other writers, including Mr. Beard and Daniel Defoe (of *Moll Flanders* and *Robinson Crusoe* fame), was, in full, *The Compleat Gentleman: The Truth of Our Times and the Art of Living in London*. Peacham begins by urging certain legal reforms with regard to gentlemanly status: that the gentleman be given certain emoluments from the state "before the common people." For instance: "His punishment ought to be more favorable and honorable upon his trial, and that to be by his peers of the same noble rank . . . . [A]nd then imprisonment ought not to be a base manner or so strict as others." His was not a democratic age.

The main part of the book is an annotation of Castiglione, albeit with some very English additions, such as this advice on fishing, an anticipation by several decades of Izaak Walton: "You must not keep your live baits all together, but every kind by itself, and feed them with such things they delighted in when they had their liberty." This meant your red worms should feast on "moss and fennel cut small," which is altogether a very enlightened view. A first-edition copy of *The Compleat Gentleman*, in "contemporary limp vellum" and with inscriptions on a flyleaf from the owner into whose hands the book had passed circa 1828, was recently offered at just under $3,000. A steal.

There is an interesting sidelight to the life of Henry Peacham. A portion of *The Compleat Gentleman* was devoted to the importance of the arts in a gentleman's life. Wishing to provide his novices with what amounts to an Elizabethan *Dummies' Guide* to contemporary literature, Peacham included a list of those who, "in the time of our late Queen Elizabeth, which was truly a golden age," were the greatest practitioners of "poesie with their pennes and practice." The list includes some names familiar to us today (Philip Sidney and Edmund Spenser, for instance), but excludes the name of William Shakespeare. Why? Because according to some, Shakespeare was merely the pen name of Edward de Vere, the Earl of Oxford.

Oxfordians, as they are known, gather dispositive evidence to support their claim that de Vere was the author of the greatest plays ever written, and the strength of their arguments rests largely on the accumulation of individual facts that taken alone would be unconvincing. They ignore the contradictory. Peacham's list of poets, which was itself lifted almost word for word from an earlier work (George Puttenham's *The Arte of English Poesie*) includes de Vere and excludes Shakespeare. But then he also fails to mention John Webster and Ben Johnson, both of whom were in their time more famous than those others whom Peacham singles out. An Oxfordian might argue that Webster and Johnson were excluded because they were still alive in 1622 when *The Compleat Gentleman* was written, but then how does one explain the conspicuous absence of Christopher Marlowe? Marlowe was by far the greatest Elizabethan dramatist in the eyes of his contemporaries, and he had been dead longer than either Shakespeare or Oxford when Peacham wrote his book. To Oxfordians, the segregation of Shakespeare is proof of de Vere's authorship of the "Shakespeare" plays, but they fail to speculate about Peacham's failure to name Marlowe. Perhaps the Earl of Oxford wrote his plays as well.

In any case, the man who wrote *Hamlet* was surely acquainted with discussions about the character of a gentleman and with the classical sources that had been bonded to chivalry in order to make this new exemplar. He caught perfectly the qualities of this man, expressed by Hamlet about his friend Horatio:

> Since my dear soul was mistress of her choice
> And could of men distinguish, her election
> S'hath sealed thee for herself, for thou hast been
> As one, in suff'ring all, that suffers nothing;
> A man that Fortune's buffets and rewards
> Hast ta'en with equal thanks; and blest are those
> Whose blood and judgment are so well commedled
> That they are not a pipe for Fortune's finger

To sound what stop she please. Give me that man
That is not passion's slave, and I will wear him
In my heart's core, ay, in my heart of heart,
As I do thee.

As in so much of Shakespeare, we hear echoes of the compleat gentleman's heroic, Stoic virtues: at heart a prince, but a plain man too; an artist and an athlete and a melancholy man resolved to treasure fleeting happiness. Above all he is a man of honor dedicated to duty and ready to die to fulfill it. And, as it happens, he's pretty good with a sword.

Lord Chesterfield

In less than a century, this heroic aspect of the gentlemanly character would begin to be lost in the mystification of mere manners.

In the 1720s, William Darrell wrote in *The Gentleman Instructed* that some gents manage to get by without benefit of courtesy books. These few are nature's own gentlemen: "Their Extraction glitters under all Disguises; it sparkles in Sackcloth, and breaks through all the Clouds of Poverty and Misfortune; there is a *je ne sçay quoy* in their whole Demeanour, that tears off the Vizor, and discovers Nobility, though it sculks incognito."

Of course even Mr. Darrell is quick to admit that if the qualities of gentlemanly refinement were inborn there would be no reason for manuals of courtesy such as his. Most of us "must acquire Behaviour like any other Art, by Study and Application."

His peculiar French notwithstanding, this notion of the *je ne sais quoi*, which is reminiscent of Castiglione's *una certa sprezzatura*, anticipates the soul—if we may call it that—of Lord Chesterfield's argument, for whom no gentleman could properly be "natural," since proper behavior is altogether artificial. Chesterfield (who met his maker in 1773) is the much-maligned author of a series of famous letters to Philip Stanhope, whom the very proper H. D. Sedgwick called Chesterfield's "young kinsman and godson" and others have termed his "natural" son, and who was in fact his bastard. This book of letters is notorious as much for the great Samuel Johnson's view of it as for the many disingenuous adages it contains. Chesterfield was keen to patronize—and then to have dedicated to his august self—Dr. Johnson's *Dictionary*. Johnson refused, telling friends that the word "patron" belonged in a sequence: "Pride, envy, want, the patron, and the jail." Whether or not the good doctor might have been more amenable to a grant at the start of his long labor, he certainly had no need of help to complete a work that was already finished. But the friends of Chesterfield pressed, and James Boswell records Dr. Johnson's famous dismissal: "Johnson having now explicitly avowed his opinion of Lord Chesterfield did not refrain from expressing himself concerning that nobleman with pointed freedom: 'This man (said he) I thought had been a Lord among wits; but, I find, he is only a wit among Lords!' And when his Letters to his natural son were published, he observed that 'they teach the morals of a whore, and the manners of a dancing master.'"

If there was ever a more poisonous comment about a book, I've not come across it. But was the good doctor correct?

First of all, Johnson always believed that a gentleman was born, not made. He looked upon his era's courtesy manuals the way we view the recent glut of self-help books as sound and fury, signifying nothing. Second, Johnson was genuinely offended by Chesterfield's avidity, so much so that one senses more in the famous words than just the great man's stubborn integrity. There was at work here a kind of pride that is not virtuous.

Still, Chesterfield was—for all his supposed influence upon

generations of young men—mostly the sort of courtier Shakespeare lampooned in the character of Osric in *Hamlet*. He says all the right things, behaves exactly as he ought to, and is utterly insincere.

There was something too glib about so much of Chesterfield's counsel. "I am convinced that a light supper, a good night's sleep, and a fine morning, have sometimes made a hero of the same man, who, by an indigestion, a restless night, and rainy morning, would have proved a coward." Spoken like a man who was never called upon to be brave. As if all a soldier needs to steel himself for battle are three squares and a decent bowel movement.

One can certainly see what John Henry Newman, writing in the next century, would find objectionable. Cardinal Newman's famous observation that a gentleman is one who never knowingly causes pain—which the cardinal did not *really* consider a virtue—comes from his reading of comments such as Chesterfield's that a gentleman "makes people pleased with him by making them first pleased with themselves." That's mere flattery. Newman knew, if Chesterfield did not, that heaven is not populated by "agreeable, well-bred men."

Indeed, the whole of Chesterfield's book is like the whole of the admonitions of Polonius to Laertes in *Hamlet*. Many of the observations taken out of the whole may sound just right, but in their human context they are a bitter parody. "To thine own self be true," Polonius says, and was ever better advice given? Yet we know the old schemer lacks commitment to the inherited wisdom he mouths. (The prince, on the other hand, speaks beautiful words, too, but they come from his heart, not his head: "To be, or not to be.")

"Never seem wiser, nor more learned, than the people you are with," Chesterfield told the young man whose mother he would not marry. "Wear your learning, like your watch, in a private pocket: and do not merely pull it out and strike it; merely to show that you have one." How paltry a compensation such words must have been for the love young Philip never received from the great "gentleman."

The Victorian Age

Joseph Addison, Samuel Richardson, and Richard Steele used their novels and essays as media for understanding and for satirizing the gentleman. Addison and Steele especially, in a series of articles in the *Spectator* (published in 1711 and 1712), helped to define the various aspects of gentlemanly virtue; however, with Chesterfield they created a dubious legacy because they pacified the gentleman.

The successor of the knight increasingly became a man with no martial skills and an accommodating attitude. Between 1800 and 2000, wars would spike revivals of the gentleman's embrace of militancy, but his once proud coat of arms was mostly degraded to a blazer patch, the profession of arms supplanted by "manly" sports of which he was often merely a spectator himself. This is hardly the end of the world—at least it was not then— and the new gentleman was not merely a dandy, "a Clothes-wearing Man," as Thomas Carlyle described the wholly denatured knight, "a Man whose trade, office, and existence consists in the wearing of Clothes. Every faculty of his soul, spirit, purse, and person is heroically consecrated to this one object, the wearing of Clothes wisely and well: so that as others dress to live, he lives to dress." But although he had become more of a lover, the Victorian man was, speaking in the broad measure of history, remarkably domesticated—and more of a monk. The Victorian gentleman was astonishingly well versed in the classics; he was only rarely a fighting man.

On the other hand, recognition of a man as a gentleman became more democratized. Education and refinement became the primary standards by which a man was judged, regardless of his birth.

No doubt it is because we are closer in time to the Victorians that we observe their awareness of class more clearly than we do that of the medievals. This is due in no small measure to the nature of the literary record from the two ages. Most educated people have read—or seen film versions of—some of the works of the great Victorian writers, whereas few have read anything actually written in the Middle Ages. In any case, it does not matter if you are a close reader of medieval texts, since those books and poems and plays are by and large lacking in the kind of sociological detail about which nineteenth-century writers were quite obsessed. The names of the great authors of the early to late 1800s, especially in England, evoke the upstairs-downstairs, town-and-country, gentleman-and-bounder fixations of the age: Carlyle, Tennyson, Arnold, Newman, Coleridge, Scott, Eliot, Gilbert and Sullivan, Thackeray, Fielding, Dickens, Disraeli, Hughes, the Brontës, Trollope, Meredith, Butler, Gissing, Ruskin, Kipling, and Chesterton.

Thackeray, who never could quite see himself as a true gentleman (he argued with Dickens that a writer can never be one), remarked during a lecture that to be a gent is "to have lofty aims; to lead a pure life; to keep your honour virgin; to have the esteem of your fellow-citizens and the love of your fireside; to suffer evil with constancy; and through evil or good to maintain truth always." Although he was not one of Thomas Arnold's students at Rugby, Thackeray's was a very apt description of the great schoolmaster's "muscular Christianity."

The greatest schoolmaster of his age, Thomas Arnold believed that "character training" was the essence of education and that the goals of the program at Rugby, where he was headmaster, were, first, that a boy should be a Christian, second, that he should be a gentleman, and third, that he should have knowledge of the classics. (Of his son, Matthew Arnold, it has been said that he stood for disinterestedness rather than partisanship, cosmopolitanism rather than provincialism, and traditionalism rather than faddism, which makes him the very model of the modern gentleman, though not exactly his father's boy.) As Thomas Hughes has Squire Brown, father of the hero of *Tom Brown's School Days* (1857), say: "If [Tom will] only turn out a brave, helpful, truth-telling Englishman, and a Christian, that's all I want."

Thanks in part to Arnold, the tradition of classical education thrived in England and in North America. As a result, the ancient Greeks and Romans, especially the Stoics—where do you think that "stiff upper lip" comes from?—had considerable influence upon Victorian gentlemen, whereas they had little or no influence upon the knights of the Middle Ages. Those knights were not particularly well educated (they were barely literate, in fact), and in any case the ancient writers had not yet been rediscovered, as they would be during the Renaissance. Throughout most of the eighteenth and nineteenth centuries, the education of gentlemen was largely a liberal education, rooted in study of the classics. Thus the American Founders "could command a gentlemanly tradition as intellectually respectable as it was long," in the words of Edwin Harrison Cady, who cites, as did the Founders, such classical influences as "Plato, Aristotle, and Isocrates; Quintilian, Cicero, Horace, Juvenal, Theophrastus, Plutarch, and Ovid." And Forrest McDonald, speaking of that American gentleman who was "first in war, first in peace, and first in the hearts of his countrymen," describes George Washington as a man passionate about a "classical" view of honor, especially as exemplified in

English playwright-essayist Joseph Addison's drama *Cato*. The real-life Cato was an exemplar of Stoic virtue—and a champion of the republic—in the time of Julius Caesar. He was the perfect subject for Addison, whose essays in the English periodicals the *Tatler* and the *Spectator* throughout the early years of the eighteenth century often promoted his view of the gentleman as a detached, broadminded Christian man of the world. *Cato* was Washington's favorite play, and he made frequent references to it throughout his life. From several of the characters in the drama, Washington gleaned the importance of honor. As McDonald writes: "True honor, he [Addison] says, 'though it be a different principle from religion, is that which produces the same effects. . . . Religion embraces virtue, as it is enjoined by the laws of God; honour, as it is graceful and ornamental to human nature. The religious man fears, the man of honour scorns to do an ill action.' The one considers vice as offensive to Divine Being, the other as something beneath him; the one as something forbidden, the other as what is unbecoming."

As I wrote in chapter one, the American Republic—at least as envisioned by its Founders—is the gentleman writ large.

At Rugby and then at Cambridge and Oxford, at American preparatory schools and then at Yale and Harvard, education meant gentlemanly formation. This is why the most famous of all Victorian pronouncements about the gentleman is contained within a book entitled *The Idea of a University*.

John Henry Newman (1801–1890) was of a class of Englishmen who in the nineteenth century were *ipso facto* gentlemen, at least when he was still an Anglican vicar. (He converted to Roman Catholicism in 1845.) Along with military officers, certain government officials, and, of course, the propertied aristocracy, clergymen fit the mold, as defined by author Samuel Smiles, whose *Self-Help* (1859) had in its time a popularity akin to Castiglione's *The Courtier*, though none of that earlier book's elegant resilience.

Smiles was perhaps a step above Polonius (although his frontispiece epigraph is the "To thine own self be true" quotation), but he was still a very able advocate of a kind of religion of individuality—albeit the Whig, not the Tory version. (The book was wildly trendy in Japan in the 1870s and remains popular with libertarians today.)

Cardinal Newman possessed as elegant a mind as anyone in the past several centuries; Smiles's glib tales of humble men rising to achieve greatness in government and industry must have seemed to him a bit shallow—especially considering that the story he lived by was of a king born in a stable who was rejected and executed, but then rose from the dead.

When Smiles wrote that "riches and rank have no necessary connexion with genuine gentlemanly qualities. The poor man may be a true gentleman—in spirit and in daily life. He may be honest, truthful, upright, polite, temperate, courageous, self-respecting, and self-helping; that is, be a true gentleman. The poor man with a rich spirit is in all ways superior to the rich man with a poor spirit," Newman may have agreed, but with some suspicion. And when Smiles wrote that

> . . . [g]entleness is indeed the best test of gentlemanliness. A consideration for the feelings of others, for his inferiors and dependants as well as his equals, and respect for their self-respect, will pervade the true gentleman's whole conduct. He will rather himself suffer a small injury, than by an uncharitable construction of another's behaviour, incur the risk of committing a great wrong. He will be forbearant of the weaknesses, the failings, and the errors, of those whose advantages in life have not been equal to

his own. He will be merciful even to his beast. He will
not boast of his wealth, or his strength, or his gifts. He
will not be puffed up by success, or unduly depressed by
failure. He will not obtrude his views on others, but
speak his mind freely when occasion calls for it. He will
not confer favours with a patronizing air. . . .

Newman may have been impressed, yet he surely was skeptical.

Newman, as much as anybody, understood the differences
between mere courtesy and real chivalry. Men such as Smiles,
Chesterfield, and Charles Kingsley (whose attack on Newman
led to the latter's greatest book, *Apologia Pro Vita Sua*) put forth
a particular view of gentlemanly decorum that for Newman
lacked . . . blood.

I do not mean that the intense and ascetic Newman believed
men needed to live more by the sword than by their wits. Only
that the gentleman described by these others was to him blood-
less, a whited sepulcher. Kingsley is often (incorrectly) given
credit for coining the term "muscular Christianity," but in fact it
was a term he disliked; he probably doesn't deserve to be associated with Chesterfield and Smiles. Still, Kingsley certainly was a
proponent of sport as a means of promoting manliness, which
Newman must have considered just more bluster.

Newman was a neo-Aristotelian, and he layered his description of the gentleman in the Eighth Discourse of *The Idea of a
University* with reflections that are at once candid and guarded,
much as was Aristotle's description of the *kalokagathos*, the "great-
souled man." Newman says that the ideal university (his thoughts
were originally lectures delivered in the early years after he became the first rector of Catholic University in Dublin) is not
meant to propagate "any narrow or fantastic type, as for instance,
that of an 'English gentleman.'" Rather, higher education is in

the liberal arts, knowledge meant to make a man free. Paradoxically, he calls the ideal curriculum "gentleman's knowledge."

He lists some of the characteristics of a gentleman: "a cultivated intellect, a delicate taste, a candid, equitable, dispassionate mind, a noble and courteous bearing in the conduct of life." I think it is clear that he considered this catalog admirable. That is—as he said—"as far as it goes."

Newman's portrait is by no means an endorsement of the man of manners, the one "mainly occupied in merely removing obstacles that hinder the free and unembarrassed action of those about him." That man is no Stoic; he is not a man committed to truth and beauty. He is an ambitious poseur. In his most elegant and Stoic conclusion, Newman insists that the ideal gentleman is "patient, forbearing, and resigned, on philosophical principles; he submits to pain, because it is inevitable, to bereavement, because it is irreparable, and to death, because it is his destiny."

Akin to Castiglione (and, again, to Aristotle), Newman's gentleman—now we're talking about the real thing, not the gentleman manqué—has the quality of "understatement" (the Greeks called it *eironeia*), which, according to Ronald Begley, is the same as Newman's sense of "reserve": "The portrait of the gentleman in the Eighth Discourse is one of several portraits from Newman's pen in which reserve figures prominently. Newman not only sketches a portrait of a reserved figure, but he also presents the sketch with reserve." Newman was not asserting a new version of *sprezzatura*, so much as demanding that we understand that what makes the true gentleman special is that which we can neither see nor define. It is something concealed and ineffable. It is that the gentleman "discerns the end in every beginning." He possesses the first among the theological virtues—prudence. He's a good fellow, the cardinal might have said; he's just not a saint.

Victorian America

Charles Dickens once quipped: "I do not know the American gentleman. God forgive me for putting two such words together."

Of course, he was wrong, although in the way certain talkative modern author-celebrities are often wrong: they thrive on provocation. Dickens traveled widely in the United States, and he met many of the nation's leading citizens. His comments were no doubt as much a reflection of his own struggles with gentlemanliness as of any ill will toward the Yanks.

From its earliest days, America has been an incubator of moral ambition. The aspiration to be good—to be the best—has run the gamut from the obsessive honor of dueling Tidewater patricians to the acrimonious moralism of New England preachers. The so-called Puritans referred to themselves as Goodman (for men) and Goody (for women). In reading American literature through at least the 1920s, one is struck by the number of times that the word "Sir" is used and by the number of times (countless) that men are called "gentleman," both amiably and bitterly.

America's founding generation had a healthy respect for religion (even if many of the Founders were themselves not devout), and in no country has there been more interest in the distinction between the Christian gentleman—which concept will be examined briefly in chapter six—and the "fine" gentleman.

In his tidy summary of civility as a theme in American writing (*The Gentleman in America*), E. H. Cady notes: "No one really pretended that every Christian man was automatically a gentleman. But it was held, most strongly at the popular level, that the true gentleman began by being a Christian."

The "fine" gent, on the other hand, was probably a faithless cad, and the litany of adjectives to describe him was seemingly endless: dude, swell, dandy, fop, spark, macaroni, blade, popin-jay, coxcomb. This was, as Cady suggests, a fashionable attitude in its way, and yet there were always American gentlemen who refused to subsume customary civility to religious creed. Urban-ity was not a strictly European attribute.

The appellation of "gentleman" was as much desired by Americans as it was by Englishmen. Writing in the May 1898 issue of the *Atlantic Monthly*, S. M. Crothers observed that

> . . . though the average man would not be insulted if you were to say, "You are no saint," it would not be safe to say, "You are no gentleman. . . ." [A] gentleman, if not the shape that every man actually is, is the shape in which every man desires to appear to others. It is needless to re-mark that this aspiration is not always adequately fulfilled . . . . All this is but to say that the word "gentleman" rep-resents an ideal. Above whatever coarseness and sordid-ness there may be in actual life there rises the idea of a finer kind of man, with gentler manners and truer speech and braver actions.

The divergence of this true gentleman from the fop is played out in the fluid genres of romance and satire, and American litera-ture bristles with the distinction, from Nathaniel Hawthorne's *House of Seven Gables* (1851) to Tom Wolfe's *A Man in Full* (1998).

The debate was also carried on at the very founding of the nation. It is the nineteenth- and not the eighteenth-century gentleman that I wish to conjure here. But it is worth noting that what defined our ideal man in 1900 had also defined him in 1800, and even in 1700. The long and entertaining correspon-dence between John Adams and Thomas Jefferson proves the point.

They were enemies at the dawn of the republic who became friends in the waning of their years. "Where Jefferson was anxious that the way be cleared for the true natural gentleman," Cady writes, "to rise and provide able leadership for democracy, Adams believed grimly that nothing on earth could stop their rise and only the firmest and canniest of governmental structures could contain both them and republican liberties."

The matter remains unsettled to this day and forms the basis for disputes between "liberals" and "conservatives"; between those whose preference is for democracy and those who believe in republicanism; between men who think mankind is perfectible and those who are certain that man is fallen.

On the question of differentiating the gentleman from the mob, nearly every prominent writer, thinker, politician, and celebrity of the last two centuries has had a say, from Ralph Waldo Emerson to Emily Post, from Robert E. Lee to H. L. Mencken. Ever the delightful cynic, Mencken defined a gentleman as "one who never strikes a woman without provocation." Which, as Cardinal Newman might have quipped, is good as far as it goes.

But Mencken stood at the end of a long line of commentators; anyway, he was twenty-one years old as the nineteenth century came to a close and derisive of every single aspect of American life, sacred and profane. That's his charm. (To be fair to him, Mencken said of himself: "It is inaccurate to say that I hate everything. I am strongly in favor of common sense, common honesty, and common decency. This makes me forever ineligible for public office.")

Less charming, but unfortunately more influential, was the sainted Emerson, the Sage of Concord, or, as the poet Allen Tate called him—and I think more accurately—"the Lucifer of Concord," a prime contributor to the devaluation of American character, a "light-bearer who could see nothing but light, and was fearfully blind." Few have been so prominent in the movement to make "gentleman" a democratic concept. Like Jefferson, Emerson was enamored of the notion of "nature's gentleman," but he gave the idea a positively Nietzschean interpretation: "Repose and cheerfulness are the badge of the gentleman, repose in energy."

Now that seems positively lighthearted until you realize that by "energy" he means force of will. "Power first," he elaborated in his essay "Manners," "or no leading class . . . My gentleman gives the law where he is; he will outpray saints in chapel, out-general veterans in the field, and outshine all courtesy in the hall." Meet the American *Übermensch*.

The trouble with Emerson is very much the trouble with Chesterfield. Aphoristic writers are often quoted with appreciation by people who have no grasp of the heart of the authors' actual philosophies. All Emerson's incessant tongue wagging about individuality really adds up to a ruthless selfishness that willingly tramples any tradition he finds inimical to his own pleasure. Witness the following scribbling in his *Journals*: "As long as our civilization is essentially one of property, of fences, of exclusiveness, it will be mocked by delusions. Our riches will leave us sick; there will be bitterness in our laughter; and our wine will burn our mouth. Only that good profits. which can taste with all doors open, and which serves all men." He out-Rousseaus Rousseau. He would have the gentleman be Savonarola.

Emerson gave lip service to the democratic character of gentility, and yet—despite his own patrician status—he was convinced that the rich lacked the proper spirit of, as he liked to call it, self-reliance. In a kind of mocking parody of Christ's warning about the difficulty of "rich" men finding heaven, Emerson assumed that the Brahmins of Boston and the Grandees of Charleston were less likely to have gentlemanly virtues than the salt-of-the-earth farmers and working men in post-bellum America. Had he lived to witness the *Titanic* disaster, he might have reconsidered.

Raising Titanic

On the night of April 14–15 of 1912, it was the middle- and upper-middle-class men who, statistics would indicate, behaved most like gentlemen: their survival rate on *Titanic* was lowest. Proximity to the lifeboats and a practiced aggressiveness—which nonetheless may not have been unethical—account in part for the better survival of first-class men; however, the gentlemen in second class almost certainly acted with the most courage, restraint, and self-sacrifice.

In James Cameron's *Titanic* movie, true grit is shown mostly among the third-class men, but on the real ship this may not have been the case overall. That there were heroic third-class passengers no one will doubt, but it is striking to learn that those men had a survival rate twice that of those in second class. Mr. Cameron makes bollix of the story by perpetuating the slander that the poor immigrants from steerage were actually locked below decks and thus prevented—often at gunpoint—from reaching the lifeboats. No such thing transpired, although the progress of passengers from the lower decks was slowed by difficulties of language, by their reluctance to follow the instructions they did understand, by their tendency to carry with them in the evacuation all the possessions they had brought on board, and finally by the sheer distance they had to travel to the ship's upper deck, the only area from which lifeboats could be manned. These obstacles make the survival of equal numbers of male and female passengers from third class all the more remarkable, especially given the striking disparity between the sexes in the other classes.

Nearly three times as many first-class women lived as first-class men. In second class, it was nearly five times. So for equal numbers of third-class men (seventy-five) and women (seventy-six) to have survived may indicate that a different set of "crisis criteria" were at work in this group. (Also conspicuous is the fact that all the children in first and second class—with but one exception—were rescued, but fully two-thirds of third-class children died, although the actual number of surviving third-class children was highest among the three classes.)

All this probably indicates a reversal of the popular version of the *Titanic* saga, the one embodied in Mr. Cameron's cinematic fantasy, which—as Stephen Cox describes it in *The Titanic Story*—is this: "if you have money, then you are very probably deficient in morality; and if you have morality, you are very probably low on cash." That's the received notion all right, but it is hardly the truth.

I have no doubt that at least a part of *Titanic*'s ongoing popularity is nostalgia. Much as was the case with the lore of chivalry and the allure of the Middle Ages, a modern industry has sprung up to satisfy our every nostalgic whim with regard to the Age of Victoria Regina. There is—to my knowledge anyhow—no organization comparable to the Society for Creative Anachronism, no group of Victorian activists attempting to recreate the latter half of the nineteenth century at the start of the twenty-first. But there is an active business providing Victorian-style wedding dresses and other clothing, which are useful at Victorian-style nuptials, that apparently many people choose, no doubt, because the collective memory insists marriages back then had more gravity and were more enduring. How many of our great-grandparents divorced?

Again, the Internet is our Baedeker and catalog. At vintagewedding.com, you can get the scoop on how to make 2009 seem like 1899. The wedding dresses offered there, and at a number of other retailers, are quite lovely, and I especially love the hats recommended for brides and bridesmaids. These days beauty is all about hair. But hats framed a woman's face in such a way that her loveliness was given a special elegance, one we rarely see anymore.

For very serious, academic information about the span of the queen's long reign, from1837 until 1901, students may consult victorianweb.com, a project organized by Professor George P. Landow of Brown University. Considering that its many essays come from mostly Ivy League contributors, the content of the Victorian Web, as it is more formally known, is remarkably commonsensical.

But my favorite Victorian site is Victorian Adventures (victorianadventures.com, of course). Among other things, this outfit runs a summer Victorian Day Camp, one for girls aged eight to twelve and one for teens. The younger group from a previous camp session is pictured in hoop skirts and bonnets, and the Victorian Adventures staff—they are a "Georgia-based limited liability company"—promise that campers will get a "glimpse into the life of a girl in the mid-1800s," presumably without smallpox scarring or outhouses.

Southern Honor

It would be wrong to imagine that America's conception of the gentleman has always had a democratic character. For one thing, the very notion presupposes inequality. For another, the English and French beliefs concerning "gentle" birth as a prerequisite came to North America with the earliest settlers. In churches there were special pews for the elite; at Ivy League schools the sons of gentlemen had their own section in college meetings. Still, from 1600 until the present, America never had anything like Europe's feudal system. Well, that's not quite true. There were the Dutch patroons of pre-Revolutionary New York, and, of course, the slave owners of the Old South. Yet men such as Stephen Van Rensselaer and Thomas Jefferson, respectively the most famous patroon and slaveholder in American history, were noted for their efforts to democratize the nation's life. Van Rensselaer founded the college that still bears his name and still offers education free to deserving students. As to Jefferson, it is sufficient simply to quote the epitaph he wrote for his own tombstone: "Here was buried Thomas Jefferson, Author of the Declaration of American Independence, of the Statute of Virginia for Religious Freedom, and Father of the University of Virginia."

Jump ahead now to America at the end of the nineteenth century. In 1885, more or less, a Harvard professor, himself born in the eighteen-teens or twenties, looked out upon the eager faces in the lecture hall at young men in jackets and stiff-collared shirts and dark ties, and said, "Probably none of you young men have ever even seen a gentleman." (Emerson had made a similar quip, saying that gentlemen are rare: "I think I remember every one I have ever seen.")

The anecdote is told by Henry Dwight Sedgwick, who was probably a student in that elderly professor's class and was sufficiently struck by the comment to write a book on the subject, *In Praise of Gentlemen*, published in 1935. "And now even the ideal is gone," Sedgwick observed gloomily, "like an old fashion in dress, not spoken of but to be laughed at."

There is in Sedgwick's version of the gentleman rather more of Chesterfield and less of Newman, or, as we shall see, of Robert E. Lee. He spoke of a Guild of Gentlemen—not latter-day Templars, mind you, not a cabal of scheming Masons, but a confederation of decent fellows, much as I remember my grandfathers (born in 1888 and 1890) to have been. These were men who possessed "courtesy, self-restraint, a nice regard to the rules of etiquette, a command of speech, an elegance of dress, a familiarity with the habits of the leisure class, a respect for appearances, for outside things, a desire to make the passing moment pleasurable."

I picture men in straw boaters punting on the Charles River on a late summer's afternoon; 1935 may as well have been1835. The Great War fades from memory, and the bad news has yet to come from Pearl Harbor. It is, you might say, perpetually December 6, 1941—or September 10, 2001. There is no reason not to swallow ever-greater helpings of democratic sludge and call it ambrosia. The world is so safe that the response to moral flabbiness is mere irritability.

Times change. I found myself chuckling the other day when I noticed the bumper sticker on the automobile ahead of mine: "Give War a Chance." Civil War veterans were few when Sedgwick wrote his book. American involvement in WWI had lasted barely two years; those veterans were in their forties and fifties and happy to recall the horrors of war nostalgically, convinced that it really had been the war to end all wars, and that they who once were warriors could forge their swords into fountain pens and watch the parade pass by. They were in the "lee of the world," like the conversationalists at Urbino in *The Courtier*.

The world changed so fast that it was transformed even as the old men died: Lee (1870) and Grant (1885), Sherman (1891) and Longstreet (1904). The officer as gentleman survived through the 1914–1918 war, and the Pershings and the MacArthurs were esteemed. But the fundamental association of combat with the chivalric ideal was severed. Worldwide there was a great sigh: good riddance! The "sword" became an implement of children's stories. Very few duels have been fought in the twentieth century.

Thank God, we may say, and who can argue? And yet with the pax comes a pox: honor has become indefensible. We swallow pride rather than stand up for it.

Obviously the needle indicating the temperature of my moral engine is tipping over into the red space, and it's as much for what's to come as for what I've written so far. What's next is a defense of the Old South, of that chivalric, gentlemanly sensibility that seems doomed by its association with slavery.

There has recently been some cleansing dialogue concerning the infamous N-word. I agree that no one who is not African American has any business ever using the word, and some of the best black minds reject using the word under any circumstances. It is a particular kind of ugliness that we can do something about; we can eradicate it by individual refusals ever to use the word. In a similar vein, I understand African American objections to the endurance of the Confederate stars-and-bars on state flags in the South. For them the Southern Cross is a purely racist symbol.

The trouble is that the flags have complicated antecedents, of which the association with slavery is only one. There is a danger that the rejection of a historical symbol can become the rejection of history itself—that the reduction of a complex symbol to a single connotation smears generations of men and women whose lives are of inestimable value. I think especially of Robert E. Lee.

I have not said it yet in this book and I will not say it again, but Lee was a compleat gentleman. (I disdain naming others, because I have no wish to become the Mr. Blackwell of this subject, yearly publishing my list of the Ten Best Gentlemen or Ten Worst Cads, the way Blackwell for years rated Hollywood's glamorous and ghastly.) Lee was not simply the South's paradigm of chivalry; he was America's as well. As Bertram Wyatt-Brown has written, Lee exemplified the "three graces of gentility": sociability, learning, and piety. And he was, of course, one of our greatest warriors. Like so many men of his era, Lee proffered his own definition of a gentleman:

The forbearing use of power does not only form a touchstone, but the manner in which an individual enjoys certain advantages over others is a test of a true gentleman.

The power which the strong have over the weak, the employer over the employed, the educated over the unlettered, the experienced over the confiding, even the clever over the silly—the forbearing or inoffensive use of all this power or authority, or a total abstinence from it when the case admits it, will show the gentleman in a plain light.

The gentleman does not needlessly and unnecessarily remind an offender of a wrong he may have committed against him. He cannot only forgive, he can forget; and he strives for that nobleness of self and mildness of character which impart sufficient strength to let the past be but the past. A true man of honor feels humbled himself when he cannot help humbling others.

We might be tempted to say that there are strong echoes here of John Henry Newman, except that Lee made these comments some years before Newman made his.

Here clearly was a man willing to fight for what he believed was right; we remember him as one of America's great warriors, even though Lee's embrace of the Confederate cause was never wholehearted. As has often been remarked, Lee was offered command of Union forces but took control of the Confederate Army of Northern Virginia instead, because he considered himself a Virginian more than an American. Virginia was to Virginians the center of the universe. According to Rollin Osterweis: "The Southern cult of chivalry developed principally from a fusion of the tradition of the 'Virginia Gentleman,' with those medieval notions best exemplified in the writings of [Sir Walter] Scott and with certain ideas drawn from the current fervor for Greece. A number of minor cults combined to make up the whole. These focused on manners, women, military affairs, the ideal of the Greek democracy, and romantic oratory. The planters believed that their society approximated the social order of the chivalric period." Like Washington and Jefferson before him, Lee cherished these conventions and like them he also condemned one part of the tradition: dueling.

Of all the aspects of antique chivalry, the *brittleness* of honor may be hardest to fathom. Edmund Burke lamented that ten thousand swords were not raised to defend the honor of Marie Antoinette, and we recall how William Marshal, when accused of adultery, called upon his enemies to defend their charges in a trial by combat. For nearly a thousand years men fought duels whenever the old escutcheon was blotted.

The first duel in America was fought in 1621, and the last— well, perhaps it has yet to be fought—although the practice seems to have disappeared after the Civil War.* "Judicial combat," as it was sometimes known—ironically, since it was generally illegal— was governed by the twenty-five rules of the Code Duello, established in Ireland just after the American Revolution. So popular did dueling become in the states, though, that in 1838 the governor of South Carolina, John Lyde Wilson, felt compelled to revise and update the code for a specifically American milieu.

---

* The list of American duelists is distinguished indeed: Button Gwinnett, signer of the Declaration of Independence; Vice Presidents Aaron Burr and Alexander Hamilton; future president Andrew Jackson; Senator Thomas Hart Benton; Commodore Stephen Decatur; Senators Henry Clay and John Randolph; Senator James Westcott; and assorted governors and justices. In 1842, Abraham Lincoln accepted a challenge from James Shields. Given the choice of weapons, Lincoln, ever the frontier ironist, at first opted for cow pies, which angered Shields all the more. So Abe chose cavalry swords. When Shields realized the 6'4" Lincoln's superior reach gave the future president a distinct advantage, the duel was postponed. Indefinitely.

The 1804 duel between Alexander Hamilton and Aaron Burr, fought along the banks of the Hudson River in Weehawken, New Jersey, is the most famous in American history. But many other prominent Americans also dueled. Andrew Jackson was nearly killed in a duel. Charles Dickinson shot at the future president but only wounded him. Jackson swooned and collapsed, but not before he aimed and fired. Dickinson fell dead, and a good thing too. He'd previously killed twenty-six of his fellow citizens in duels.

The code included provisions for apologies after the first shots were fired. If the quarrel was settled with swords, and the man challenged to the duel won but spared the life of the challenger, the dispute was settled—unless, that is, the challenger wished to revive it. "Rule 23. If the cause of the meeting be of such a nature that no apology or explanation can or will be received, the challenged takes his ground, and calls on the challenger to proceed as he chooses; in such cases, firing at pleasure is the usual practice, but may be varied by agreement." A sense of civilization is in there someplace. At least the Code Duello protected bystanders from barrages of bullets in taverns and on Main Street—until the Old West gunfight became popular, anyway.

But our beloved General Lee would have none of it. His sense of honor was exactly the old *franchise* of the knights, as we see in this excerpt from a letter he wrote to his son:

> You must study to be frank with the world. Frankness is the child of honesty and courage. Say just what you mean to do, on every occasion, and take it for granted that you mean to do right. . . .
>
> Never do a wrong thing to make a friend or keep one; the man who requires you to do so is dearly purchased at the sacrifice. Deal kindly but firmly with all

your classmates; you will find it the policy which wears best. Above all, do not appear to others what you are not.

If you have any fault to find with any one, tell him, not others, of what you complain; there is no more dangerous experiment than that of undertaking to be one thing before a man's face and another behind his back. . . .

Duty, then, is the sublimest word in our language. Do your duty in all things like the old Puritan. You cannot do more; you should never wish to do less. Never let your mother or me wear one gray hair for any lack of duty on your part.

If that sounds like Polonius, listen more carefully. This is a man speaking his *own* words from his *own* heart.

When Lee died, the *London Standard* wrote: "A country which has given birth to men like him, and those who followed him, may look the chivalry of Europe in the face without shame; for the fatherlands of Sidney and Bayard never produced a nobler soldier, gentleman, and Christian."

G. K. Chesterton called Lee "the last of the heroes." As the old general expired, his last words were, "Strike the tent!"

Manners over Man

Throughout the nineteenth and early twentieth centuries, the idea of the gentleman was vigorously debated and dissected—so much so that the concept began to suffer from being too familiar and too fastidious. (In a marvelous bit of ironic understatement, the author of the entry on the gentleman in the 1930 edition of *The International Encyclopedia of the Social Sciences* put it this way: "In general the plain man distinguishes morality from immorality; the gentleman distinguishes immorality from scandal.") The number of books and articles written about manliness and gentle-manly conduct was truly staggering, and there was a clear descent into legalism. In part, this was what caused uneasiness in Cardinal Newman.

But not all the many books were completely silly. Some were silly and sage at the same time. Among the most famous, at least in the United States, was *Etiquette* (1922) by Emily Post. Mrs. Post was quite as pompous in her rules for Americans as Polonius in his instructions to Laertes. Where Shakespeare's sly fool says: "Neither a borrower nor a lender be, / For loan oft loses both itself and friend, / And borrowing dulls the edge of husbandry," Mrs. Post wrote: "A gentleman does not, and a man who aspires to be one must not, ever borrow money from a woman, nor should he, except in unexpected circumstances, borrow money from a man."

One might heed such advice, even if one winks knowingly at the tediousness of the advisor. The old man's final gem ("This above all—to thine own self be true, / And it must follow, as night the day, / Thou canst not then be false to any man.") is good counsel, but Mrs. Post managed to do him better and define the American gentleman as well as anybody ever has:

> Far more important than any mere dictum of etiquette is the fundamental code of honor, without strict observance of which no man, no matter how "polished," can be considered a gentleman. The honor of a gentleman demands the inviolability of his word, and the incorruptibility of his principles; he is the descendant of the knight, the crusader; he is the defender of the defenseless, and the champion of justice—or he is not a gentleman.

Still, no matter how the early twentieth-century former

Colonials tried to style themselves as proper fellows, it was the English who continued to define the type.

In writing about the affection for British culture among Europeans, Ian Buruma says that it was not aristocracy they admired but "something more liberal and bourgeois" than "the gentleman, whom André Malraux once called England's *grande création de l'homme*. A bourgeois man with aristocratic manners, a tolerant elitist who believes in fair play: the image of the English gentleman, bred rather than born, appeals to snobbery and liberalism in equal measure." I'm not sure I agree with Mr. Buruma that snobbery and liberalism are properly contrasted as opposites, but I take his point.

Another British liberal, Harold Laski, best summed up this view: "The gentleman," Laski wrote, "*is*, rather than does; he maintains toward life an attitude of indifferent receptivity."

So far so good, but there is less here than meets the eye.

The gentleman, you see, "is interested in nothing in a professional way. He is allowed to cultivate hobbies, even eccentricities, but he must not practise a vocation. He must not concern himself with the sordid business of earning his living; and he must be able to show that, at least back to his grandfather, none of his near relations has ever been engaged in trade."

There is more—about riding and shooting and fly fishing—but these outdoor pursuits (as well as membership in a good club and the Conservative Party) cannot rescue the poor fellow described from our assumption that he is a ninny. Reading Laski's witty representation of the ideal, one is reminded of Cervantes' view of chivalry, that not too far beneath the veneer of sarcasm lay a more solid grain of admiration. Published in *Harper's* in 1931, "The Danger of Being a Gentleman," to which Laski gave the subtitle "Reflections on the Ruling Class of England," was imagined a decade before his nation's gentlemen fought the Axis in World War II, and it seems to me that his judgment of the gentleman's role in English society has been proved wrong by events during and after the war. Until his death in 1950, Laski was in the thrall of socialism, which helps to explain his bizarre claim that the gentleman is "too individualist to welcome organization and too self-confident to welcome ideas." This is not even a fair description of Bertie Wooster (the upper-class twit of the P. G. Wodehouse *Jeeves* books), let alone the men who crushed the Nazis and launched the modern corporation.

But it does help explain the truth of the first sentence of Shirley Robin Letwin's superb book, *The Gentleman in Trollope*:[†] "The gentleman has become a figure of fun." This is the fact I observed in the theater that day my son and I saw *Titanic*.

• • •

As we have seen, war has been an essential element in the history of chivalry. At the very start, the code was devised in large measure as a means of pacifying the ferocity that is potential in every warrior.

Strict adherence to a chivalric code was always more or less limited to the officer corps, but by 1900 that cadre was no longer limited to the sons of the aristocracy. (This is a theme beautifully explored in Jean Renoir's 1937 cinematic masterpiece, *La Grande Illusion*.) To be an officer was to be a gentleman—at least if you were a good officer—and through World

---

[†] Letwin's 1982 study of the greatest English novelists of the Victorian era is so much more than mere literary analysis. As one reviewer wrote: "Letwin is an American living in London who has a fondness for some British institutions and manners. But she gets exasperated when good old class–ridden England takes to the egalitarian bottle and has tipsy affairs with such foreign whores as socialism, sociology, scientism, and others who when you go to bed with them pick your pocket."

War I, and then especially during World War II, the men who served at the highest echelons of military leadership were often of humble birth. I cite Dwight David Eisenhower to prove the point.

Ike's father was a mechanic at a Kansas creamery, and the future Supreme Allied Commander's earliest memories were of him and his five brothers trying to scratch sustenance out of the dusty garden in back of their prairie home. He attended West Point not because he longed for a military career but because the education there was free. He was a student of modest accomplishments, and graduated in 1915, sixty-first in a class of 164. But the experience of military life and leadership so transformed him that when he attended the Army's Command and General Staff School in 1926 and then the Army War College in 1928, he finished first in his class both times. The rest is history.

Although Ike was, especially as president, often a "figure of fun," the dignity, restraint, and sense of honor he brought to the Oval Office were remarkable, especially by the standards subsequently set. He did not come to the presidency directly from war but from the leadership of Columbia University. He was a much more intelligent and studious man than he was given credit for by the media during his presidency and since, and he was a loving husband, father, and grandfather. That he was a warrior no one can doubt. As Chesterton observed (in *A Handful of Authors*), there is "no such thing as being a gentleman at important moments; it is at unimportant moments that a man is a gentleman." Ever the master of paradox, G. K. C. provides his own rejoinder: "At important moments he ought to be something better."

What is better than a gentleman? Well, like Ike, a gentleman warrior.

And that leads us to the next chapter.

CHAPTER FOUR

The Warrior

How to Die With Your Boots On

Malcolm: *Nothing in his life*
            Became him like the leaving it; he died
            As one that had been studied in his death
            To throw away the dearest thing he owed
            As 'twere a careless trifle.

Duncan: *There's no art*
           To find the mind's construction in the face;
           He was a gentleman on whom I built
           An absolute trust.

                        –WILLIAM SHAKESPEARE, *MACBETH* (CA. 1603)

It may or may not be obvious from what has gone before that the chivalric heritage of the compleat gentleman demands that even today he possess a martial spirit, but that is one of the major premises of this book; whether this literally means he must be a warrior, a latter-day knight—one ready, willing, and able to sacrifice his life in defense of honor—is what this chapter will consider.

It is as easy to state that the idea of the gentleman was born in the echo of the twelfth-century knight as it is difficult to assert that the twenty-first-century gentleman *must* be a fighter, a Lancelot, a Gawain. But it may very well be that the waning of the gentlemanly ideal is directly a consequence of the gentleman's pacification over the course of some seven centuries. Although it may be an overstatement, it seems likely that as the gentleman became less a warrior he became more a fop, a dandy, a fraud, a fool. And nobody aspires to be a fop except a fop. Literature is filled with stories of well-born villains and ne'er-do-wells who fail to fulfill their destinies or to command respect from their peers because they lack honor and courage, if not also prowess. Authors of every conceivable philosophical orientation have reveled in pronouncing judgment upon the ignoble coward and artless brute alike: "Sir, you are no gentleman."

Death before Dishonor

All this would have been self-evident to the medieval knight, at least in theory. (We will not rehash here the question of the degree to which the knight's aspirations were matched by his actions.) If one tenet of the contemporary worldview represents a heretical break with tradition, it is in the confident assertion that nothing is worth fighting for—which is to say, dying for. Implied in this is the assumption that peace is always preferable to war, and life is always preferable to death, and here the compleat gentleman dissents—militantly—even if he himself is not combat-ready.

It would follow that if, contrary to the popular view, there are things worth fighting for, then there will be conflict (we are always living in either a postwar or a prewar era), and somebody had better be capable of fighting.

I had the privilege some years ago to be the editor of the autobiography of the American philosopher Sidney Hook, *Out of Step: An Unquiet Life in the Twentieth Century*. Professor Hook was first among that illustrious cadre known as "cold war liberals," whose anti-communism so nettled Marxists and others on

the Left sympathetic to statism. I convinced Professor Hook that
we should include as an epigram in his memoir a quotation of
his that did not appear in the manuscript, but for which he was
justly famous—or infamous, if you happened to be an "anti-war
liberal" or an "anti-anti-communist." Throughout the cold war
period, one often heard it said: "Better red than dead." The appeal of this pithy maxim was enormous; it seemed the essence
of American commonsense. And it was frighteningly hollow.
Here is Sidney Hook's retort:

> It is better to be a live jackal than a dead lion—for jackals,
> not for men. Men who have the moral courage to fight
> intelligently for freedom have the best prospects of avoid-
> ing the fate of both live jackals and dead lions. Survival is
> not the be-all and end-all of a life worthy of man. Some-
> times the worst thing we can know about a man is that
> he has survived. Those who say life is worth living at any
> cost have already written themselves an epitaph of in-
> famy, for there is no cause and no person they will not
> betray to stay alive. Man's vocation should be the use of
> the arts of intelligence in behalf of human freedom.

No better statement can be made about the gentleman-war-
rior's view of his place in the scheme of things, unless, perhaps, it
is made by the example of one of the great gentlemen-warriors
of our time—James Bond Stockdale.

Admiral Stockdale, who was for eight years a prisoner of war
in Hanoi, did not fare very well as the vice-presidential running
mate of Ross Perot; however, that unfortunate episode hardly
tarnishes his Congressional Medal of Honor or his twenty-six
combat decorations, among which are two Distinguished Flying
Crosses and two Purple Hearts.

Many people know something of Stockdale's prison experiences, which have been chronicled by him in such books as *In Love and War* (written with his wife Sybil) and *A Vietnam Experience: Ten Years of Reflection*, but most are likely unaware of the extent to which he drew strength during his captivity from the works of Epictetus, the great Greco-Roman Stoic philosopher.

At one point, on the eve of yet another interrogation and beating at the hands of his Vietnamese captors, Stockdale recalled the words of the philosopher concerning the importance of never begging: "For it is better to die of hunger, exempt from fear and guilt, than to live in affluence with perturbation." Here are these two great philosophers, Epictetus and Hook, separated by two thousand years but arguing the same thing: it is better to die courageously than to live spinelessly.

Strength and Honor

Must the modern gentleman really embrace this militant, Stoic approach to life and death? I believe he must. Without descending into a splenetic tirade about the reasons for the decline of American "values," I think it is fair to say that one pervasive characteristic of our current collective state of mind is a conviction that accommodation is always better than conflict. Nothing in the last decade of my life has forced steam from my ears as much as the reports of my sons about sessions at school in which administrators and teachers and so-called facilitators have attempted to teach kids about "conflict resolution." Have we really come to a point at which we actually believe that the natural state of humanity is peace and that peace is maintained by conciliation? That there is some negotiable middle ground between good and evil? Perhaps we—the collective "we"—have (witness the recent machinations at the United Nations over . . .

"everything"). But no compleat gentleman can accept such premises.

I acknowledge the efficacy of peacemaking, especially in the hothouse climate of so many American schools. However, strength and honor more dependably keep the peace than palaver about psychic posture and moral equivalence. (Besides, in my experience, kids learn to "play" the conflict-resolution game, just as they "play" the safe-sex game and the substance-abuse game. It's not that the best kids aren't just, sexually responsible, and drug free, but that they make their own decisions and are far less influenced than people like to believe by all the high-profile hectoring. Indeed, I fear that DARE and other drug-abuse-resistance educational programs are to the new generation what *Reefer Madness* was to my parents'—although not so seductively lurid.)

There is simply no substitute for strength of character, and in boys, or men, this requires two things increasingly rare in our time: knowledge of the past and a vision of the future. Of the former much has been written, and no compleat gentleman will deny that history is the most essential aspect of a sound education. Having a vision of the future is nothing more than possessing the ability to apply the lessons of history to the shaping of an emerging present. Tempting as it may be for the schools or the armed forces to take on the burden of character development, it ought to be obvious that the process begins and matures—although not necessarily to completion—in the home. If it does not happen at home, it probably never will.

Be Prepared

At the start of this book I suggested that there are not many men who willingly embrace the burdens of chivalry, and this aspect of militancy is one reason why. When James Stockdale's philosophy instructor at Stanford University first gave him a copy of the *Enchiridion* of Epictetus, he told him that "the Stoic demand for disciplined thought naturally won only a small minority to its standard, but that those few were everywhere the best."

Most of the time, of course, the compleat gentleman will not be called upon to fight, but he will always be prepared. If this sounds a little like the Boy Scout motto, well, that's not so bad. A good man will not be surprised when somebody grins at him and exclaims, "You are such a Boy Scout!" He will be neither surprised nor flustered, because the intention of the comment is essentially good; it means that he is morally upright.

Winston Churchill was a big fan of Robert Baden-Powell, founder of the Boy Scouts, and of the gentlemanly qualities of early scouting, which Churchill considered "an inspiration, characteristic of the essence of British genius, and uniting in a bond of comradeship the youth not only of the English-speaking world, but of almost every land and people under the sun." Baden-Powell's 1908 book, *Scouting for Boys*, stirred sentiments of "knightly chivalry, of playing the game—any game—earnest or fun—hard and fairly, which constitute the most important part of the British system of education." Churchill went on to say that scouting was not militaristic, and so "no one, even the most resolute pacifist, could be offended" by it. But that is a half-truth at best. Scouts aren't armed, and scouting eschews combat training per se, but the structure and practice of the Boy Scouts is otherwise quite martial.

As Heather MacDonald has written, Baden-Powell envisioned "a new organization that would draw on wartime scouting lore and ancient codes of chivalry to teach boys the Victorian virtues. King Arthur's Round Table, Baden-Powell understood, resonated in boys' souls, for it symbolized the marriage of strength and goodness, by contrast with today's 'gangsta' culture, which defines manliness as violently predatory."

It may seem ironic that, after decades of decline and in spite of recent bad press, the Boy Scouts are thriving, especially in America's inner cities. It may seem remarkable to imagine any modern American kids pledging to be "physically strong, mentally awake, and morally straight," but they do, even if, like NASCAR and the martial arts, their commitments (and Scouting's popularity) have tended to fly beneath media radar.

I do not believe that our gentleman Boy Scout should obsess about combat. But I do think he ought to be concerned about combat readiness. A man, however hard he works for peace, must always be ready for war. Not all gentlemen will be suited for combat in the usual sense, but all will be prepared to oppose vigorously the enemies of liberty and justice. The component of physical fitness is in my view important but not essential. But the fact remains—life is a martial art. It is, anyway, if you do it right. As the Stoics of ancient Rome used to say, *Vivere militare!** How can our modern knight protect the innocent and punish the guilty unless along with his courage and honor he has prowess?

"Manliness," Baden-Powell wrote, "can only be taught by men, and not by those who are half men, half old women."

Codes of Honor

If the compleat gentleman has always been akin to the warrior, it does not follow that he has always been a soldier. When duty calls he will be a fighter, but his martial skill may be practiced with his wits rather than his fists. In World War II, for instance, many men contributed to the war effort without ever taking up a gun or getting behind the controls of a plane. Code

_____

*From the Stoic writer Seneca: "To live is to fight."

breakers and quartermasters played essential roles in the victory over tyranny. This will always be true. That said, it remains the case that a proper gentleman will usually do more than simply cultivate a martial spirit. So long as God and nature allow, he will keep himself fit for battle.

In their early teens, my sons attended summer sports camps at West Point, New York, run by the coaches and staff of the United States Military Academy (USMA). To be on the campus at West Point is to experience a kind of culture shock—at least if you have experience of other American colleges. Obviously I'm not referring to the stunning views of the Hudson River from Trophy Point, or even to the fact that the verdant hills in and around the campus disguise ranges for artillery training and venues for war games. What makes the academy so remarkable is the bearing and attitude of its students. It is tempting to suggest that they benefit in comparison because they are America's best and brightest. Well, I'm uncertain how one defines "best" with regard to seventeen to twenty-seven-year-old men and women, but it is fairly certain that the academy's cadets are measurably—by standardized tests, anyway—not the "brightest." Admission standards at all the academies (naval, air force, coast guard, as well as USMA) are demanding (in addition to the usual competitive academic exams, there are also physical tests), but the "brightest," at least as measured by SAT scores, mostly end up at the "elite" colleges: the Ivies and the Seven Sisters, the big research universities, and the chic liberal-arts colleges.† What the academies get is a group of highly motivated, academically excellent, morally upright young people who will either blossom or shrivel under the discipline and rigor of the program.

---

† *Forbes* magazine recently rated West Point the nation's #1 public university.

It may be argued that the cadets who do thrive under conditions that would make the average college kid whine, swoon, and skedaddle simply reflect the "self-selection" inherent in the USMA's admissions process. There is some truth in this, just as it's true that the success of Harvard students has as much (or more) to do with native intelligence and competitiveness as with the school's curricula and pedagogy. Still, West Point's diverse cadet corps, including the lowliest plebes, is universally enthusiastic, gracious, and robust, both physically and intellectually. I'm convinced this is not only self-selection but also a consequence of the academy's standards (this is true of the other service academies as well), which in regard to honor are higher than at any other American educational institution.

Now that could be damning with faint praise, but it isn't. Outside Washington Hall, the massive cadet mess hall where all four thousand cadets can be served in under half an hour, there is a marble slab on which is inscribed the academy's honor code: "A cadet will not lie, cheat, steal, or tolerate those who do." Those are a dozen words to live by.

This conception of honor may seem to be closer in spirit to the Victorian gentleman's than to the medieval knight's, since it does not explicitly embrace prowess or loyalty or liberality or courtesy. But we need to recall that *franchise* was the knight's signal virtue; it meant not only honesty or frankness but also honor, defined as "nobility of mind." The honor code at West Point is a seed that will take root and grow in the cadet's mind—it is hoped—to flower perennially in his or her life. I admire James H. Toner's definition of character, which is essentially the same as *franchise* or honor: "Most of us struggle to know right and then to do it. There, then, is the property of character: one has character who struggles (perhaps not always successfully) to do what should be done."

Vivere Militare, *Indeed!*

The outpouring of pride and affection for veterans that we beheld after the Gulf War (and are again witnessing in the ongoing battles in Iraq and Afghanistan) stands in stark contrast to the reception of soldiers, sailors, airmen, and marines returning from combat in Vietnam. Therefore, one might conclude that the warrior was actually more popular at the start of the twenty-first century than at any time since WWII, and there is some truth in this. The most recent opinion research indicates that the military is the institution in which we have the most confidence—more than we have in the police, the Supreme Court, or even our churches, and *way* more than we have in either Congress or the presidency. The larger truth, however, is that esteem for the military life is very high only in certain segments of the population, while in other segments the armed forces‡ are not so much despised as they are dismissed. Start with the fact that enlistments have been down—this despite the fact that after the Gulf War there was a serious contraction in the size of the active armed forces. Participation in ROTC is down. Early retirements are up. The pundits proclaim that this is the result of protracted economic expansion. Throughout the eighties and nineties, more and better jobs were available in the private sector, causing the allure of the military to decline even among the economically and educationally disadvantaged kids for whom it has always been one of the surest means of upward mobility. Still, today's recruits are more likely than their predecessors to say that

---

‡ Although I don't think it affects the overall argument made here, it's important to note that recruitment goals have been achieved over the last several years and that re-enlistments are up.

money—and not honor, duty, or patriotism—is the main reason for joining up. The failure to attract more technically talented (and especially college-educated) warriors has meant that an increasing amount of military work is "outsourced": it's not just an adventure, it's a job. (How many of the nation's recent military undertakings have seemed almost the work of a mercenary force?)§ Attitudes concerning the new American warrior are a far cry from our view of the citizen-soldier of Gettysburg, the Meuse-Argonne Offensive, D-Day, or even Khe Sanh.

"We" like what "they" do—at least when they do it well—but we don't want to be them. In the short run this does not matter—the armed forces will fulfill their missions with or without broad-based support among the American people. In the long run, however, the decline of regard for the profession of arms is a very dangerous matter indeed, and the recent stunning successes in Iraq should not mislead us.

Our republic functions under the aegis of democratic elections, which means that—the Constitution and other fixed principles notwithstanding—national policy may come over time to reflect the whims of shifting majorities. This has haunted the imaginations of conservatives and liberals alike since the days of Madison, and yet history has been kind to the American experiment. The All-Volunteer Force (AVF) has worked extremely well so far (although not without some problems), but by its very nature it depends upon a spirit of enthusiastic voluntarism among young men and women. If general attitudes about the military begin to deteriorate seriously, there is a risk that young people will look elsewhere for a productive beginning to adult life. That's bad enough, but imagine the political nightmare if national security subsequently demands a return to the draft.

---

§ I was thinking here of the American incursions into Sudan and Bosnia.

Indifference to personal service reflects the wider conviction that the most essential American ideal is the pursuit of happiness and the not so essential American heresy that happiness is the result of self-interested pleasure seeking. All religion and the best philosophy—beginning with Plato, Aristotle, and the Stoics, and continuing right through Kant and Wittgenstein, Popper, and Hook—have refuted the assertion that self-interest is the same thing as self-satisfaction. What fulfills hunger is not necessarily what promotes health, and fitness is superior to satiety. This is true for both body and soul.

When I was a boy—of the first generation after World War II—American culture (at least in my small Ohio town) was suffused with the military values of honor, courage, patriotism, and self-sacrifice. It may seem frivolous today, but we kids grew up playing war: we were equipped with our fathers' surplus equipment, as well as with their stories of fighting in Europe and the Pacific, and we looked upon the military as a mechanism of male fulfillment.

Attitudes about the military life matter very much to the state of attitudes about the chivalrous gentleman, because the two ideals share so much. If a person looks upon the figure of a U.S. Marine Corps colonel standing ramrod straight in his dress blues and thinks, "Now there's fascism on the hoof," he'll almost surely look upon a well-dressed man with impeccable manners and think, "Now there's repression manifest."

As Robert G. Kennedy, a management professor from the University of St. Thomas, told a conference of top brass meeting to discuss military ethics, "There is reason to believe that the gap between military and civilian cultures is not a result of the failure of the armed forces to keep up with the progress of the larger culture, but a consequence of its resistance to participate in the deterioration of that culture." He's right. We have so few chivalric models anymore. Legal authorities lie; religious leaders sin; teachers propagandize; athletes cheat; pop stars lip sync. The litany of hyp-ocrites and counterfeits seems endless, and the media loop it all 24/7 for our edification. Have we become a nation of voyeurs and enablers? Not entirely, to be sure, but whereas the more subtle evolutionary changes in style and decorum have always—and I mean throughout history—made earlier generations wince un-easily to glimpse the future, they must now make our forebears re-coil painfully from our prospects. Above all, they must look down upon us and be aghast at our passivity.

Perhaps it is not surprising that as we finally and properly begin embracing cultural diversity we also feel compelled to give a hug to moral equivalency. I have a friend who, when the news brings us the story of yet another prevaricating politician or ped-erast priest, likes to joke: "It doesn't make him a bad person."

Sam Damon and Leadership

The importance of a seasoned, professional military has always been evident. When amateurs, including politicians, get into the di-rection of war, disaster awaits. Take the case of Eleanor of Aquitaine's first husband, Louis VII of France (1137-1151). When he was dissatisfied with the recalcitrant province of Champagne, he decided to lead a force of soldiers, including mercenaries, against the little town of Vitry-en-Perthois, where the local count had his headquarters. Louis had no rapport with his commanders, and his commanders had no control over their troops. The siege became a rout, which became a conflagration. The terrified residents sought shelter in the cathedral, which was torched with more than a thou-sand residents inside, all killed when the roof collapsed.

Louis did nothing. He was paralyzed by fear and self-loathing, because he knew he had not understood his men nor been able to anticipate the consequences of his own orders.

Good commanders are cool under pressure. They care about their men and their mission and are at peace with the tragedy of their calling, because they realize that "it is difficult to remain both at peace and free. Peace is man's most fervent hope but war represents his surest experience." Those are the words of Gen. John W. Vessey Jr., in his foreword to the recent reissue of *Once An Eagle* by Anton Myrer. Myrer's novel deserves a short digression here.

The reason the book is worth considering—aside from the fact that it is a fabulous yarn (though not necessarily "America's War and Peace," as its admirers have hailed it)—is its eminence: it has become the most popular book among our armed forces, and that's an understatement. Myrer deftly traces American military progress from the years before WWI up through the Vietnam catastrophe. (He was prescient about the political futility of that conflict.) The hero of the novel, Sam Damon, who rises through the ranks from private to general, has become the ideal that military men aspire to in our time. First published in 1968, *Once An Eagle* received modest acclaim, which was revisited when it became a TV miniseries in the 1970s.

But then the book went the way of most books: its sales diminished to a point at which the publisher allowed it to go out of print. Thus was born a cult classic. The phrase "What would Sam do?" has become the standard in military decision making. "Sam Damon" or simply "Sam" is scrawled on tanks and aircraft, and the publisher has reissued the book under the aegis of the United States Army War College in Carlisle, Pennsylvania. A new edition was essential since the book has become required reading at the academies and at several postgraduate combat schools for their courses in leadership.

Once An Eagle is a curious icon for the military in the era of the All-Volunteer Force. For one thing, it has properly been described—and by military men at that—as a "consummate anti-war book." The book's view of the armed forces in peacetime is especially acidic, although its descriptions of command decisions in war are nearly as tart. Still, Sam Damon is above all a man of honor, a latter-day knight whose prowess, loyalty, largesse, and courtesy equal those of any medieval paladin. Just as the virtuous Sam has entered the psyches of our officer corps, so has the "anti-Sam" of *Once An Eagle*, Courtney Massengale, an ambitious, by-the-book West Pointer without concern for anyone but himself. A young man can be denied a promotion these days when one of the higher-ups refers to him as a "Courtney Massengale type." I can't say to what extent the spirit of Sam Damon has actually entered into the hearts and minds of today's officer corps, but to the degree that it has we have a more compassionate, commonsensical armed forces. Nearly every article of appreciation written by soldiers about *Once An Eagle* cites the tender moment in which Sam gives advice to his son: "You can't help what you were born and you may not have much say about where you die, but you can and you should try to pass the days in between as a good man."

My Own War and Peace

I would be distressed if what I've written here leads a reader to suppose I was a military man—not because I would be anything but proud to have served my country, but because I am ashamed that I did not.

I grew up in Ohio in the 1950s and had a passion for the United States Army. My father was a veteran of World War II, and I recall standing in the halls of the elementary school I attended—I was ten at the time—and saying to a pal (now a Vietnam vet), "I hope when the next war comes I'm old enough to fight." As the saying goes, be careful what you wish for.

Long story short, I was caught up—my moral house in those days being built upon the sand of too little knowledge of history (and I was a history major!)—in the anti-war enthusiasms of the late sixties. Several weeks before the official date of my graduation from college I received "greetings" from my local draft board. I will not go here into the sordid details of the philosophical confusion I was feeling at the time. I impulsively took the counsel of well-meaning friends and determined to "defect" to Canada. I got as far as Connecticut. There the American Friends Service Committee put me together with a psychiatrist who wrote a letter for me to deliver to my draft board, the sense of which was that I was psychologically unfit to serve. (The letter reasoned that my intense disapproval of the war meant I'd be unable to follow orders.) This was high water in the "anti-war movement," and honor meant nothing; ends justified means.

Amazingly—and against its own rules—my local board granted me conscientious-objector status. As I understand it, I was the first and only person ever to receive such a change *after* an induction order had been issued. Apparently, the board thought I was sincere, perhaps proving that sincerity is a much-overvalued quality.

In any case, I did my alternative service. Then I read *The War Against the Jews: 1933–1945* by Lucy Dawidowicz (1975).[††] I had recently converted (from amorphous Protestantism) to Roman Catholicism and picked up the Dawidowicz book simply because the atmosphere of the church had rekindled my interest in history. You must understand that I had settled nicely into a self-image that was very much tied up in a belief in pacifism and

---

[††] When I was literary editor at *National Review*, I called Prof. Dawidowicz's office at Yeshiva University to see if I could convince her to write a book review. I don't recall the book in question—probably because of the shock I felt when the voice on the phone told me she'd died about an hour before I called.

the essential goodness of Man. War will end, I used to say, only when good men refuse to fight. Honestly, the truistic banality of this pearl was lost on me, that is, until I read Dawidowicz, at which point I realized that: 1) human beings are not basically good (the Nazis settled that); 2) there will always be reasons to fight (history proves it); and 3) some of those reasons will be good ones (as, for instance, defeating a tyranny before or after it begets world conflagration).

I've read some terrific books in my life, but only *The War Against the Jews* truly changed my life. The process was gradual, and I fought it as best I could, but by 1980 I was a conservative.

Certainly duty does not trump conscience, and the dilemmas of Vietnam—and of most armed conflicts—have raised and will continue to raise serious questions about national and individual responsibility. But the men and women who served in Vietnam served with honor. I and many other dissenters often acted dishonorably: sincerity is not the same as propriety. You live, and learn.

Body and Soul

A compleat gentleman seeks a harmonious union of body and soul; if his will—his soul—is strong then his body ought to be strong as well. I've emphasized earlier that physical fitness is not absolutely a requirement of gentlemanly character, but it is close to being one. I don't see how a man can consider the nature of things in the world—the violent, selfish, criminal nature of things—and not believe it necessary to be fit for battle. Yes, we have the police and the armed services to protect us, but that protection is mostly a general deterrent. In the specifics of assault against our communities and ourselves, our reaction against evil must sometimes be immediate or it will fail.

Am I recommending vigilantism? Am I giving comfort to

the militia movement? Certainly not. Loyalty demands respect for law. *Largesse*, in the sense of compassion, demands respect for the rights of others—for the innocent, of course, but even for the criminal.

Nor am I suggesting that any gentleman should consider himself like David Dunn, the character played by Bruce Willis in M. Night Shyamalan's 2000 film, *Unbreakable*. Dunn is a real-life superhero who goes forth into his community to do battle with evil. A gentleman does not possess superpowers, but he does posses the martial virtues of strength, courage, honor, and—if he is serious about it—prowess. He will thus be equipped to avoid the fate of both dead lions and live jackals, and his presence in the community will be a deterrent to mischief.

The founder of modern karate, Gichin Funakoshi, wrote that the truth of the martial arts is "that in daily life, one's mind and body be trained and developed in a spirit of humility; and that in critical times, one be devoted utterly to the cause of justice."

Some will worry that—concerns about militant lunacies aside—all this amounts to an incentive to violence. Well, a gentleman really must face the reality of violence and not reject it; like any warrior he will turn to violence only as a last resort. So often when violence is depicted in literature or on film the combatants are portrayed as filled with rage: eyes are wide as the trigger is squeezed, overkill is achieved. Hollywood especially has tended to believe that the warrior is a dysfunctional individual. This may be changing, however, as the technicians of cinema become more interested in and respectful of the techniques of combat. These days the warrior is a little more likely to be portrayed as one cool customer: violence is his business, but, hey, it's only business. There is some ambivalence here, and audiences may be left wondering if the 1970s' psychopath has simply been replaced by the 2000s' sociopath.

But the truth is that all great warriors have always been dispassionate in combat. Ernest Hemingway famously defined courage as "grace under pressure." Better is the observation of the Roman historian Sallust: "In battle it is always those who are most afraid who are exposed to the greatest dangers; courage acts as a protecting wall."

In martial arts training, one learns quickly—and sometimes painfully—how emotion befouls the execution of sound technique. The karate teacher's advice to "always plan your work and work your plan" comes from the rather obvious fact that uncertainty leads to anxiety, anxiety to fear, and fear to anger, and that anger is always the worst reason and condition for fighting.‡‡

The Way of All Flesh

I often hear it said that violence is not inevitable, and, therefore, that the warrior's attitude and training are unnecessary. I once thought so, too, but I grew up, and now the pacifists and I are simply moral strangers. I came to grasp what Conrad Hensley, hero of Tom Wolfe's *A Man in Full*, comes to understand when he reads Epictetus in prison. Only Epictetus, Conrad realizes, "began with the assumption that life is hard, brutal, punishing, narrow, and confining, a deadly business, and that fairness and unfairness are beside the point. Only Epictetus, as far as Conrad knew, was a philosopher who had been stripped of everything, imprisoned, tortured, enslaved, threatened with death. And only Epictetus had looked his tormentors in the eye and said: 'You do what you have to do, and

---

‡‡ In my case, the hardest thing for me to learn when sparring was simply to relax. Relaxation comes from confidence (which itself comes from training), manifest in easy breathing, and is the key to being an effective fighter.

I will do what I have to do, which is live and die like a man.' And he had prevailed."

Let us, please, be sure to understand that what is being discussed here is not a Stoic replica, not a style to be imitated by affected gestures, by role-playing. This is not about being a "tough guy" or evoking martial imagery. Men who retreat to the woods with cases of Bud Lite and paint their faces like Plains Indians or the Scots of *Braveheart* are clowns, not warriors. To be sure, every true warrior has a warrior "within," but he also has, as my sons like to put it, "skills." There is an "inner" warrior, but he exists because the "outer" warrior is actually capable of battling his enemies. It doesn't matter whether the fight is a battle of wits or fists, but the true warrior—the true gentleman—is no mincing pacifist. Or, if he is a pacifist, he has courageously accepted his vulnerability in the face of evil and is willing to use his body, albeit passively, as a weapon of choice in the battle against his enemies.

It may be that certain saints have no enemies because they selflessly love all men. They may go singing into the ovens. Their example may even transform the hearts and minds of their murderers, although the historical evidence for the assertion is slim. Not to deny the humanity of even the most ruthless killer (whose homicidal motives may be personal or political), but the best method for vanquishing him is neither sweet reason nor passive resistance, but a dagger in his heart, a bullet in his brain, or a punch in his nose—you pick your weapon. Would that it were not so, but it is so.

And here is refutation of the sage observation that the pen is mightier than the sword. There is truth in this pithy maxim, although to be literally true it ought to read: "The pen is *sometimes* mightier than the sword." Both the pen and the sword are tools, appropriate in certain situations. When the pen is most suitable, the sword is inappropriate. But when the sword is necessary, the pen may be dangerously inapt, as writers discovered who waved their editorials at Nazi or Soviet tanks. It's not that talk is cheap (although it may be), but that words simply aren't bullets. Words, especially brave words, may endure to inspire future generations, but there are times when—to fall back on another cliché—actions speak louder.

To be a warrior is to live in readiness, not just the readiness to fight but also the readiness to die, in battle or in bed. Men have always feared death, but our prototypical knight feared death much as any one of us might fear sparring with someone we know is stronger, quicker, and more skilled. You fight the fight knowing you will lose, but you fight honorably. To our knight, death was the enemy—but a noble enemy, and there was no shame in losing the fight. Death was respected and—as in this paragraph—personified. Death was a Man in Black, and possibly a friend, even if you wished you'd never meet him.

But now death is a monster. Death is a scandal and—to secularists, anyway—a sin. Once death was near; now we want death as far as possible from our lives. Few of us feel differently. Not only do we expect long lives, we are scandalized by early death. To most people, it seems positively ghoulish that Victorians sometimes photographed their dead children and kept the pictures as treasured memories. Until this century, death touched humanity at every age—not simply in old age. Babies died, children died, teens died. Pestilence and war and poverty were death's agents, and every one of them seemed as inevitable as death itself. But, in America especially, we are not so besieged by the agents of death as other countries are today or as every country once was, and death is pushed more and more to the margins of consciousness. When I was a boy, a death at fifty was considered premature. Now that I am past sixty, death at seventy seems untimely, believe me.

I'd like to think that my mates at the gym are there in order to stay strong and healthy, but I think many of them exercise in order to stay young, which of course they cannot. As the Baby Boomers have turned fifty, many have speculated that the entire cohort would experience a kind of psychic meltdown: how can the Youth Generation cope with being middle aged? In fact many of us are fitter at fifty or sixty than we were at twenty, and so long as you squint when you look in the mirror you can fantasize that nothing has changed. But, God willing, we will all turn ninety, and then what? We can plausibly think of fifty as young, but ninety? Even Baby Boomer optimism and self-delusion have their limits.

"The man whose end is approaching," Georges Duby writes about the death of the greatest of all knights, William Marshal, "must gradually rid himself of everything, and before all else, the honors of this world." The approach of death was seen by the medievals as an unfolding. Too often, of course, it came with the suddenness of an arrow in the night. But when a man was blessed, as Marshal was, to observe death's approach, his own *exitus*, from the haven of his own bed, he could aspire to a very real tranquility, because "the ritual of death in the old style . . . was not an evasion, a furtive exit, but a slow, orderly approach, a careful prelude, a solemn transfer from one condition to another, to a higher state, a transition as public as the weddings of the period, as majestic as the entrances of kings into their fine cities." It is a way of dying, Duby concludes, "that we have lost, and, that it may well be, miss."

Can a man honestly say he is *willing* to die—for anything? Does it matter? Certainly we don't need fellows going about proclaiming their willingness to make the ultimate sacrifice. No compleat gentleman would; *sprezzatura* disallows it. There is never really any reason to risk death—except honor. To be sure, this is honor broadly construed to include diving into river rapids to save a drowning man, because it would be dishonorable to watch him go down, or refusing to betray a comrade or one's country even in the face of torture. Of course not every gentleman can swim, and such heroes as John McCain and Everett Alvarez and James Stockdale have all testified that even the strongest, most Stoic prisoner of war could—indeed probably will—break if his tormentors are persistent. And older men may not have the strength to fight effectively against younger thugs. But the point is that they fight on.

What is so striking in Duby's description of Marshal's death is the way in which old William approaches his end—with utter courage. He seems to welcome it, if only because he knows he can't avoid it. His courage allows him to do what is right, which is not to cling to the world he is leaving. It's not that men such as William Marshal were completely congenial to the actuality of death; they were men after all. But they were altogether less likely to divorce themselves from it; their view of the world embraced it. Indeed, there was an art of dying, a drama in which a man's performance revealed the final and best measure of his life.

The old knight gathers around him the people he loves and gives to each some part of the bounty of his life. In some cases it is land; in other cases it is money; in each case there is also a bequest of wisdom. In the end William has nothing left to give, which means he leaves the world with exactly what he had brought into it.

Poignant above all is William's bequest to Anselm, his youngest son. The boy will be, like the famous Prince John—whom William had helped succeed to the throne—a lack-land, and must, as his father put it, "live long enough to become a knight . . . [and] ride errant till he win honor; then he will find someone who will cherish him and do him great honor." In this, young Anselm is like most modern men—and like William Marshal was himself: We make our own ways in the world; we are without privileges other than our God-given rights and talents. In some manner we must be apprenticed and then earn such wealth, power, happiness, and wisdom as diligence and fate will allow.

At the very end, William Marshal is dressed in the white cloak with a red cross that is the habit of the Templars. This is the first time he has ever worn the garment. He had pledged himself to the semi-monastic Templars thirty years before, and now he is fulfilling both his promise to their order and to the order of life itself. Leaving the earthly plane, he is no longer a warrior or a baron or a husband or a father. He has become a monk.

No doubt he knew how clay-footed even the Templars could be, but he also surely knew that their failures were the common failures of all men. But their victory! Theirs was the exceptional triumph of men who aspire to holiness in everyday life.

As in the knighting ceremony of Saladin by Hugh of Tiberias, priests did not control the rite of William's last hours. As Duby observes, historians barely comprehend this knightly morality. We're familiar with Christ's admonition to be "in the world but not of it," but we are unaccustomed to the claim that we ought to be in the church but not of it. On his deathbed, William complains that the churchmen "shave us too close," and when the priests gathered around his bedside urge him to give his expensive wardrobe to their religious communities, the old warrior stirs himself long enough to snarl at them to get the hell out. He gives his fine garments to his comrades-in-arms. And if there aren't enough of William's outfits to go around, the dying knight tells his closest friend, "Send again to London to buy what is lacking." Duby concludes: "A good seigneur thinks first of his own people."

For Marshal his clothes were the outward symbols of power and authority, whereas for modern men being well-dressed is more a reflection of good taste and self-respect. But the gentleman has always been well turned-out, albeit in a restrained style.

As Trollope, who knew a thing or two about gentlemen, wrote: "I hold that gentleman to be the best-dressed whose dress no one observes." This is the somewhat paradoxical motto of nearly all the best tailors in the world.

William Marshal was praised—and even loved—by the most powerful men and women of his time. He was called the bravest and the wisest of knights ("the flower of chivalry"), and he may have been in his day the most exalted commoner of all time, a parvenu extraordinaire—possibly the model for Lancelot in several versions of the Arthur story. He was almost a superhero, but he was always only a man, albeit a very brave man.

·　·　·

Fearing death is not cowardly per se. But death will come, and the question is: How will a man face death? In this, the warrior and the monk are of a single mind. The warrior's way is the way of the dojo: he spars with death, brother against brother. When death wins, the gentleman graciously bows in defeat. The monk's way is the way of the cloister, where death walks the corridors, sits at the table, and works in the gardens alongside his living brothers. When death takes a brother, it is as if the dead monk has entered a room in the monastery from which the living are prohibited; he remains in the community awaiting his brothers, who will join him one by one.

We do not control the order of the universe, and we cannot know the exact moment of our dying. But we can live in recognition of that moment, in readiness.

Be prepared.

CHAPTER FIVE

The Lover

Romance and Folly

Chivalry is not an obvious idea. It is not as plain as a pike-staff or as a palm-tree. It is a delicate balance between the sexes, which gives the rarest kind of pleasure to those who can strike it.

        –G. K. CHESTERTON, *THE NEW JERUSALEM* (1920)

Don't confuse "courtly love" with Courtney Love, queen of grunge and décolletage. Courtly love is the accompaniment to chivalry; it is a worldview that introduced romance into the West and began the process of taming male sexual aggression. This, anyway, is what the academy considers the unsophisticated view, and they ought to know.

Courtly love—or, as the medievals themselves called it, *fin amour*—surely was part reverie and part reality, and few are entirely certain where to draw the line between fantasy and history. Because it seemed to promise the liberation of women and failed to deliver, many scholars dismiss its impact. But one of the most elegant of contemporary academicians, C. Stephen Jaeger, of the University of Washington, insists that it "was not merely some high-flung dream-vision masking a crude, brutal reality." It was a force that rivaled religion itself in a time when the force of religion was unrivaled.

The model courtly lovers are Lancelot and Guinevere—and Arthur, who must be included because the philosophy, if you can call it that, was predicated upon the so-called *eternal triangle*. As we shall see, it was a view of love and sex fashioned to an unprecedented degree by women, powerful women, in reaction to a variety of forces and opportunities, a similar confluence of which would not appear again until the twentieth century.

If it was not exactly a proto-feminist movement—most of its champions were men—courtly love definitely was inspired (and certainly encouraged) by some of the most dynamic women of the second thousand years after Christ. Although its genesis is in the first centuries of the second millennium (recall that we are in the first years of the third), it was a remarkably modern institution in that it was an outgrowth of leisure, affluence, and liberty, and—like many of our twentieth- and twenty-first-century social innovations—it was in its time simultaneously hailed as a kind of salvation and decried as damnation manifest. It would take a shelf of books to detail the trends in medieval society that made 1100 a propitious year for a revolution in manners. I'll try to shrink it all down into a paragraph.

Early medieval marriages—at every level of society—were usually arranged and frequently loveless. The Crusades had snatched away many of Europe's husbands (much as the twentieth-century's world wars would), leaving aristocratic wives especially with time on their hands. And there were all those younger brothers we considered in chapter two, men trained for knighthood but lacking land and prospects; they, too, had time to kill. Add to this mixture two very disparate ingredients: the spirit of Arab culture (especially its love poetry) brought back from the Crusades; and the elevation of Mary, the mother of Jesus, to centrality in religious life. (It seems as though every church built in France from AD 1100 on was named *Notre Dame de* whatever.)

New ideas, whether they are truly radical innovations or simply novel versions of tradition, are like a virus. The virus and the symptoms it causes may be deadly or benign, but either way everybody's in a sweat.

The Great Game

According to the French medievalist, Georges Duby, *fin amour* was a game played thus:

> The protagonist is a man, a "youth.". . . This man besieges and tries to take a lady . . . a woman who is married and thus inaccessible, impregnable, a woman who is surrounded and protected by the strictest prohibitions. . . . At the heart of this model lies danger, and this is where it should be. For on the one hand, the whole spice of the affair came from the danger involved . . . on the other hand, it was a test in the course of a continuing education, and the more perilous the test, the more educational it was.

It was, Duby explains, the "exact counterpart of the tournament." Diane Ackerman makes a fair point indeed when she writes: "Courtly love is actually a form of decoration. What's being decorated is lust. Over and over, succeeding generations have discovered courtly love as a way to cleanse sexual attraction of its carnality." Some historians have pointed out that we don't really know the extent to which the relations between a knight and his lady were carnal, and a few writers have argued that adultery in the Middle Ages was probably quite rare. This is why modern theorists tend to dismiss the observation of C. S. Lewis that courtly love was "Humility, Courtesy, Adultery, and the Religion of Love." As one scholarly publication forewarns students about the book (*The Allegory of Love*) from which the Lewis quote comes: "Charming, but use with caution; some ideas are a bit dated."

If some academics consider Lewis "dated" (perhaps even poisonous: "use with caution"), it is not so much that his scholarship was flawed as the traditional Christian view he takes of the matter. Jesus famously warned that a man and woman who simply exchange lustful looks have already committed adultery. Of course, consummation will likely be more complicated—after all, his ogling won't make her pregnant—but the sin of lust is grave nonetheless (first among the Seven Deadly Sins, in fact). Thus courtly love became a principal reason for reciprocal enmity between the knights (with their ladies) and the church; in one way or another, adultery was a matter of faith to courtly lovers.

Contemporary scholars do have a valid point in urging caution when weighing medieval testimony about actual infidelity: the price of adultery was so severe in 1100 (banishment or castration or death) that fornication was probably uncommon, or, rather, less common than it is today. Nonetheless, monks and priests—their own hypocrisies notwithstanding—were scandalized by the flaunting of mortal sin inherent in the behavior of the swells at court. There have always been tales of ribaldry—homosexual and heterosexual—swirling about medieval monastic life, and not just in Boccaccio's *Decameron*. But it was in the nature of the cloistered life that such sins were clandestine and contained. Here were these rascal warriors and their wanton women actually parading their licentiousness, making it into a kind of holy rite. This the churchmen found not only degenerate, but blasphemous as well, and theirs was an age in which blasphemy was considered the greatest of all sins—liable to grievous penalties both spiritual and worldly.

Thus two of the era's notable literary men, Andreas Capellanus and Chrétien de Troyes, engaged either in subtle parody or downright sabotage—or so it is alleged—in order to distance themselves from the great works of romantic love they wrote under the eyes of their patronesses, Queen Eleanor of Aquitaine and her daughter Countess Marie of Champagne.

Irony, History, and Parody

The Art of Courtly Love by Andreas and the Arthurian romances of Chrétien may very well have been written under duress. Andreas (aka André the Chaplain) wrote a gloss of the Roman poet Ovid's satirical handbook of adultery, Ars Amatoria. As John Jay Parry wrote in the introduction to his edition of The Art of Courtly Love, "the men of the Middle Ages thought they had his [Ovid's] approval for the dictum that the best partner in a love affair is another man's wife." Chrétien, of whom Colin Morris wrote that he "has a reasonable claim to be the first exponent of romantic love," was "forced" to add the tale of adultery to the story of Lancelot and Guinevere in order to satisfy the lustiness of his wealthy patronesses—or so they say. I'm not so sure, by which I mean I don't think the matter of the author's intent is or can be finally settled.

There are aspects of The Art of Courtly Love that strongly suggest parody, but there are also elements of the book that read like reportage. For instance, Andreas describes one meeting of the so-called Court of Love in which the judge is apparently none other than the great Queen Eleanor herself. The Court of Love was a kind of parlor game, but one with a didactic purpose—to educate men about love and courtesy. In this case a knight pleads to the queen, in effect: *I won from this fair lady the pledge that I would be her lover if and when she ever lost the adoration of her beau. As it happens, Majesty, she married the man. Naturally, I stepped forward to claim her promised love, but she has rebuffed me. She claims she loves her new husband, her former lover, and so has not lost his adoration!*

Is this not a violation of the Rules of Love? Eleanor decides that it is, citing as precedent an earlier opinion of her daughter's: "We do not dare oppose the ruling of Countess Marie, who has decreed that love can exercise no power over husband and wife. We therefore pronounce it proper that the lady grant you her favor."

In *The Art of Courtly Love*, Andreas had listed thirty rules, the first of which is: "Marriage is no excuse for not loving." He did *not* mean—as it may sound to the modern ear—that a husband and a wife must not allow the love that joined them to cool with time and under the pressures of married life. No, he meant (ironically or otherwise) that marriage is not an impediment to the wife's *affaire de coeur* with a knight who is not her husband. After all, everyone understood that marriage and love were incompatible. The sense of the rest of the rules is that lovers are delirious and that their delirium is intensified by denial and danger. Sexual intercourse may actually have seemed the negation of courtly love (the chaplain's book is no *Kama Sutra*), since relieving the tension might cool the ardor. "Consummation" might be nothing more than a few stolen moments alone in the lady's bedchamber, intimate but sexless, or possibly a brief glimpse of her naked body, a cruel reward indeed for the poor ardent knight.

Much of *The Art of Courtly Love* does read like a protracted joke, albeit one that is essentially humorless. But this story of Eleanor and Marie has about it the ring of truth; at least I think so. It moves me in the same way as the New Testament story of Christ's healing of the man who was blind from birth. Suddenly sighted, the man says, "I see men as trees walking," which phrase has about it the inimitable clarity of an actual anecdote. There were Courts of Love all right, and the ladies really did lord it over their men. If Andreas was overly ironic and blandly witty, it was in part to justify his engagement in so un-Christian an enterprise. He was a priest, after all.

Still, we need to admit that irony and parody are meaningless unless there is a reality against which the presentation is made. Something was going on in the baronial mansions and ducal courts. There is a reason why men and women, then and now, have found such power in the stories of the famous triangle at Camelot and of Tristan, Isolde, and King Mark (which is nearly the same tale and prototypical for the former). It hardly matters—in fact it matters not at all—whether or not copulation was an accompaniment to the "adultery" of courtly lovers, although as we shall see, Queen Eleanor herself was a woman whose sexual appetites were probably not constrained by marriage.

Of Chrétien's intentions—let alone his personal feelings— we know little. But we know that he, like so many writers in his time, was unlike modern scribblers who produce work—or claim to—strictly to satisfy their own creative impulses. Chrétien, like the *trouvères*, the troubadours whose poetry was sung and recited at all levels of medieval society, wrote to please a patron. While Chrétien was working at the court in Poitiers, he was cranking out his romances to satisfy Eleanor and Marie, two women we may confidently assume demanded satisfaction. But Chrétien did balk at fulfilling their fantasies when he took on the story of Lancelot and Guinevere. This was the last piece he composed for the grand ladies, and he left it unfinished. Speculation has it that he decamped in disgust to the more comforting, more masculine patronage of Philip of Flanders, because he could not stomach Marie's insistence that he glorify adultery. One scene he did write is so ludicrous in its historical context as to suggest biting sarcasm: Lancelot genuflects to the empty bed in which he and the queen have just coupled. This blasphemous act by Chrétien was akin to a prisoner of war's employment of a middle-finger gesture toward his captors during a propaganda film.

The Queen of Romance

The French have pretty much always had an international reputation as lovers. This is why the voice of actor Charles Boyer is today mimicked whenever Americans want to make light of the suave and stylish Continental lover, burlesqued even by kids who have never seen a Boyer film. That's thanks to Pepé le Pew, the amorous skunk of all those Warner Brothers cartoons, whose voice imitates Boyer's. What's marvelous in this is the echo of reality, and it's a very distant echo indeed, because the French probably did "invent" romantic love. If you had to acclaim the one person deserving credit as mother of the brainchild, you could do worse than name Eleanor of Aquitaine. Of course the truth is no single individual ever "invents" a powerful emotion. But Eleanor was among those who, with a kind of ferocious élan, encouraged the embrace in the West of the idea of romance.

"Romance" itself is an interesting word. By now we think of it almost exclusively as indicating the feeling of passionate wonder akin to wooing or courting. However, it originally meant words, whether written or spoken, in vernacular, Latinized French, as opposed to legal, literary, or ecclesiastical Latin. It meant the language of the common people, or the subject people, if you happened to be part of the Roman occupying force. One may be easily confused by the similarity between "Rome" and "romance." The latter word is derived from the Latin *Romanicus*, essentially the language of the common people of Rome (as distinguished from *Latinum*), but it comes more directly to us through the Old French *romanz*. Many of the tongues of Western Europe (Italian, French, Spanish, and Portuguese) are referred to as the "Romance languages," meaning that they were local and vernacular adaptations of spoken Latin.

Historians are divided in their opinions about Eleanor, who lived from 1122 to 1204, and whom we met briefly in chapter two. Nearly all agree, generally, that she was extraordinary, but they disagree, specifically, about the facts that made her so re-markable. Some declare, for instance, that around this great lady the principles of chivalry and courtly love coalesced. Others maintain that nobility, in the moral sense, was a stranger to her and her houses, and that we moderns who believe the tales of valiant knights and fair ladies are victims of some of the best and earliest press agentry. There is truth, I believe, in both claims.

Eleanor's story is pure prime-time soap opera, with bewilder-ing convolutions of plot and character. The trouble begins with her country, Aquitaine, which at the time was not actually part of France. It comprised a huge chunk of what is today south-central France and included such vassal states as Gascony, Périgord, Poitou, and Limousin. But in no way did the Aquitanians, the Gascons, and the rest think of themselves as French. When we think of France, we think of the nation we know today, and when we read of one of the early kings of "France," from Charles Martel right up through most of the many Louis, we can't help imagining them all as sovereign over the geography that is mod-ern France. But in and around the year 1100—our signal year—"France" was just one among several dominions in the area, and it was neither the largest nor the strongest. Aquitaine, Normandy, and Anjou were bigger and more powerful; Burgundy, Brittany, and Champagne were richer and more famous; and the political ascendancy of France, such as it was, had mostly to do with the rise of Paris. Times being what they were, the dukes of the other regions recognized the need for a union of security. The French suzerain was an attractive leader, in no small measure because he was *not* the strongest, which is why he got the title "king." But the political unification of the French nation would not come about until after the Hundred Years War—some two-and-a-half centuries following Eleanor's death, a period we know from Shakespeare's *Henry V*, from Joan of Arc and all that. Until that time, French kings maintained a very frail hegemony in the region, primarily because they had no armies to enforce their jurisdiction—only a few garrisons strategically placed but far outnumbered by the armed vassals of the local ducal warlords.

In Eleanor's day, the people of Aquitaine (sometimes called Occitania) were as much Spanish as French. To be precise, they were part Basque, a clan that to this day defies easy classification and covets its separate identity. Eleanor's native language was Occitan (also called Langue d'Oc, after the word for *yes*, which was "oc"). In the Provence region of France today some writers and artists, especially the more provincial ones, use Occitan or a modern version of it called Provençal.

We really don't know what Eleanor looked like, except that she was beautiful. The troubadours who came to her court and wrote songs about her sang of her loveliness in terms that were beyond glowing. Though we can't see the face the balladeers saw, we can hear their songs. There is a superb recording (on the Harmonia Mundi label), called *Troubadours*, which contains some of the original *"cansos"* (songs) of men such as Bernard de Ventadour, who said of his patroness Eleanor that she was the very embodiment of charm.

The alternately sprightly and haunting music sounds almost North African—at least as performed on the CD by the Clemencic Consort—and the language more Spanish (or Basque) than French. It's all fiddles and tambourines and flutes and booming drums, with warbling voices such as one might hear calling from a minaret. There's that Arab influence.

Eleanor was the granddaughter of the greatest of the warlords and perhaps the very first of the troubadours, the Duke of

Aquitaine, Guillaume IX (or William, as we English speakers would call him). He was a very unusual man. Crusader, poet, politician, lecher, he was excommunicated from the Catholic Church—twice. Although Eleanor was just five when he died, William's spirit was very much with her throughout her long life. William was an enthusiast of Ovid, *Ars Amatoria* being among the most widely read books during the Middle Ages. Other Roman ideas were in play as well, and, as C. Stephen Jaeger puts it, court-liness "is medieval Europe's memory of the Roman statesman, of his humanity and urbane skillfulness in guarding the state and facing the trials of public life." His antique humanity and urbanity, his attachment to the exotic East, his tenderness toward Moorish Spain, and his ardor for Provençal women—all led William to be condemned as a heretic and a pornographer, and these animadversions surely influenced the proud Eleanor, who by heritage and instinct, was a woman of radiance and passion.

At fifteen, she was also the most eligible woman on the Continent, and shortly after the death of her father—also a William, the tenth of his line—she became the bride of the seventeen-year-old French dauphin, shortly to become King Louis VII, with whom she would have two daughters but no happiness, because he was a man of gloom and prudery. Louis was not supposed to be king; the honor of succession should have gone to his older brother, but that poor prince was thrown from a horse and died. So Louis was taken out of the cathedral school in Paris, where he was training to be a priest—surely one day to become a bishop, or even pope—and told that he must prepare instead to become king and to marry the richest woman in France, whose lands were vastly larger than his own. Louis was, by all accounts, thunderstruck by her beauty and vivacity, and she found him and her new status almost charming: he was well educated, thank God, and she was soon to be a queen, not just a duchess.

She sounds like a woman born to love Paris; however, it was a different city then, a massive, malodorous, muddy town, by twelfth-century standards, filled with philosophers, priests, and pedants, and she disliked it from the start. The only true pleasure she took was listening in on the disputations of the brilliant students (such as John of Salisbury) of great teachers (such as Peter Abelard). (Salisbury would in later years come into conflict with Eleanor's second husband over the fate of Thomas Becket, but it was a small world back then.) Eleanor listened to these scholars argue, spent the king's money, and longed for the blithe freedom and green beauty of her true home in sunny, southern France. She pilfered Louis' purse and made him the object of ridicule among such Provençal courtiers as she had in Paris, and the king loved her more and more.

But Eleanor felt as though she were wasting away. Her baby daughter, Marie, gave her consolation, but she was growing increasingly estranged from the pious Louis, whose personal dullness was exceeded only by his sexual indifference. The end of the marriage might certainly have come sooner if the pope had not called upon Louis to lead the Second Crusade.

As a way of shoring up their crumbling marriage, the royal couple decided to go to war together, and Eleanor and her ladies (noble women with glorious French names such as Mamille, Sybille, Florine, Torqueri, and Faydide) rode to a recruitment rally dressed in the costumes of Amazons, which certainly means that they themselves were armed for the battles ahead and possibly that they rode topless, the better to inspire the Christian soldiers preparing to march off to dislodge infidels from God's holy places, especially Jerusalem. This did not endear her to the pope and to the other powerful clerics (most notably Bernard of Clairvaux), who sought to instill different, more elevated passions in the crusaders. But the success of the Crusade depended upon the enthusiastic participation of the troops from Aquitaine, and, besides, the king had no intention of leaving her in France where lustful men might invade the royal bed.

In any event, Eleanor wanted to go—she needed the adventure—and she threw herself with energy and commitment into preparations for the great quest. If you imagine a melding of Eleanor Roosevelt and Carole Lombard on tour in 1942 to sell War Bonds for that later Great Crusade, you get a sense of Eleanor home in Aquitaine raising men and supplies for the long journey east.

Queen Bee of England

When they reached Antioch (in modern-day Syria), where one of her father's brothers, Raymond, was prince, Eleanor was so ecstatic at the wondrous sensuality of the place that she became her uncle's lover—or so said the wagging tongues. Disgusted, the dour Louis kidnapped her and dragged her off to Jerusalem and then home to France, where—after she had begun an affair with the father of the man who would become her second husband—Eleanor was granted an annulment on grounds not of adultery (which was considered) but of consanguinity: she and Louis were fourth cousins. Louis, his love now sere, and the pope, his patience with this particular royal melodrama at an end, were only too happy to be rid of her; they and much of officialdom were convinced she was the devil's own daughter. And there was one additional factor. In the interim between their return from the Crusade and the annulment, Eleanor had given birth to a second daughter, called Alix. Her failure to produce a male heir was probably as much as anything an impetus for the separation, since, unlike England, France never permitted the succession of women to the throne.

Geoffrey Plantagenet, her future father-in-law and present lover, was just nine years her senior. He may have been among the crusaders who had accompanied the quarreling royals to Antioch, and she is said to have remarked to him that "I thought I had married a king, but he is merely a monk," whereupon she fell into his arms. There was nothing monkish about Geoffrey.

He had two nicknames. He was known as "le Bel," which is usually translated as "the Fair," because he was tall and handsome. The other nickname was, of course, *Plantagenet*. This was not his surname.

The sobriquet, as the French would say, was derived from Geoffrey's habit of placing a sprig of broom flower in his hat. Some books mistakenly credit his son Henry with this little innovation, but it was Geoffrey. The botanical classification for the yellow broom is *planta genista*.

He was Count of Anjou and the husband of Matilda, widow-empress of the Holy Roman Emperor Henry V, and, as daughter of the late King Henry I of England, pretender-queen of Britain. Matilda had only recently ceased warring to regain the English throne that her cousin Stephen had seized with the help of the barons, the ones whose sons and grandsons would eventually wrest from her grandson John, a document, the Magna Carta, that in one way or another helped inspire modern notions about civil and human rights. But all this was in the future.

Queen Matilda was nearly a dozen years older than Geoffrey and was probably used to his dalliances. It's even likely that she cared not at all or even that she approved, especially if the fields her husband was furrowing might advance her cause in England, although she no longer hoped to rule herself. Now her ambitions fell upon the eldest of the three sons she'd had with Geoffrey. This was Henry Plantagenet, Duke of Normandy (but also known as Henry of Anjou), who was nineteen in 1152 when his mother arranged to have him wed to the thirty-year-old Eleanor, just eight weeks after the annulment ended her marriage with Louis. The rakish Geoffrey had died the year before, so Eleanor never had too many uncomfortable moments with father and son, lover and husband, as well she might have. In any case, she forgot Geoffrey pretty much the instant she met Henry.

An interesting footnote: back at the time of the Crusade, Geoffrey had tried to convince Louis that Henry ought to be wedded to Louis' and Eleanor's older daughter Marie. Such arranged marriages were common, of course, and no doubt Louis must later have wished he hadn't said no, but he did refuse—ironically, on grounds of consanguinity.

Although still a very young man, Henry was truly a real man. Unlike the ascetic Peter O'Toole, who played Henry to Katharine Hepburn's Eleanor in *The Lion in Winter*, the real Henry was a fitness fanatic, one of history's earliest. He had a tendency to put on weight, and so he frequently exercised and fasted, remaining pretty much in fighting trim until the end.

Not only was he a kingly figure, but he could read too. (Among his tutors was Geoffrey of Monmouth, Arthurian raconteur.) It was said he could read most known languages but spoke only French and Latin. Although he was to become one of England's greatest kings, like all English rulers in the two centuries after the Norman Conquest, he was hardly an Englishman at all. But unlike his son and successor, Richard I the Lionheart, he was a master of administration and governance, and he cared about England. Henry was king for thirty-five years and devoted most of his reign to making England one the most efficient, progressive nations in the world. Richard, on the other hand, was king for a decade, during which time he spent just six months on English soil. The rest of the time he was off making war against somebody somewhere.

Given her appetites, Eleanor could not have been more pleased with her new young husband. She and Henry were very much alike, sensual and ambitious. They made babies—eight in all, three daughters and five sons—and for the next four decades were Europe's most powerful and influential couple.

Henry became king of England in 1154 and for a fair time—nearly a dozen years—he and Eleanor got along very well indeed. But after the birth of John in 1167, Henry lost interest in his forty-five-year-old wife (he was not yet thirty-five) and began to spend all his time with his mistress, Rosamund Clifford. Eleanor left England and returned to France, to Poitiers, where she very consciously created a court similar to her grandfather's. This was in 1170. Some people believe that on a visit to England in 1176, she arranged to have Rosamund's wrists slit as the king's cocotte bathed. Some say Eleanor herself did the slashing. Historians, who are not moved by the story's dramatic potential, insist that Rosamund died of tuberculosis. In any event, Rosamund was dead and Henry would spend the next—the last—dozen years of his unhappy life fighting the sons that Eleanor turned against him. She even arranged for support of her boys' rebellion from her former husband, the king of France. She pales all the willful, wicked heroines of every novel ever written. She outlived all but two of her ten children and died at the age of eighty-two. There is much truth in the statement of Polly Schoyer Brooks, author of a biography of Eleanor written for young adults, that the great queen "won respect for women and made gentlemen out of crude knights."

Sinners, Saints, and Secular Life

Of the elegant troubadours and chivalrous knights who clustered around Eleanor's courts, it has been said that they "deified women, according them superiority over men, and laid down codes of courtesy, chivalry, and gentlemanly conduct. . . . Thus were born the ideals of honour and courtship that in the centuries to come would permeate European literature and culture to such a degree that their influence is still with us today."

How true is this? To what extent do these ancient folk have influence over us now? And what do Eleanor and courtly love have to do with the modern gentleman?

The short answer to the last question is this: any compleat gentleman is part of a lineage that begins with the ideal knight of chivalry and courtly love. Besides, the troubadours of the courts of Eleanor, her grandfather William, and her daughter Marie had a tremendous impact on secular culture. They spread the "gospel" of chivalry, and they preached the virtues of romance, which comes down in the end to respect for women.

As the great Viennese historian Friedrich Heer observed, "Europe's conversion to the courtly way of life . . . was an attack, both open and concealed, on the old . . . idea of a Holy Roman Empire with Charlemagne as its patron saint; it was also anti-Roman and anti-monastic." Almost literally, Eleanor and her troubadours attempted—and to a great extent succeeded—in installing Woman in the place of the Church. It was the invention of a credible secular life.

Love is all about confluence, the meeting of a man and a woman and the mingling of their thoughts and dreams and bodies. In the history and literature of courtly love, there was a meeting of Islamic literature and art—brought into the courts of Europe both through contacts with Cordoba in Spain, then Europe's most enlightened city, and by Muslims encountered during the Crusades—with Roman literature about love, such as Ovid's work, which was also brought to Europe by Arab scholars. This sensual and largely secular poetry collided with Christian ideas concerning love, marriage, and the authority and beauty of Mary, mother of Christ, and finally with the evolving concepts of chivalry, which until this point had been a strictly martial rule.

These ideas about love had many different literary expressions, but the most consistent features of its "philosophy" were the certainty that love ennobles man, that the woman he loves is superior to him, and that his longing for her will never be satisfied.

Satisfaction was even more elusive than now. We mustn't forget how dreary medieval marriage often was. It would be an overstatement to say that nobody married for love, but it is certainly the case that few did. And since there was no active tradition per se of husbands giving loving attention to their wives, it isn't hard to imagine love-hungry women and men being "caught up" in the rhetoric of the troubadours and the postulates of courtly love. Husbands had the authority and backing of the church, which—sad to say—had not a happy view of women, but, in fact, saw them as both inferior and dangerous. Of course there are men today who will say the same, but few of them believe it deeply. Husbands in 1100, however, were likely to view their wives as chattel and to believe them, as daughters of Eve, capable of the most grievous sins. While the so-called "cult of Mary" was in the long run beneficial to the status of women, in the short run it was proof that only a sexless woman was worthy of admiration and adoration.

Romantic love, for that's what courtly love comes down to, was the invention of this period, and it was born out of the woman-as-saint/woman-as-slattern duality. The ancients never really believed that "love" was a factor in the relations between men and women. Passion was a kind of affliction, of insanity. Whom the gods would destroy, first they make carnal. The church agreed, although it believed the cause of the madness was the devil. The sport of the marriage bed was an unfortunate necessity, and its pleasures were overwhelmed by that necessity: procreation. Sex merely for the sake of pleasure was sinful.

The courtly love tradition can be seen as a first step in giving voice to a woman's desires. "Courtliness and courtly humanity," as C. Stephen Jaeger writes, "were, next to Christian ideals, the most powerful civilizing forces in the West since ancient Rome." If they came into conflict with the powerful Roman church, that should come as no surprise.

"Troubadour poetry was totally non-Christian," H. B. Parkes has written. "It glorified adultery and denied any possibility of love between husband and wife. But it transformed the whole meaning of sexuality, changing it from an animal appetite to an instrument for promoting self-control, respect for women, and an appreciation for cultural values. Thenceforth the warrior nobleman was expected to be not only *preux* [valiant] but also *courtois* [gracious] and endowed with a 'gentle heart.'"

Heretics in Love

Love in the Western World is a portentous tome written in 1940 by the Swiss philosopher Denis de Rougemont. Rougemont believed that romantic love, which he considered foxfire, was more or less invented in Europe by those twelfth-century troubadour poets, although their *fin amour* was actually a disguise for their real beliefs, the heresy known as Catharism (aka Albigensianism). So, anyway, said Rougemont. Scholars now pretty much pooh-pooh the idea (although *Love In the Western World* remains on the reading lists of most elite universities, as does the equally "discredited" *Allegory of Love* by C. S. Lewis), but it seems to me that there is both more and less here than the academics are willing to admit or than Rougemont ought to have concluded.

Briefly, the Cathari (a term that comes either from the Greek *katharos*, meaning "pure," or from a German insult having to do with kissing a cat's backside), or Albigensians (or Albigenses, from the town of Albi near Toulouse in what is today southern France), were possibly the most significant heretical sect in the history of the Western Church. Setting aside the ongoing and pervasive heresy of modernism, Catharism was surely the most widespread. Albigensianism, as the heresy was known in what amounts to the territories of Queen Eleanor, was a daughter to the older Manichaeism, itself a variant of Zoroastrianism, the mother of all dualisms. Manichaeism had been ably refuted by Saint Augustine after his conversion, in the mid-fourth century, from Manichaeism to Christianity, and there is a legend that says it was brought to Albi by one Fontanus, whom Augustine himself may have debated face to face.

The Cathari believed that the world is held in tension between Good and Evil: two equal forces represented by God and Satan respectively. God is ruler of heaven and the world of pure spirit, and Satan is ruler of earth and all muddy reality. They believed that Jesus, the one who walked among us, was literally an apparition. As such, he had not really died and had offered no actual redemption, but only ethical instruction. They believed that salvation, which was unity with God, came through renunciation of the flesh and the repudiation of material structures such as civil authority, and, especially, the Catholic Church, which the Albigensians considered Satan's right arm. Suicide was a popular form of Catharist self-denial, as were celibacy, pacifism, and vegetarianism.

One may wonder how such views could possibly be compatible with the sensual dogma of courtly love. The answer is that, in practice, there were two kinds of Cathari: the "perfect" (*perfecti*) and the "believers" (*credentes*). From the former group came the sect's leadership, and they were, as you might suspect, aspirants to purity: chaste, serene, ascetic. The believers, however, were often libertines. The path to purity for the *credentes* ran through a dominion of excess, the notion being (much as in the tantric sects of Hinduism and Buddhism) that, paradoxically, earthly desires may be extinguished through debauchery. At the end of all his drunkenness and fornication (adultery and even incest were tolerated), a believer might (and should) embrace perfection in the *consolamentum* ("consolation"), a ritual that compressed baptism, confirmation, ordination, and last rites into a single ceremony. Deathbed *consolamenta* were common, since most *credentes* figured they couldn't handle the *perfecti*'s rigid rule except in the span of life's last, precious moments. Indeed, if a dying believer recently elevated in extremis to lofty perfection were to recover his health, his concerned brethren might lovingly poison or suffocate him in order to prevent backsliding. That sexual excess was assumed to be common among the *credentes* may be deduced from the evolution of the word *buggery*, a popular euphemism for sodomy, which comes from the association between Catharism and Bulgaria, of all places, from whence it was believed the heresy had sprung.

In fairness, it must be said that nearly everything written about the Cathari in their time—and much subsequently—comes down to us from their enemies, and it's hard to know how much of the reports of scandalous shenanigans is fact and how much is smear.

In any case, Catharism was a complicated worldview, to say the least, but one aspect of its credo is especially important in terms of its similarities with courtly love: it embraced women among the *perfecti*. This is not to say that women commanded equal status with men in every aspect of Albigensian culture. But set against the exclusion of women from the Catholic priesthood and their general inferiority in medieval life, the "heresy" must have had considerable appeal for many women. At least one hardheaded modernist scholar, Meg Bogin, has plainly stated that the heretics of Albi "considered women and men equals; women converts to Catharism, in which women were allowed to preach, vastly outnumbered men."

Much of Queen Eleanor's vast constituency was in the thrall of Catharism (as were large portions of the rest of Europe) and would remain so until the so-called Albigensian Crusade, which in one form or another went on for a century after 1200 and resulted in the disenfranchisement and death of nearly all Cathari. The warrior abbot leading an attack on one Albigensian stronghold (the walled city of Béziers) is said to have replied to concerns about how crusaders would differentiate Catholic from Cathar by saying, "Kill them all. God will recognize his own." This infamous quip may be apocryphal, but it's a fact that the abbot later wrote to Pope Innocent III: "Twenty thousand . . . were put to the sword, regardless of age and sex. The workings of divine vengeance have been wondrous!"

With the echo of steel and the stink of smoke still hanging in the Provençal air, the Inquisition was born. It was very specifically the Albigensian heresy that led Pope Gregory IX to establish his New Tribunal through the Council of Toulouse in 1229. My old edition of *The Catholic Encyclopedia*, bearing the imprimatur of Francis Cardinal Spellman, archconservative archbishop of New York, ruefully admits that "the Inquisition has come to stand in the judgment of many historians as a symbol of cruelty, intellectual terrorism, and religious intolerance. The attempts of certain Catholic apologists to exonerate the medieval Church and Inquisition of those charges have been futile."

One need say no more about it than to recall the chilling fact that heretics who did not end in ashes were forced to wear crosses stitched to their clothing—yellow crosses no less, proving that the Nazis were scrupulous students of medieval history.

An annotation to this and the earlier discussion of chivalry in chapter two involves the Knights Templar. They seem to turn up whenever there is a whiff of medieval mystery and conspiracy. Internet searches reveal interest in Catharism among some contemporary homosexuals, as well as assertions that Templars and Cathars made common cause (then, and if you believe these Web sites, now), both spiritually and sexually. The official suppression of both groups was indeed concurrent, but claims that the Holy Grail and the Shroud of Turin were smuggled out of Albi by gay Templars and lesbian Cathari seem farfetched, although I suppose it might be God's own irony if the Grail were found sitting on the mantle of a Greenwich Village loft.

The bloody end of Albigensianism is often identified as the end of troubadour poetry as well, and, to a lesser extent, the end of *fin amour*. If Rougemont were right about the troubadours' adherence to Catharism, their extinction in the slaughter of the Albigensians would make perfect sense. But more recent scholarly work has proved that the troubadour tradition continued well after the end of the Cathari persecutions, and this indicates what is probably right and wrong about the association of Catharism and courtly love.

When asked where he got the ideas he wrote in the Declaration of Independence, Thomas Jefferson famously remarked with a shrug that they were "in the air." That the sensuality of both *credentes*-style Catharism and courtly love should emerge at the same historical moment is hardly surprising. You might say love was in the air. So were budding ideas about sexual equality.

But it's obvious that not all troubadours were Albigensians and that Catharism was not a required antecedent of sensual, romantic love. History—like the history we're living now—is a stew, but it's a stew no one actually makes. Thus we never know exactly which ingredients give each soupçon of time its particular flavor.

Credentes Catharism, chivalric idealism, absentee husbands, and primogenital angst were like atoms colliding and fusing in a reaction that exploded in the medieval imagination to create the first stirrings in male minds that women were actually the superior sex. Don't take this to mean that in halcyon days our knights believed what subsequent generations failed to continue to believe; that—with apologies to Alan Jay Lerner—we cannot "let it be forgot / that once there was a spot" where women achieved respect and equality, only to see that momentous juncture crushed in its infancy by the force of male-dominated history. The truth is that other women did not share the power over men exercised by Eleanor of Aquitaine, because there was no one else like her. Again, Meg Bogin: "If women were among [courtly love's] most important patrons, it is principally because they stood to benefit from men's new 'courtly' attitudes. Aristocratic women in Occitania had the power to support a movement that appeared to offer them prestige. But the degree to which the veneration of the lady was a veneration of the lady for her sake remains extremely questionable." And yet from Eleanor's time and her court did come the kind of deference toward women that has led so many men, such as those on *Titanic*—to act, they believed, as gentlemen—to surrender their lives in defense of women. This deference is probably a precedent necessary to the evolution of social and legal equality between the sexes, and contemporary feminists who disparage the chivalric attitude among men must explain how history would have conspired to bring us to a point of relative sexual equality without it. Biological inequalities between the sexes are a natural impediment to fair play, and the development of male-female social equity can hardly be seen as inevitable. On the other hand, chauvinistic men who think that this equity is not now an inexorable force are lost in a reactionary hallucination.

Amazons in Love and War

I'm inclined to agree with the comment of classicist Jane Harrison that to be "womanly is one thing, and one only; it is to be sensitive to man, to be highly endowed with the sex instinct; to be manly is to be sensitive to woman." This is especially so with regard to compleat gentlemen. Obviously (and I believe this is what Professor Harrison meant) there is much more to each woman than her sexuality alone; it's just that—and here's a truism if ever there was one—her sexuality is what distinguishes her as a woman. A woman's other qualities are sexless, which is true as well of a man. This should be obvious to anyone possessing just a modicum of objectivity. In business, sports, politics, and in every other conceivable activity, the qualities leading to success and failure have nothing whatsoever to do with sex, which is to say that intelligence, strength, perspicacity, and every other conceivable human quality are sexless. Of course there are observable differences between men and women, which are related—usually hormonally—to sex distinctions, such as top-end speed and top-end strength, but this does not change the fact that the qualities themselves are identical. The strongest man may be stronger than the strongest woman, but she, in turn, is far stronger than most men. This may not have been clear in the past when women's roles were limited, but it is obvious now. Even in parenting and family life, where much is made of feminine nurturance and masculine governance, the administration of love and discipline is extremely fluid. But it is in sport and war that traditional sex roles are truly being transformed.

Indeed, we are fast coming into the era of the woman warrior. Since the 1970s women have been admitted to America's military academies, and there is a steady and compelling chorus intoning the mantra of combat equality.

And what about it? There is tremendous political pressure imposed upon the armed forces to extend full equality to women, and this has no real gravity unless it means allowing them to serve in combat units on the front lines during war. This may seem a slightly tangential issue for the present book, but, in fact, it is central, for nothing promises to change male-female relationships so much as shared combat experience. In the past, chivalric attitudes and practices were fundamentally dedicated to the protection of women, and this was based in part upon the assumption that women were essentially weaker than men. If this assumption is true, then the old ways have the logic and force of truth. If true.

At the Olympic games in Sydney in 2000, women competed in weight lifting for the first time. The top woman in the games, Ding Meiyuan of China, set a world record in the snatch—the lift in which the athlete yanks the bar from the floor straight up over her head, catches it in a crouch, and then drives up to a standing position. That record is nearly 300 pounds (135 kilos, to be exact). I'll wager that among the elite men who serve in the Army's Rangers or Green Berets, the Navy's SEALs, the Marine Corps Force Recon, and Air Force Special Ops there is but a handful who can lift what Ms. Ding lifts. I would be surprised to learn that any of those proud, brave men can run as fast or jump as far as Marion Jones—with or without steroids. And that is what matters.

Sure, neither Ms. Jones nor the 2008 Olympic champion, Veronica Campbell-Brown, can out-sprint male Olympians such as Usain Bolt or Richard Thompson, but they can beat the vast majority of men. There was a time when certain feminists were boldly proclaiming that, with world-class training methods finally available to women, the gaps between men's and women's world records would disappear in time. We now know that this is false. To be sure, it is true that the gaps shrank dramatically as full participation by women was achieved. For instance, when

Florence Griffith-Joyner set the one hundred- and two hundred-meter women's world records at the 1988 Olympics in Seoul, she ran faster than all male Olympic champions had up until the days of Eddie Tolan and Jesse Owens in the 1930s and faster by far than, say, ninety-nine and a half percent of all the men in America could today. But does the athletic superiority of some women to most men make these women and others like them prepared for the rigors of combat? Could they endure elite-force training?

Consider the Navy's SEALs, whose program of preparation is prohibitively difficult, a little bit of hell on earth, in fact, done on very little sleep (maximum four hours per night), and with very big men screaming at you, daring you to quit. And this is just phase one. You don't even want to know what comes in phases two and three.

Could a woman cut it? Women are currently not admitted to SEAL training on the assumption that they can't endure. But is this true? Well, given the demands placed upon candidates, it's hard to imagine anyone cutting it, and, despite the rigorous self-selection that precedes actual admission, a large number of trainees do fail. But I think there are quite obviously a number of women—surely including some already in the navy or attending Annapolis—who are as qualified and capable as most of the men. Perhaps the time has come to give them a shot.

The point of all this should be clear. Modern women can meet the physical demands of combat. Not most women, but then those demands don't suit most men either. If the physical requirements of war were the only ones that matter, that would be an end to the debate about women in combat. But there are other things to consider: cultural, psychological, and biological assets and liabilities. It's pretty clear that men and women must face a degree of discomfort if assimilated in combat. Some men may feel emasculated. Some women may feel complaisant. Some men and some women may feel anxious and confused regarding libido. If and when women are fully integrated in front-line units, there will be problems such as these, since the psychological realities arising especially from cultural traditions do not easily respond to change, well-intentioned or not. But since soldiers, sailors, marines, and aviators are meant to be gentlemen and ladies, we may hope that honor will overcome initial resistance.

However, it is unimaginable that pregnant women could serve in combat positions. Some proponents of women in combat have argued that, due to the stresses of warfare training and actual battle, elite women fighters would become amenorrheic, and thus could not get pregnant. But this is ideological poppycock. Various stresses may diminish the likelihood that a woman will conceive, but they hardly guarantee that she will not get pregnant. A combat-ready soldier who discovers that she is with child would be lost to her unit for about a year. This would lead to some operational and administrative difficulties, but presumably these could be dealt with since all fighting units are by definition prepared for losses. In this sense, there is no difference between a pregnancy and a broken leg. But what if the woman is unaware of her pregnancy until after her detachment has been deployed in hostile territory? We're used lately to short-lived engagements, but we have no clue what the future will bring. In a protracted conflict, such as we experienced in the two World Wars of the last century, combat units can be in place for months at a time. It may be that the risk of pregnant women in the line is not worth the probable cultural and psychological benefits of "equality." War is not politics (no matter how much politics goes on during war), and what may be judged beneficial in peacetime may turn out to be disastrous when armed conflict ensues.

If the bold experiment is to be undertaken—as, it seems, it

inevitably will be—then let it happen immediately so the armed forces will have as much experience as possible of the consequences before we face again the horrors of war.

But let us also accept the implications of the discussion. Women are ever more capable of taking care of themselves in the most extreme situations. As a consequence, many women will resent the actions of a chivalrous man, since they will infer that those actions are "sexist," which is to say that they reflect male superiority. And the question becomes: Does this—should this—lead a gentleman to change his behavior toward women? The answer cannot be made absolute, for there are some situations in which the answer is yes, others where the answer is no.

In the dojo where I have studied karate, there are a number of women who are skilled enough to stand up in a brawl with any man I know—any man, that is, who isn't a first-rate martial artist. For the men with whom they train to show these women deference during sparring would be a perilous imbecility. It would also be an insult to their skill as martial artists, and that would involve any number of transgressions against gentlemanly decorum. So, in the limited combat of the ring, neither I nor any other man will give quarter to these women warriors.

But I still allow them to precede me through a door. They find this odd, perhaps even a little obnoxious, but the truth is that I usually let other men go first as well. It's a matter of courtesy, although probably one I make with a tad too much scrupulosity. As a rule, I think it's the best way to live, so long as I'm not asked why. If I'm asked to defend myself, I shrug, silently invoking my right of *sprezzatura*.

If I seem too casually optimistic about sexual equality, I offer the following cautionary note from Rachel Trickett, late of St. Hugh's College, Oxford. She calls the sort of sexual equality I've outlined above "inevitably anarchic" and worries that the evolved rules of behavior between men and women cannot be jettisoned except at a great price: "When all ideas of a code of conduct collapse, when the concept of courtesy disappears, a condition of primitivism prevails, and its principle is, inevitably, brute force. There is no other way in which to assert some sort of predominance, some sort of pack leadership. And in this situation men will inevitably prevail for the simple, biological reason that they are stronger than women. So that women, without some code of deference or respect, become increasingly victims, however much they try to compete with their superiors in strength." This is not far from the view taken by Christine de Pizan (1364–1430): true love is a disaster without the virtues of civility.

Even in the rarified atmospheres of elite combat units and world-class athletic competitions—and certainly in everyday life situations—there needs to be a common code of courtesy.

Practical Romance

In *Orthodoxy* (1908), G. K. Chesterton speaks of the human need for that "mixture of the familiar and the unfamiliar" we know as romance. This romance—or, as G. K. C puts it, "practical romance"—is again a mixture of "something that is strange with something that is secure," of "an idea of wonder and an idea of welcome." The key thing is to be held to account for the risks and rewards of the romantic adventure. Chesterton writes: "If I bet I must be made to pay, or there is no poetry in betting. If I challenge I must be made to fight, or there is no poetry in challenging. If I vow to be faithful I must be cursed when I am unfaithful, or there is no fun in vowing. . . . For the purpose even of the wildest romance results must be real; results must be irrevocable." Marriage, he says, is the ultimate example of a real and irrevocable result.

Our courtly lovers practiced a kind of adultery in a time when marriage was a contract, not a covenant. I am convinced they did so at least in part out of a new respect for women, and this is what the modern gentleman must emulate. He respects his wife in the only way that has any meaning: he lets her be what she wishes to be.

Courtliness comes down through the ages to us today—or more precisely, yesterday—as *courting*, that lovely, languid dance of a man and a woman preparing themselves for marriage. I say yesterday, because there isn't much courting these days. Relationships are rather more informal; commitments are desultory. Why? The reasons are manifold. As Leon Kass has written, the so-called sexual revolution has led to an "erosion of shame and awe" with regard to sexuality, with all the familiar consequences: so many abortions, so many unwed parents, so many fatherless children, so many divorces, so much infidelity, so much voyeurism. In all, a popular culture that "celebrates youth and independence not as a transient stage en route to adulthood but as 'the time of our lives,' imitable at all ages, and an ethos that lacks transcendent aspirations and asks of us no devotion to family, God, or country, encouraging us simply to soak up the pleasures of the present."

Whether or not one agrees with the whole of his assessment, Professor Kass has certainly captured the dark mood of our time. More simply stated, we live in a hedonistic society, one in which restraint is anathema. With Burke, we might lament that, not only is chivalry dead, but romance is moribund as well:

Never, never more shall we behold that generous loyalty to rank and sex, that proud submission, that dignified obedience, that subordination of the heart, which kept alive, even in servitude itself, the spirit of an exalted freedom. The unbought grace of life, the cheap defence of nations, the nurse of manly sentiment and heroic enterprise is gone! It is gone, that sensibility of principle, that chastity of honour, which felt a stain like a wound, which inspired courage whilst it mitigated ferocity, which ennobled whatever it touched, and under which vice itself lost half its evil, by losing all its grossness.

On this scheme of things, a king is but a man, a queen is but a woman; a woman is but an animal, and an animal not of the highest order. All homage paid to the sex in general as such, and without distinct views, is to be regarded as romance and folly.

So wrote Burke in 1790.

• • •

No matter who is to blame for this state of affairs, the compleat gentleman is called upon to make things right—although only in his own life, since only there can romance be real and irrevocable. In this he may be edified by the story of Sir Gawain and Dame Ragnelle, among the most popular of all Arthurian tales in its time, and a proto-feminist story if ever there was one.

The origins of the tale are Welsh and versions of it appear in the work of John Gower and in the tale of the Wife of Bath in Chaucer. Though elements of the story differ, the sense is always the same.

King Arthur loses a test of skill with a knight near Carlisle and will forfeit his life if he fails within the year to answer the knight's remarkable proto-Freudian question: *What does a woman want?* Arthur is stumped; all of Camelot is stumped, and—365 days having passed—as the king rides despondently to meet his fate, he comes upon a hag (usually referred to as a "loathly lady") who asks him why he is so cheerless. He explains. The ugly old woman laughs her toothless cackle and says, "I can answer the question." Arthur perks up and promises that if she saves him he'll grant her anything. Well, her answer—and it's the correct one—is that what a woman wants most is to have her own way. So the king is delivered, and he couldn't be happier until he hears the hag's quid pro quo. She wants a knight of the Round Table for her husband.

Now of all the noble knights at Camelot, none was nobler than Sir Gawain and he steps forward, ready to fulfill the king's promise to the hag. Gawain and Dame Ragnelle, for that's the loathly lady's name, are married, and on their wedding night, which Gawain has been dreading, she tells him that she is actually a beautiful woman—the most beautiful—and she may appear so half the day. It's a curse, of course. She is transformed before him, and he is indeed stunned by her splendor. So, she says, you must choose: *Shall I be lovely during the day and loathly at night, or loathly in the sunshine and lovely in moonlight?* Gawain scratches his chin. *Well,* he thinks, *would I rather make love to the ugly her in the darkness of our bedroom—I could keep my eyes closed—and be at court with the beautiful her in the daylight for all to see? Or would it be better to make love to my beauty by candlelight and endure the horrified stares at court during the day?* Either because of his inability to decide or because inspiration has broken through to the medieval male mind, he tells Ragnelle that she should decide. As it happens, this is exactly right: the curse is lifted, and she is beautiful forever.

Men and women don't have to be equal, exactly, but a gentleman does have to allow a woman to be what she wants to be. This as much as anything ought to inform a man's ambitions. I admire Katherine Kersten's description of ideal manliness from the standpoint of a "conservative feminist." She will teach her sons that "while strength is good, the strong have a special responsibility to assist and protect the weak and less fortunate." She will insist that her boys "understand the importance of behaving with honor under all circumstances, achieving self-mastery, and cultivating restraint." She "does not wish her sons to grow up believing that, by virtue of being male, they are guilty of the oppression of women. Nor does she wish them to affect to be more 'caring' than the next man in a demeaning effort to impress women who condemn them for the fact of their manhood. True manhood, she counsels them, means accepting responsibility for others and making their welfare a primary focus of life. It means developing a capacity for judgment, courage, honesty, generosity, determination, public-spiritedness, and self-denial in pursuit of a larger good."

It's not for me to comment on a woman's goals. I'll let Mrs. Kersten do that. Her ideal woman—and mine—is "the architect of her own happiness," which she finds in her efforts to "fulfill her responsibilities, to cultivate wisdom, to develop her talents, and to pursue excellence in all her endeavors," and that "no matter how frustrating others' behavior may be, she refuses to seek solace in a life of rage and self-pity."

Who better for a gentleman than such a gentlewoman?

CHAPTER SIX

The Monk

The Ear of Your Heart

They can never have known old monks, wise, shrewd, unerring in judgment, and yet aglow with passionate insight, so very tender in their humanity. What miracle enables these semi-lunatics, these prisoners of their own dreams, these sleepwalkers, apparently to enter more deeply each day into the pain of others? An odd sort of dream, an unusual opiate which, far from turning him back into himself and isolating him from his fellows, unites the individual with mankind in the spirit of universal charity!

—GEORGES BERNANOS, *THE DIARY OF A COUNTRY PRIEST* (1937)

N ow, the reader may well wonder, can a gentleman be a warrior, a lover, and also a monk? The first two seem naturally compatible, the chivalrous medieval knight—practitioner of bloody battles and courtly love—being our model, but the last one must seem fundamentally antagonistic. In the Middle Ages there were "warrior monks" (recall the Templars or Friar Tuck of the Robin Hood legend), but at any time have there been "lover monks"? Well, setting aside considerations of ecclesiastical hypocrisy or of mystical ecstasy, the answer would seem to be no, certainly not as a class. But looked at another way, the monk is very much a lover—of learning and of truth. He is also a man of silence, a man reconciled to his own death, and it is these aspects of the monastic character that dovetail with the character of a compleat gentleman.

The word "monk" comes from the Greek *monakhos*, meaning solitary, and there has always been among monks a conviction that they must be isolated from the rest of us, that only in silence and solitude can the worldly cacophony be tranquilized. If—as religion insists—this is a God-made world then we err if we live without embracing that fact, and a God-centered life must inevitably be offensive to lives fixed on anything else. In the twenty-first century, what is secular has fairly overwhelmed what is spiritual. Sure, folks may profess faith, but spiritual practice is pretty much marginalized.

This is as profound a change as any in Western culture in the past thousand years. Writing of medieval monasticism, Friedrich Heer insists that the monk's pursuit of perfection was influential at all levels of society.

> This is something of far-reaching political and social importance, which must be appreciated, and without it even the Reformation cannot be properly understood. People outside the monasteries, noblemen, peasants, bishops, church dignitaries, village priests, caught in the toils of secular conflicts and passions, were only too well aware that their lives fell far short of the highest Christian standards. . . . All the hopes, prayers, and demands the medieval Christian set on the monks and the monasteries were centered on one expectation: that they would achieve the complete sanctity of a perfect Christian life.

Perfection, of course, is not given to any man. But an awareness of perfection—of the highest possible standards in every aspect of life—is possible. Once again we confront an enduring human aspiration—significant not so much for our success or failure in achieving it as for our awareness of it.

How remarkable is the contrast implied in Heer's statement between the monk's status in the Middle Ages and in our own time. The monastic life is not a topic that comes up often in conversation these days, and I suspect that when it does the bemused response of most people would be: *You mean to say there are monks living in the world today?* And they would wonder why. Why would a certain cadre of religious men and women repair to the wilderness, so to speak, when our cities and towns offer so many delights, including even houses of worship? Can't a spiritual person do more good living "in the world"? *Oh sure,* some may say, *we understand that there are monks in Tibet, but why would an American remove himself so far from the action?* We are a brash and busy people, and there is something suspiciously *outré* about the idea of monasticism in these United States. What can a man gain from some knowledge of or association with monks?

Plenty.

Because he is not a man under vows, the compleat gentleman, seeker of the chivalrous life, will not follow precisely the monastic injunction to be "in the world but not of it." Indeed, he will rather be thought of as a "man of the world," although this does not mean that he will be "worldly" in any base sense. To be a man of the world is to be one who is comfortable in most situations and among most people, and odd as it may seem to those unacquainted with monks, this is actually true of many of those who live cloistered lives. The reasons for this are, first, the monks' education; second, the perspective on their learning provided by contemplation; and third, that faith makes them open to all men of good will. Hospitality is the hallmark of monasteries East and West, just as a generous spirit is the seal of gentlemen everywhere.

But it is the quiet gravity of a monastery, especially in the monastic friendship with death, which separates monks (and, perhaps, compleat gentlemen) from the herd of other men. Monks possess a dignity that roots them even as it sends them soaring.

As the poet Peter Levi describes them: "What marks the monks in the course of their long lives is a silence of the spirit, a childish innocence, an apparently meaningless goodness. They become like good children playing at being good. Their simplicity is more obvious than their depth." This doesn't sound much like a gentleman, does it? If not, we need to look a bit deeper.

The Three Orders

It was one Adalbero, Bishop of Laon, who was among the first to describe (circa 1025) the three orders of feudal society. They were: the *oratores*, the ones who pray; the *bellatores*, the ones who fight; and the *laborares*, the ones who work. "The house of God, which appears as one, is three-fold," the bishop wrote. "Here on earth, some pray, some fight, and some work. These three belong together and are not separated. Thus on the work of one rests the achievement of the two others; each one in turn helps all. This threefold link is therefore a single thing. As long as this law prevailed, the world has been at peace." We may think of Adalbero as an early sociologist and reckon that his theorizing served him no better than it does today's academic canons. It is certainly the case that many contemporary scholars dispute that *trifunctionalism*, as it is sometimes called, was ever an actual matter of substance. Or they assert that it was all too real and was, in fact, the ideology of feudal oppression.

But if Adalbero was an agent of privilege and hierarchy, he was also a genuinely democratic voice, which in the first decades of the second millennium was a rare thing indeed. To be sure, he was not at war with a social structure that rigidly assigned positions in society according to "class" (like just about everybody else, he saw these castes as inevitable, even God-ordained), but he was also aware of the rights inherent in the very existence of every individual.

There are two legal spheres, he argued: the laws of the state and the laws of God. Of the latter Adalbero makes clear that divine law makes no distinctions among its ministers: "according to it, they are all of equal status. The son of a worker is not inferior to the heir to the throne." No prince is exempt from God's judgment.

In the same way, the character of the compleat gentleman, which was beginning to be formed in Adalbero's lifetime, is trifunctional. These parts of his identity correspond—more or less—to the old notion of "orders" or "estates," except each is truly integrated with the others within a single personality. I have chosen to call these personal estates the monk, the warrior, and, in the third case, the lover rather than the "worker." Your average medieval man on the street—or man on the mud path—was unlikely to see himself as trifunctional. Nevertheless, his view of the world was—more than our own, I suspect—defined by war, religion, and sex: war, because it was a looming and brutal political reality; religion, because it was the defining intellectual and emotional verity; and sex, because it was both the biological imperative and his only escape from war and religion.

In every medieval person's life there were almost certainly two foci of attention: the manor and the monastery. Each in its way stood for a person's very survival, body and soul. From the manor or castle of the local suzerain came the legal and military authority that was alternately a blessing and a curse, and from the local monastery came the religious and spiritual authority that gave life its order and hope. The legacy of the manor is debatable, although chivalry and courtly love are inconceivable without it. But the monastery gave us an unambiguous and enduring structure for modern life, especially in education and government.

Benedict and Modernity

The high point of monasticism came in or around our signal year, 1100. At that point, the great Benedictine abbey at Cluny in France was the headquarters of a truly multinational corporation of faith, education, diplomacy, and enterprise with branch houses—one thousand of them—located all over Europe. The democratically elected abbot of Cluny was the most powerful person on the Continent after the pope, who was himself the only earthly person to whom the abbot had to answer. Half a dozen popes during the age were formerly Cluniac monks.

Cluny was a Benedictine house—founded by one of Eleanor of Acquitaine's forebears—but it gave rise to the Cistercians, who in turn gave rise to the Trappists. Bernard of Clairvaux, of whom we spoke in chapter two, expanded the Cistercian order from which the Trappists sprung; the Cistercians—named for the site of their first house at Cîteaux—themselves were an offshoot of the Benedictines of Cluny. Whereas the Benedictines wore black habits, the Cistercians wore white. The Trappists wear a black cowl over a white habit. The Knights Templar were essentially Cistercians by rule and wore the order's white habit, albeit emblazoned with a red cross. The Cistercian abbeys have been called "nurseries of saints," because so many of their order have been canonized. Each new order represented an impulse to reform monasticism, the church, or even faith itself, and behind each new shake-up was the imperative to live up more faithfully to the rule, the spiritual and organizational guide created by Benedict of Nursia in the sixth century.

St. Benedict may be the most underestimated man in the history of the West. To be sure, he is the patron saint of Europe, and yet I'm amazed at how few people know anything at all about him—including the Europeans themselves. He was not the first monk, but he was certainly the greatest, which is why Joseph Ratzinger chose the name Benedict when he was elected pope in 2005.

The earliest monks were *anchorites* (from the Greek meaning "retiring one"), men of the fourth century who took to the desert alone. If they had any interaction with others, it was usually with hermits like themselves, with whom they might join for Sunday Mass. A few were itinerant and lived off alms. Just as Christianity was becoming an established religion, emerging from centuries of persecution, it was entering into its first great period of reform, the ultra-personal reformation of hermit monks.

A little later, a handful of *cenobitic* houses were formed. The word comes from the Latin for "common life." An Egyptian convert, St. Pachomius, founded the first monastery in 312, and by the time he died in 348 there were three thousand monks living in nine monasteries, mostly in what we now call the Middle East. The rule he wrote to govern their common life was a primary source for the later statutes of St. Benedict. The rule of Pachomius was translated into Latin by St. Jerome, who also created the Latin, or Vulgate, Bible, and St. Augustine—of *The Confessions* and *The City of God*—who used the rule in organizing his North African monastic community. But it was Benedict's expansive and compassionate rule that struck the soul's tuning fork and has kept it vibrating ever since.

Benedict was a monk—an anchorite, in fact—for some years before he became part of a community and adapted several popular monastic constitutions into his rule. His first brother monks grew restless under his influence and even attempted to poison him, or so the legend goes. But when Benedict blessed the tainted wine offered to him, the goblet shattered. A saddened and disgusted Benedict headed for the mountains.

He promulgated his famous rule at the monastery he built on Monte Cassino, near the Rapido River in central Italy. Few men before or since have had so clear a sense of the strengths and weaknesses of the human heart. The Rule of St. Benedict balances autocracy—the authority of the abbot—with democracy—the individual voices of the monks. It unifies manual labor and higher learning. It has been said of the Benedictine monks that they saved European knowledge and literature during the instability of the so-called Dark Ages, and to the extent that this is true, the credit belongs in large measure to their founder. But there is more.

Monasticism was the dominant cultural force in Europe for the millennium from 500 to 1500, and the Benedictine rule was the most widely read and studied non-biblical work during that period. Moreover, it was in this momentous age that the first-nation states were formed and the first universities and guilds founded. Each innovation in its way owed a great deal to lessons learned from the governance, education, and organization developed in Benedictine houses. We may begin to wonder if Benedict ought not to be the patron of modernity itself. Of the good parts, anyhow.

The rule begins with a prologue: "Listen carefully, my son, to the master's instructions, and attend to them with the ear of your heart." What follows is Benedict's *via media*, a "middle way," a plan of life less harsh than earlier monastic rules, which among other things, had called for the monk to refrain from retiring to his bed until he was actually asleep standing up. What does not follow is the familiar priestly trilogy: poverty, chastity, and obedience. The last was first in Benedict's new rule, but its brother concepts were silence and humility, with greatest emphasis on humility. Benedict laid down rules concerning the recitation of prayers, since a monastery is first and foremost a "school for the Lord's service." The rule also prescribes work: each monastery ought to be self-sufficient.

From earliest times there was debate among the monks themselves concerning the central aspects of the religious vocation. For many it was prayer, contemplation, liturgy, and nothing else. For others, it was those things but also a rich cultural life in which education, the arts, and even industry were essential. (The debate goes on unabated: Thomas Merton, an American Trappist monk who died in 1968, never ceased complaining that the "cheese-makers" at his monastery in Kentucky detracted from its meditative spirit.) The monks were not only, in their scriptoria, the meticulous copiers and translators of ancient texts but also builders of libraries, founders of universities, and patrons of science and the arts.

Monasticism began in the desert and by some interpretations has never left it. Monks, wherever they are, seek "dryness," a flat and empty spirituality that leaves them utterly alone and dependent upon God. Of course, this "wandering in the wilderness" usually goes on within a stable community that shares the experience, and the role of senior monks, priors, and abbots is to stand ready with the "water of life," which is the word of God, and the cool counsel of their own itinerant years.

If you have never been to a monastery for a retreat, I recommend it—whether or not you are Catholic. Go to one of the Trappist houses—there are about a hundred worldwide—because there, for however long you may stay, you are privileged to participate in a way of life that has changed very little since the Middle Ages. There are, of course, some Trappists (they are technically the Cistercian Order of the Strict Observance; "Trappist" comes from the first of their chapter houses at La Trappe in France) who will tell you that the old ways have pretty much disappeared. But relative to the rest of modern life, Trappist observance is downright medieval.

Liberal Learning

We so often acknowledge the value of education that we have ceased to understand that it is practically a sacrament. Organized Western education arose most directly from the *studia generalia* of European monastic communities. The *studia* were open to monks and laymen alike and were a response to two forces at work in Europe during the Middle Ages. The first was an expanding interest in classical authors and ideas caused by interaction with Islam. Arab scholars were almost literally centuries ahead of their northern neighbors not only in the translation of Greek and Latin texts but also in the important work of developing the scientific theories of Aristotle, Galen, and others. The second was an expanding enterprise of monasteries, which demanded that the integration of science, the arts, and commerce be a matter of course for monks as well as laymen. Whatever the monks did—farming, winemaking, brewing, translating—they employed the latest knowledge available.

Education had been a part of the chivalric temperament (if not its practice) as far back as that earliest influence on chivalry, Charlemagne. Not only did the great king's love of learning influence the development of writing in the innovation of Carolingian script, and literature, in everything from the encouragement of troubadours to the opening of libraries, it also profoundly affected the structure and institutions of higher learning. It was very much with Charlemagne's encouragement that the English monk, Alcuin, introduced into the king's palace school a rudimentary program of liberal arts.

Above all, education came to be valued not so much for what

it could do to make man a more effective professional as for the value it had in making him a better human being. We see this in the work of clerical authors such as Chrétien de Troyes. "The earliest romances, the romances of antiquity," C. Stephen Jaeger has written, "name two themes: love and chivalric combat. But a quite different theme enters the romance in the works of Chrétien: the education or the moral formation of the knight. Mere chivalric activity without some higher motive brings a knight to ruin."

To a considerable extent, we are now living through an era now very like the medieval period. The Internet is a kind of new scriptorium,* where civilization is both preserved and created. The opportunity presents itself—to gentlemen at the very least, but perhaps also to the culture at large—for the rediscovery of the virtue of liberal-arts education, which seeks to teach a man (and a woman) how to enjoy life, not simply how to advance a career. Far be it from me to demean vocational education per se, but to be a cultured person, which a compleat gentleman surely is, is to have a liberal education because no other kind of learning truly edifies.

As we have seen, the monks of the early Middle Ages have been credited with preserving European learning. For many centuries afterward, the only schools on the Continent and in Britain were monastic schools. Monks such as the Venerable Bede and Alcuin helped make liberal learning an integral part of monastic life, just as Abelard, Aquinas, and Bacon made it the heart of the new universities.

---

* A scriptorium was the room in a monastery—usually next to the library— where scribes copied manuscripts. It was essential, since (before 1450, when Gutenberg invented moveable-type and began printing books) every volume in a library had to be handwritten. A "book" (every book was rare and precious) would come on loan to the scriptorium where a scribe would copy the manuscript—and usually "illuminate" initial letters with gold—for inclusion in the monastery's own collection.

The prototype of the European university was the ninth-century medical school in Salerno, Italy, although in its concentration on medicine it was more like an Islamic university. The first true university emerged in Bologna late in the eleventh century and was followed by foundations at Paris and Oxford. In each case the universities were extensions of cathedral schools or the *studia* of monasteries, and their curricula were focused primarily on theology and law. But as they began to attract scholars from around the world, men who brought with them expertise in a wide variety of disciplines, the universities developed programs of study in what became known as the liberal arts, liberal in the sense of free—education befitting a free man.

The University of Paris emerged from the cathedral school of Notre Dame sometime in the late eleventh or early twelfth century. As much as any institution, Paris spawned the development of the scientific method, although credit for this is usually given to Roger Bacon of Oxford. But it was the scholastic philosophers and theologians at Paris (of whom Abelard is the first and Aquinas the most famous) who embraced the Aristotelian logic that opened the door to free inquiry.

Oxford can date some form of organized teaching as early as 1096, but the university has no actual founding. Its evolution was speeded by Henry II, who banned English students from attending classes in Paris in 1167.

In our own time, students are fleeing public schools for traditional private schools, for non-traditional experimental schools, and even in increasing numbers for home schooling. As we begin—and justly—to experiment with such reform techniques as vouchers and charter schools, we must remain cognizant of the unbelievably, even transcendently important role that "free" public education has played in making American democracy work. (I put *free* in quotes, because nothing—and certainly not schooling—is actually gratis.) We may agree to one degree or another about the failure of public education, but in such discussions we may fail to recall how successful it has been and how clearly it has been a major reason for American ascendancy.

What remains at risk in education at all levels is learning for learning's sake. Cardinal Newman, writing in *The Idea of a University* (which, as we've seen, is justly famous for its well-reasoned comments about the unsound popular definition of the gentleman à la Lord Chesterfield and Samuel Smiles), makes clear his conviction that the tool of diverse curricula must never degrade a university's goal: an educated whole man. Newman, of course, believed that what was wrong with much thinking about higher education, as about the gentleman, was the absence of a truly higher learning and higher living, which meant too much specialization and too little religion. Newman was right that education without a vision of its proper end is mere dilettantism, and he was right that a gentleman without chivalry is merely a dandy.

In our time it is not likely nor is it appropriate outside of parochial schools for faith to be the ordering principle of education. But what about chivalry? Could it be the new and proper goal of higher learning? Well, no. Most schools are wholly unprepared to produce chivalrous men. Even at the schools, such as the service academies, where chivalry is seen as an end, the number of graduates who truly embody chivalry is no doubt small, so insistent is the drumbeat of vocational specialization and canine self-interest.[†]

The closest thing we have to an academy of chivalry is the monastery, and how close is that?

[†] One exception of particular interest to the author is Montfort Academy in Katonah, NY, which describes itself as "a classical high school for young men." The academy requires its students to take a year-long course in chivalry. I'm very pleased that *The Compleat Gentleman* is the textbook.

The Great Silence

I first came to Our Lady of Gethsemani Trappist Abbey one cloudy winter morning in 1974. I drove down from a Catholic seminary in Cincinnati along roads made slick from the previous night's ice storm. Power lines were arched ominously under the weight of icicles. Bare tree limbs were bowed but glistening. As I turned onto Kentucky 247, a few miles south of Bardstown, my hands gripped the wheel so tightly my knuckles were white, especially when I saw a yellow caution sign warning that the curving road was about to dip. I worried that the tires on my old Nash Rambler might not have the traction to climb the hill up after the hill down, but the rise was gentle, and as I made the east-west curve and came onto the last flat straightaway, I saw the monastery spire and saw that there was a patch of blue sky above the abbey and that the border of gray clouds around the blue was rimmed in fiery gold. Sunlight streamed down in ribbons on the monastery, and I was actually frightened that I was witnessing some message from God, that this retreat was meant to be the beginning for me of a vocation to the monastic life. I almost turned the car around and drove away.

It was a momentous stay for me. As I recall, it was a Monday to Friday retreat—because I realized I was not cut out to be a monk, however much I admired the monastic life and might try to emulate it in my worldly existence. I did not mind rising at three in the morning and collapsing into bed at eight in the evening, and, though as a visitor one does not participate in the work of the house, I would not have minded the farming I saw the monks doing—I'd spent summers in high school working on a farm. I did not mind the silence, which in any case is not particularly burdensome for a visitor. What I minded was the absence of women, and if you miss the girls you know you are not made for monkhood. I shared my thoughts with the guest master and told him about the omen of sunlight that had greeted my arrival. I wondered if I were missing God's call. The monk looked at me for a moment and then, barely suppressing a chuckle, he asked:

"You mean to say you think God arranges the weather for you?"

Then we both had a good laugh.

"Anyone who takes himself too seriously always runs the risk of looking ridiculous; anyone who can consistently laugh at himself does not," Václav Havel wrote in *Disturbing the Peace*.

I had not expected to realize so quickly that I was not cut out for the monastic life, and in the years following I could not help feeling that I had missed something essential on my visit. I did not marry for another decade, and until I did, I would wonder if I had overestimated my passion for women—this despite considerable evidence to the contrary. I'd tell friends the story of my retreat: the ride down, the portentous sunlight, the day-long process of prayer, the hiking in the woods, the hours in the library studying the Rule of St. Benedict.

"Tell me about that rule," a friend said once. "You were reading it then and there. Did the Trappists seem to be following it?"

I said I thought they surely were, and my pal wondered what that meant.

"'Ne quid nimis,'" I replied.

"Which means what?" he asked.

"Nothing to excess."

Well, he was flabbergasted. He demanded to know how cloistered men praying incessantly and living in silence and solitude can be considered anything but excessive. I replied that those words from the rule seem to govern life at Gethsemani, that the monks seem to float along on a cushion of equable poise. They were unflappable.

"Stoic?" he asked.

Exactly.

Had I been twenty-seven and brought my sorry self before most "men of the cloth," I likely would have received advice along the lines I've often heard and read in subsequent years: *Perhaps the parting clouds rimmed in gold were meant by God to signify the wedding ring you'll wear one day.*

I've rarely met a "counselor" whose eagerness to please has not made him the prisoner of shibboleth. But the Trappists were capable of speaking directly, simply, and without homily. They possess the compassion you expect but also a detachment that takes you by surprise. That's the stillness that on first encounter seems downright eerie. I tended to glamorize it, imagining that the monks really were floating by, feet off the ground, carried along by angels. But they were just going here and there, and they knew exactly where, and, in fact, they were always already there. The guest master spoke to me plainly, and his words were wonderful because they were created only for me. He gave me his precious time, and in the minutes we shared he was able to see me with a heart and a soul and a mind uncluttered by the bumptious intrusions of television and movies, car payments and mortgages, women and children, war and peace. If your retreat into monasticism works, it works because you share a week on the edge of eternity. The monk's day seems to be ruled by the clock, although in the form of bells, and the order of his life is more structured than a corporate manager's:

3:15   Rise
3:30   Vigils (the first stage of the Divine Office)
4:00   Scripture study, private prayer, and breakfast.

6:30	Lauds (Divine Office, II)
7:00	Mass
8:00	More scripture study and private prayer
9:15	Terce (Divine Office, III)
9:30	Work
11:45	Sext (Divine Office, IV)
Noon	Lunch
1:45	None (Divine Office, V)
2:00	Work
4:30	More scripture and prayer and supper
5:30	Vespers (Divine Office, VI)
6:00	Scripture and prayer
7:20	Chapter (the monks meet), followed by Compline (Divine Office, VII)
8:00	Retire

There is, obviously, very little wiggle room here for insinuating modernity—if by modernity we mean whatever is the latest pop rage. Thomas Merton remarked on the paradox that the monks, who have none of the pleasures of the world, "have all the happiness that the world is unable to find." In his history of the Trappist order, *The Waters of Siloe* (1949), Merton wrote of the monks that

> . . . there is something in their hearts that tells them they cannot be happy in an atmosphere where people are looking for nothing but their own pleasure and advantage and comfort and success. They have not come to the monastery to escape from the realities of life but to find those realities: they have felt the terrible insufficiency of life in a civilization that is entirely dedicated to the pursuit of shadows.

I was a great admirer of Fr. Merton in my youth but have come to question much of his political and moral sense, especially at the time of his death. But nobody ever wrote with such authority and elegance of the monastic life. His work was always meant to be a bridge between the cloister and the world outside, and the message was clear: the "world" can give little to the monk, but the monk can give the rest of us the precious gift of silence. This silence is not simply tight lips and an empty head. It is, as in the rule, a *via media*, a middle way of balance and discretion.

Modern Trappists and Cistercians and Benedictines—following Benedict's Rule—are all engaged in some sort of for-profit work, producing goods and services that help fund monastery operations. At Gethsemani in Kentucky, the monks make cheese and fruitcake; at Christ in the Desert in New Mexico, the monks do Web page design; at Mepkin Abbey in South Carolina, the gift shop offers "Earth Healer" compost tea bags. Among the most famous of Trappist products are the ales and beers produced at Abbaye Notre Dame de Scourmont in Belgium, which are marketed under the Chimay brand. Each of the three styles, red, triple, and blue, are unfiltered, unpasteurized, and oddly spicy to the American palate. The brewery Web site (www.chimay.be) offers a wonderful guide to the ale-making process. There are six Trappist brewers in the world, all in Belgium; most of them also produce cheese.

It has been said of the monk that he is a "man who practices dying as a way of life." The Web site of Assumption Abbey (www.assumptionabbey.org), a community of Trappists in the Ozark Mountains, elaborates: "A monk dies to his egoism, his self-deception, to the illusions about who he should be and what life is all about that his upbringing and his culture have laid upon him; he dies to his compulsions and to his raw emotional responses to people and situations." That's not the most felicitous phrasing, but it succeeds in making its point; if it sounds rather like Stoicism, we ought not to be surprised.

There are communities of monks who take the business of dying to a whole different level. Consider the monks of New Melleray Abbey near Dubuque, Iowa, the house from which the monks of Assumption came. The white and gray stone monastery rises up out of the green Iowa cornfields like an apparition. The abbey was founded by a group of Irish monks who came from Mount Melleray Abbey in Ireland and who were themselves originally emigrants from the great Trappist monastery at Melleray in France. The fathers and brothers of New Melleray have organized monastic life around death—to the point that it is their industry. New Melleray is in the casket business.

There are other marvelous examples of Trappist enterprise, but one of the finest and most unexpected is the bonsai business at the Monastery of the Holy Spirit in Conyers, Georgia.

It all began with Fr. Paul Bourne (1908–1995), who grew up in Seattle and developed an early appreciation of the Japanese art of growing dwarf trees. That he would later make it the central business of his monastery is no surprise when you consider that Conyers is a daughter house of Gethsemani and that Gethsemani was the home of author Thomas Merton, whose passion for Zen gave new perspective on the contemplative life to Christian monks worldwide. As Fr. Merton became the correspondent of leading Asian, especially Buddhist, religious leaders (such as D. T. Suzuki), Fr. Bourne became the friend and pen pal of the top bonsai artists from America, China, and Japan. There are bonsai plants available from the greenhouse at Holy Spirit, but the monks' main trade is in the sundry shallow pots and tiny tools that bonsai artists require. Again the Internet, the new scriptorium, provides a glimpse of the fascinating work done at Holy Spirit, at bonsaimonk.com. It should be noted that the monks do not manufacture what they sell; they have simply become the leading American retailers of bonsai pottery and tools, mostly made in Japan, Korea, and elsewhere.

What is most striking in a retreat with the Trappists is the quiet. A monastery is a community of faith, to be sure, and its ritual of daily prayers—the Divine Office—can truly elevate one's soul. But it is the silence that grabs you. Conversations with monks can be had—after all, they are there to offer spiritual guidance to the rest of us—but as a rule, and I mean that literally, Trappists live in silence. The hours from eight in the evening until three in the morning are known as "the Great Silence."

What this means for the compleat gentleman may not be immediately apparent, but it has to do with the necessity for a kind of Stoic reserve. A part of oneself needs to be cloistered—set apart from the world's tumult and aware of perfection. The best men will seek a sort of secular sanctity in silence. Perfection is not the goal, interior calm is.

There is here a dovetailing with *sprezzatura*, about which you'll learn more in this book's final chapter. Although the primary meaning of *sprezzatura* is essentially nonchalance, I construe it to imply *restraint, appropriate silence*. Of all gentlemanly qualities, restraint—and the silence that accompanies it—is the least respected; it is the one most fallen into disuse. And that's un-American. After all, way back in 1850, Hester Prynne proclaimed in Hawthorne's *The Scarlet Letter*, "We must not always talk in the market-place of what happens to us in the forest." Why now do we feel compelled to broadcast our every dark thought and deed?

A properly monkish attitude leads one to a proper respect for silence. Some of the best advice I ever received came from a senior business associate who, taking an interest in the progress of my publishing career, gently suggested to me (after a meeting in which I'd offered some glib and fatuous insights in response to a question he'd posed) the following: "If you don't know, say 'I don't know.'"

Without knowing it, he was echoing the words of philosopher Ludwig Wittgenstein: "Whereof one cannot speak, thereof one must be silent."

The Stoic Way

The preceding has dealt very specifically with the inner calm of Catholic monasteries; however, this is not meant to suggest that Rome is the spiritual home of the compleat gentleman. Actually it is, although it's Rome before the coming of the followers of Jesus—the Rome of the Stoics.

When we think of monks—Christian, Buddhist, or of whatever other flavor—we naturally imagine men of great faith, men whose faith defines them. Without wishing to get into a contretemps concerning the "Christian gentleman," it is necessary to state that "gentleman" is not a religious concept per se. It is fine to use the particular religious adjective (Christian gentleman, Jewish gentleman, Muslim gentleman, and so on), as long as one understands that the specifics of faith do not inhere in the word modified. In this regard, "gentleman" is a kind of profession, like "accountant" or "baker." Your CPA may be Catholic and your baker may be Jewish, but there is no religious content in the bean counter's balance sheets or the other guy's cookies, unless they're kosher.

Yet if a gentleman is not per se religious, he is inherently monkish in that, like his cloistered and professed brethren, he is a man living under a dispensation of principles. Those principles may be connected to his religious faith—if he has faith—but even agnostic and atheist gentlemen (and there probably aren't many of the latter) are guided by at least one principle. Simply stated: *A gentleman is dedicated to the virtue of goodness.* He believes he ought to do the right thing.

In 1940, classicist Gilbert Murray described the secular "religion" of Stoicism: "Rank, riches, social distinction, health, pleasure, barriers of race or nation—what will those things matter before the tribunal of ultimate truth? Not a jot. Nothing but goodness is good. It is what you are that matters—what you yourself are; and all these things are not you." This is appealing—a kind of conservative liberalism: a tough-minded tolerance. But true philosophy and religion don't allow us to rush on by such grand statements without a careful scrutiny of their essential elements: What is the "good" of goodness? The Stoic answer is: the right thing. What is right (and therefore good) is the proper functioning of Man according to the laws governing his life. Christ's statement that we must "render unto Caesar that which is Caesar's and unto God that which is God's" would have appealed to the Stoics. "Good order," wrote Burke, "is the foundation of all good things."

Another classical scholar, Ludwig Edelstein, puts it this way: "It does not matter what happens to a man. What counts is that he wants the right, that he does the right, that he makes the right use of the things that befall him."

A compleat gentleman is a man who tries to do what is right and honorable in any given situation. He seeks harmony with the laws of God, or nature, and of man. Again, Murray: "A good bootmaker is one who makes good boots; a good shepherd is one who keeps his sheep well; and even though good boots are . . . [in the eyes of God] entirely worthless, and fat sheep no whit better than starved sheep, yet the good bootmaker or good shepherd must do his work well or he will cease to be good. To be good he must perform his function; and in performing his function there are certain things that he must 'prefer' to others, even though they are not really 'good.'"

If this recourse to an ancient philosophy makes the Christian faithful queasy, consider the statement of C. S. Lewis: "I reject at once the idea which lingers in the mind of some modern people that cultural activities are in their own right spiritual and merito-rious—as though scholars and poets were intrinsically more pleasing to God than scavengers and bootblacks. . . . The work of Beethoven and the work of a charwoman become spiritual on precisely the same condition, that of being offered to God."

Stoicism has had enduring appeal because it is the natural worldview of gentlemen. It has been the subject of some par-ody—and ridicule—as amounting to little more than the "stiff-upper-lip" introversion of generations of graduates from English public schools, or the "Howdy-Ma'am" taciturnity of all the American men who emulate the cowboy. But male character has been formed and transmitted across time as much through the agency of Stoic philosophers as through the more obvious reli-gious traditions. Why? As we have seen, Stoicism was the phi-losophy rediscovered in the Renaissance, and again in the Victorian Era, that seemed so perfectly suited to the martial her-itage of the best men. It was not—at least in its Roman ver-sion—fundamentally at odds with Christianity. The works of Cicero, especially—traditionally read to some extent simply as exercises in philosophy or rhetoric or Latin—became the back-ground of much spontaneous thinking about maleness. It became an interior cache of an Anglo-American passion for decency. Few men would have called themselves Stoics because they were Christians or Jews, and their God is—so they say—a jealous God.

Yet the gentleman's urbanity makes him open to the great thinkers who are not of his immediate faith—as Aquinas was open to Aristotle. John Henry Newman put it this way in his great spiritual autobiography *Apologia Pro Vita Sua*: "I understood . . . that the exterior world, physical and historical, was but the manifestation to our senses of realities greater than itself. Nature was a parable, Scripture was an allegory; pagan literature, philosophy, and mythology, properly understood, were but a preparation for the Gospel. The Greek poets and sages were in a sense prophets."

This is not the place in which to summarize the Stoic way. There are too many sources, too many ideas, too many interpreters. What matters for the present discussion is the way in which Stoicism has been adapted to the gentlemanly ideal; the ways in which influential writers and thinkers have been, since the time of Castiglione and Shakespeare, in the thrall of Stoic ideas concerning everything from national government to personal decorum. The influence of Cicero, Seneca, Epictetus, and Marcus Aurelius was profound, from the American Founding until well into the twentieth century. My reprint of the 1911 edition of the Harvard Classics, the "five-foot shelf of books" that helped to define what editor Charles W. Elliot called the "cultivated man," includes volumes devoted to, or including the most notable work of, each of the Roman Stoics (with the exception of Seneca).

Shakespeare was certainly a neo-Stoic. One sees it throughout his canon, but never more dramatically than in the several instances in which he directly states that the world is a stage and each of us an actor with a part to play. A man may play the king or the fool. It does not matter at all what role we're given, but it absolutely matters how well we perform. A later contemporary of Shakespeare named Ellis Walker wrote a poem in which he sought to define the gist of Stoicism as taught by Epictetus (or rather as reported by his student Arrian):

> Respecting man, things are divided thus:
> Some do not, and some do belong to us.
> Some within the compass of our power do fall,
> And these are they, which we our own may call.

Centuries before Cicero, Epictetus, and Marcus Aurelius, there were other Stoics, beginning with Zeno of Citium, Cleanthes, and Chrysippus, all of whom taught in and around Athens beginning in the fourth century before Christ. (The name Stoic, by the way, is derived from *Stoa Poikile*, or "Painted Porch," and refers to the actual site where Zeno and the others held their lectures—apparently a brightly decorated colonnade.) The soul of early Stoic moral teaching was harmony, austerity, and detachment; there is a Zen-like quality to the best Stoic writing. Epictetus, who lived between AD 50 and 138, is said to have lived in a small hut with just a wooden pallet, a straw mat for his bed, and a clay lamp by which he read and wrote.

Marcus Tullius Cicero (who died in 43 BC) is sometimes known affectionately in Britain as "Tully." He produced his philosophical writing late in life, in the years when he sought "*otium cum dignitate,*" leisure with dignity. Among the books he wrote then was *De Officiis* (*On Duties*), of which Voltaire said that nobody ever wrote anything "more wise, more true, or more useful."

But it is probably Epictetus who has had the most lasting impact. The finest thing about Stoicism is its insistence that a philosophy's ethics ought to conform to its physics, this is to say, that the right way of behaving in the world ought to conform to the way the world works. I regret even mentioning this, since there is not space in this book to explicate the point, but for now let it be understood that there is in Stoicism a certain elegant fatalism—a sense that things are as they are and that very little of what is, is within our control. This leads to the most famous Stoic characteristic, *apatheia*, which is not "apathy" in the sense that we use the word today (although, obviously, it is its origin). What may appear to be passivity or indifference in the true gentleman is actually the artful integration of wisdom and resignation. He is not agitated by poverty or cruelty because he has no expectation that these things should not exist. This is not to say that he will not be a good citizen and work to alleviate poverty and stop cruelty. However, his activities in this regard will tend more to quiet, individual acts of anonymous charity and personal kindness than to public displays of passion. He recognizes the important distinction between the public and the private man.

We all sense, don't we, that there is a difference between the two spheres, the public and the private? What is often missing is a proper Stoic respect for the reality involved: a recognition that the two spheres, albeit intimately related, are different, and it is not mere pretense to behave differently in each.

. . .

Goodness, according to Epictetus, comes when we live in accord with nature. This doesn't mean lots of gardening and camping trips, and it certainly doesn't mean living in teepees. It means, to put it in more familiar Christian terms, living in unity with God's will.

Stoic *apatheia* is key to a part of Castiglione's notion of *sprezzatura*. The best expression I've ever read of this "indifference" is in the Zen story told of the poet Ryokan, a Japanese contemporary of Edmund Burke. Dedicated as he was to the principles of

Zen, Ryokan lived in a simple hut with no possessions save a begging bowl and his Buddhist robe. One night as he came home to his hut from a day of petitioning and prayer in a nearby village, he surprised a burglar, who stood in Ryokan's one bare room, his eyes flashing anger at having found nothing at all to steal.

"Have you come far, friend?" Ryokan asked, but the thief seethed silently.

"No doubt you have," the monk went on, "and you will not want to leave with nothing."

And so saying, Ryokan removed his robe and handed it and the bowl to the astonished man who took the gifts and fled. Illuminated only by moonlight, the thief ran down the path toward the village until he disappeared into the dark night. The naked monk looked after him and sighed. He sat down upon the cool earth and looked up at the night sky.

"Poor, poor man," he told the stars. "How I wish I could give him this beautiful moon."

Had Ryokan been a monk trained at the Shaolin Temple in China, he might have done as he did, or—if the thief had thought to steal his few possessions before Ryokan made a present of them—he might have throttled the felon. We recall with pleasure that the very first Zen master, the Patriarch Bodhidharma, was also the "inventor" of Asian martial arts. He and his monks developed the earliest techniques of empty-handed combat as a means of defending themselves against brigands just like the one who robbed Ryokan.

Zen is certainly not tantamount to Stoicism, but both would agree with the first principle of the Stoics: that there are things in our power and things not in our power, and that the former are our concern, while the latter are not.

A chivalrous man may offer his coat to a poor man, and he may surrender his Rolex to a thief, especially if the mugger has a gun. But whatever sort of monkish calmness he has as he stares down the barrel of a .38, a gentleman will almost certainly not think charitably about the mugger. If there is a chance and if he has the ability, the monk in him will cede the moment to the warrior. To turn the other cheek, as Jesus Christ has instructed Christians to do, has always been understood to be a form of detachment from peer pressure, a refusal to be judged by others just as we decline to judge them. But just as this is not tolerance of wickedness, neither is it endorsement of pacifism.

Some would claim that resistance to the mugger is at best a necessary evil, but this is heresy. Resistance to evil through the employment of the force necessary to stop it is in fact a positive good.

If the mugger is subdued, arrested, tried, and convicted, then he ceases to be a threat to rob others. So the violence used to stop him is not only just, it is an act of loving kindness—not to the mugger, of course, but to his future victims.

Lovely as the story of Ryokan is and admirable as is his detachment, it happens to be the case that his monkish non-resistance is not precisely chivalrous. Ryokan's compassion for the lost soul who values the things of this world (the bowl and the robe) more than the truth about this world (the beauty of the moon, which is to say beauty, even truth itself)—is wonderful. But the fact is Ryokan's non-resistance empowers the thief to go forth and rob someone else. This is appropriate for a man in holy orders, since his life is a living, redemptive testimony to holiness (for all we know, the monk's example may have forever changed the thief's attitude). But the chivalrous man—no matter how much Stoic detachment he practices—cannot justify inaction, non-resistance, pacifism.

"Kindness toward the guilty," wrote the great economist Adam Smith (1723–1790), "is cruelty toward the innocent."

CHAPTER SEVEN

Chivalry in a Democratic Age

The things a man has to have are hope and confidence in himself against odds, and sometimes he needs somebody, his pal or his mother or his wife or God, to give him that confidence. He's got to have some inner standards worth fighting for or there won't be any way to bring him into conflict. And he must be ready to choose death before dishonor without making too much song and dance about it. That's all there is to it.

–CLARK GABLE, QUOTED IN ADELA ROGERS
ST. JOHNS'S *THE HONEYCOMB* (1969)

N ow the hard part.
Although tracing the paths that conceptions of chivalry and of the gentleman have followed over the last thousand years is both arduous and precarious, it is nothing compared to the pitfalls of attempting to "pinpoint" the idea for the new century. That word *pinpoint* conjures an image of a butterfly stuck up on a lepidopterist's wall, except in this case it's the grand design of this book that is splayed out—or maybe it's your author's nerve.

I'm especially aware that I have no commendation from authority—whatever arbiter one might credit—to undertake a taxonomy of the gentlemanly virtues. But, of course, there is no such authority, and so the door is left open to anyone—saint, scoundrel, or ordinary sinner—with the nerve to try. I'm no saint, and I hope no scoundrel, and—if this isn't damning myself with faint praise—my intentions are good; as for what follows, let us agree that the catalog is provisional. My uneasiness is mitigated by the motto by which for years I've tried to govern myself: it is Chesterton's genial observation (from his 1910 book *What's Wrong with the World*) "that if a thing is worth doing, it is worth doing badly."[*]

This is a thing worth doing.

The title of this chapter hints at my view of our twenty-first-century compleat gentleman or chivalrous man. He is a modern knight, a man of chivalry, a man whose virtues and vices are to some extent those of his twelfth-century counterpart, perhaps more so even than his nineteenth-century compeer. This may seem retrogressive, even undemocratic—as indeed it may be—but I beg the reader to withhold judgment for a bit. Perhaps this evolved gentleman's goodness outweighs his flaws.

The operative word here is *chivalry*. In the end I will not be crafting a new definition of "gentleman," because I am convinced that the manner of a man so defined would be too much that of a man of manners. As Cardinal Newman put it, I am "too diffident to define" this model man, too reluctant to catalog the rules and regulations of respectability. Say the word "gentleman," and one conjures fine suits of clothes and expertly mixed

---

[*] The book began for G. K. C. when the *Times of London* asked a number of distinguished authors to submit essays answering the question: "What's wrong with the world?" His essay was a letter, reprinted here in its entirety: "Dear Sirs: I am. Sincerely yours, G. K. Chesteron."

martinis and soaring insights into the complexities of baseball, and all these things may very well be characteristics of a particular gentleman, yet each is finally wool or gin or play, and what matters about the best man—the compleat gentleman—is the grit of his heart. But say the word "chivalry," and one may conjure knights in shining armor or brutes on horseback. The points of reference may be utterly old-fashioned, but at least our man is in the saddle where he belongs.

This chapter is the only one written in its entirety after the horrific events of September 11, 2001, in New York, Pennsylvania, and Washington, DC. The state of my emotions in the aftermath tends to animate these pages, although at the time of writing the first edition of this book, I had recovered from the utter shock and sadness of that awful day. In the tiny suburb of New York City where I live—Pelham, New York—we lost a number of friends and neighbors in the terrorist attacks on the World Trade Center, and the loss of each seemed a death in the family. I realize, of course, that those deaths affected most Americans in the same way. For a time we seemed a band of brothers (and sisters), if we had not been before. In 2009, I'm not so sure.

I noted some confusion about—and discomfort with, especially among the intelligentsia—the outpouring of patriotism that we witnessed in the immediate aftermath of the attacks. In media coverage of America's retaliation in Afghanistan and Iraq, I cannot recall hearing one pundit or a single man-on-the-street speak seriously of September 11 as a blow to America's honor or of the reprisals as consequences of the demands upon American honor. I have no doubt that anyone—and clearly this includes me—who would speak of honor in this context must be unwelcome in the media, because honor is retrograde.

We obsess about root causes. We need the justification of

international law. We whore after global consensus. We succumb to the allure of diplomatic compromise. We've been chasing such things for so long that there's little chance most of us don't really believe they are essential. And if we Americans are undecided about the value of our heritage, it's pretty obvious that our enemies are convinced that we are irresolute. They are depending upon the fact that we'll debate every angle of every attack and blame ourselves in the end. Liberalism—the grandest of secular philosophies—has been reduced to equivocation. We are teetering on the brink of a great chasm of relativism, swinging our arms with nothing to grab onto.

Here's the problem writ small: I once went to pick up my older son when he was in kindergarten at P. S. 87 in Manhattan. There had been a fight in his class, I was informed by a student teacher, and Bobby was involved.

"Who started it?" I asked.

The student teacher looked at me with sheer loathing. Men!

"I don't think that matters," she said coldly.

I smiled, wishing I had more Zen or more Stoicism.

"But of course it matters," I said.

"Why? So we can lay blame?"

"That's part of it. After all, there's a big difference between aggression and self-defense. Or do you want them all to be little Gandhis?"

Well, of course, she did.

"Don't you?" she asked incredulously.

"No. I want my sons to be little Galahads."

Imperfection First

Of course, Galahad has the reputation of being a practically perfect person, and you wouldn't wish that on anybody. Certainly his and his fellows' passion to find the Holy Grail, which Galahad finally did, was hell for poor King Arthur.

"Alas!" Thomas Bulfinch has the king cry after Gawain has gotten the whole Round Table to swear to spend a year searching for the Grail: "You have nigh slain me with the vow and promise that ye have made, for ye have bereft me of the fairest fellowship that ever was seen together in any realm of the world; for when they shall depart hence, I am sure that all shall never meet more in this world."[†]

Indeed, it is every bit as dramatic a moment as the king's words suggest, for just as the dispirited Arthur slumps down in his throne a hermit appears in the hall with a young man in tow, whom he introduces as Galahad, son of Lancelot, grandson of Pelles, the Fisher King, and, like Arthur himself, a descendant of Joseph of Arimathea. The boy sits right down in the Siege Perilous, which is all the proof anybody at that table needed to know that this was the pure-hearted man who would be the one to find the sacred cup. (To sit in this *siège*—French for "seat"—was death to him who was not destined to find the holy relic.) Then in the next day's tournament, Galahad proves he has prowess equal to his purity: he bests everyone except his father and Percival.

Then it's one adventure after another, with fair maidens and devil horses and many tourneys and parties for all, except Galahad who is all holy business. Some pleasures of the flesh for the other knights were a good thing since the great quest was to be fatal for half their company. Eat, drink, and be merry, for tomorrow we may die. *Certes*, as they would have said. *Depend on it.*

Of course it's all gauze, right? No Grail, no knights, no Quest,

---

[†] Not that we can say anything about governance in the mythical kingdom, but for that year Arthur alone must have had to bear pretty much every administrative responsibility.

no salvation. Their time isn't right and neither is the place. Fifteen hundred years ago, a thousand years ago, this race of brutish men cared more for gluttony and rapine than for honor or faith. Surely no band of brothers ever really went forth in search of the true and the beautiful, was attacked and enchanted by the forces of darkness, and gladly sacrificed life and limb to behold what each knew in his heart he was not worthy to witness.

Galahad, Percival, and Bors end up in Sarras, which is a place either near the vicinity of Jerusalem (which would suit Indiana Jones) or on the mystical Isle of Avalon (which would suit the Society for Creative Anachronism and fantasy novelists such as Marion Zimmer Bradley), where Galahad is visited by Joseph of Arimathea and dies rapturously.

In the end only Bors returns, and Lancelot gives him this touching pledge: "Gentle cousin, ye are right welcome to me, and all that ever I may do for you and for yours, ye shall find my poor body ready at all times while the spirit is in it, and that I promise you faithfully, and never to fail."

After all, Bors had stood by his boy.

Galahad! His "tough lance thrusteth sure," Tennyson wrote, his strength was "as the strength of ten." Why? Because his heart was pure. And that, my friends, is the fantasy. Not that men have sought (or will seek) the true and the beautiful, but that they will achieve it only through purity. As Ptah-Hotep insisted in 2350 BC: "Be not arrogant because of that which you know; deal with the ignorant as with the learned, for the barriers of art are not closed, no artist being in possession of the perfection to which he should aspire."

The compleat gentleman is not a perfect man. Indeed, if there is a first principle from which the character of the chivalrous man arises, it is this: man's fallen nature demands a radical commitment to a sort of Stoic realism. It is not a requirement that a gentleman adhere to the Judaeo-Christian belief in an actual Fall—which anyway is a canon more Christian than Jewish; but he cannot believe in the *perfectibility* of Man. Cannot, or rather must not. It is in the canard of essential human goodness that much of the cad's insincerity finds its justification. A man can hardly aspire to probity if he's convinced that whatever he does flows from a wellspring of rectitude. The conviction that we are essentially good leads to that slovenly moral view that one way of behaving is pretty much the same as every other. Recall what William A. Henry III wrote, that the unwillingness "to assert unyieldingly that one idea, contribution, or attainment is better than another" is the heart of that most dangerous of all social heresies, egalitarianism.

However much a gentleman may wish for and work for principles of legal, political, or social equity, he is by definition free of egalitarian illusions. His compassion does not delude him into a belief that bland is best, that there is no such thing as superiority. But we have certainly come to the point where the tradition of gentlemanly decorum has broken free of its sometimes belligerent connection to economic status, becoming in one sense more democratic—in that a man's birth neither guarantees nor prohibits him from being a gentleman; at the same time, the gentlemanly class remains steadfastly elitist in the sense of embracing high standards.

This is, perhaps, both promising and confusing: to say that these few, chosen from the many, ought to be good, but not too good. Perhaps there's hope here. But perhaps there's despair too. Good, but not too good: I wonder how often good men have failed to be better because they despaired that they were not perfect? As often, I suppose, as men who think themselves perfect have become evil.

This is the "existential" space in which the chivalrous gentleman lives: he consciously accepts that his calling is precarious because he is the champion of the true and the beautiful and must risk strength and profanity in their service. It is not the calling of saints. This is the characteristic of "macho" men that the contemporary chattering classes, especially feminists, abhor—which is silly, since their very liberty depends upon it. (Not that all macho men are gentlemen, of course. Far from it.)

Chivalry Today

But enough preface. The time has come to reflect on chivalry in the new millennium. We have looked at the medieval knight and at the gentleman of the Renaissance and the Victorian era, and we have pondered points of similarity between the compleat gentleman and the archetypes of the warrior, the lover, and the monk. As a result, we know that chivalry must be more than a man opening a door for a woman, even that it must be more than a single act of selfless courage, although the latter comes pretty close.

What is chivalry in 2009? It is an attitude, an interior commitment among some men to a way of life that values the martial skills used to defend the true and the beautiful, the passionate respect for true and beautiful women, the erudition necessary to comprehend true and beautiful ideas, and withal the serenity necessary, no matter what, to remain composed, restrained: *una certa sprezzatura*.

Chivalry is not so complicated an idea as its long and convoluted history might suggest. The compleat gentleman himself is merely a man; perhaps we make the process of defining chivalry too difficult because we lack the faith necessary to grasp its essential simplicity. In the end, chivalry is nothing more than putting the self second. It is the ultimate self-respect because in the moments that matter the compleat gentleman makes himself the servant of his God, his nation, his friends, and his family. He does so—is able to have the courage to do so—because he is governed by justice. Chivalry is justice manifest.

Looking again at my trusty *Shorter Oxford*, I note that the definition of "chivalrous" is as follows:

1 Characteristic of a medieval knight or man-at-arms; valorous. LME-E17. **2** Of or pertaining to (a knight of) the Age of Chivalry. L18. **3** Pertaining to or characteristic of the ideal knight; gallant, honourable, courteous, disinterested; derog. quixotic. E19.

The words in the last part of the definition are curious. "Gallantry" and "honor" may be used interchangeably, as may "gallantry" and "courtesy," yet each has its own set of conventional and distinctive reverberations as well. We might say that a gallant man is especially chivalrous with women; an honorable man is especially chivalrous in war; a courteous man is especially chivalrous in the community; and a disinterested man is especially chivalrous toward himself. That it matters to a man that he be gallant, honorable, courteous, and disinterested is what makes him a compleat gentleman. That he cares about these things in the twenty-first century may be what makes him quixotic.

He is a warrior because he will fight for the right with his body and his brains. There are warriors who are soldiers and martial artists, fighting their battles on battlefields and in the streets, and there are warriors who fight social, political, economic, and cultural battles. In both cases, the warrior knows he is in battle and employs his prowess for justice.

The compleat gentleman, as a warrior, cannot abide injustice; justice is finally the one and only thing worth fighting and dying for. Peace is justice in foreign relations; equality is justice in society; passion is justice in marriage; wisdom is justice in education; restraint is justice in behavior.

The Warrior

There is much to be said below about the importance of a chivalrous gentleman's attitude toward women, learning, and silence, and a new emphasis on these ways of thinking represents a revival of sorts. Yet of all that is old and must now be new, nothing looms so large as the man's restored martial spirit. If we are to have chivalry at all in a democratic age, we must reunite the concept with the sword it is meant to wield. Elegance alone will not suffice. A debonair man who is not also dangerous cannot be chivalrous.

To say that the compleat gentleman is strong is to suggest two things: it is to evoke the ancient chivalric principle of prowess and to invoke the indispensability of self-discipline. Among all the things a chivalrous man must be, this quality will probably be the most difficult for many to accept. After all, it is fair to wonder if a chivalrous man is really required to be physically capable and psychologically steeled for battle, which is the underlying (although hardly the only) reason for developing and maintaining physical and mental strength. I will answer immediately that he need not possess a battle-ready body, although he cannot be a flabby pacifist. He must, however, possess a martial spirit. During World War II, there were gentlemen who served the Allied cause nobly as intelligence officers and code-breakers, and it is obviously the case that the ongoing war against evil will be fought in many ways along many fronts. Some of those veterans and some of the survivors of the bloody hand-to-hand combat from that last global conflagration are still with us, thank God, and those gentlemen, now in their eighties and nineties, can hardly be required to possess still that physical prowess that once saved the world. There are also great gentlemen who—for reasons of illness or infirmity—are unable to train their bodies.

The courage and strength of the warrior are qualities that "save" society even in times of relative peace—qualities that advance the cause of justice in society. Take the case of Sidney Poitier.

Mr. Poitier, the Oscar-winning actor, is well known to movie fans around the world. If there were ever doubt that art can have an impact on life, his career should dispel it. As the young physician in his first film, *No Way Out* (1950); as the alienated teen in *Blackboard Jungle* (1955); as the escaped con in 1958's *The Defiant Ones* (which earned him his first best actor Academy Award nomination); as the idealistic young father in *A Raisin in the Sun* (1961); then in a string of films beginning with his Oscar-winning performance as the ambitious carpenter, Homer Smith, in *Lilies of the Field* (1963); as the sensitive Gordon Raife in *A Patch of Blue* (1965); and culminating in three extraordinary films released in 1967—*In the Heat of the Night, To Sir With Love,* and *Guess Who's Coming to Dinner*—Poitier changed the way movie audiences, black and white, imagined African American men. It is by now—especially after his marvelously restrained speech in accepting an honorary Oscar at the 2002 awards show—a cliché to note that he was the first bona fide black star and that he opened the door to fame, wealth, and self-respect for the generation of black actors and actresses that has come after him. What is not often enough acknowledged is that he also opened the minds of millions of Americans who are not black to the banality of racism, to what we called in my youth "race prejudice." I have a photograph in my office of Poitier, Harry Belafonte, and Charlton Heston, taken in front of the Lincoln Memorial on the occasion of the great Civil Rights March of 1963. Poitier was ever the

stalwart activist on behalf of the legal and political realities manifest in his films. He was, in fact, the prayer and the protest and
the proof: his screen presence, which was so clearly no Tinsel-
town charade, helped cauterize America's racial wound.

I am sure Mr. Poitier would wince to read this, because he is
a modest man, who when he looks back on his life, prefers to remember those who helped him rather than those whom he
helped. And it would be silly to single out Sidney Poitier in such
a way as to suggest that he, more than, say, Martin Luther King
Jr. is responsible for the end of racism. For one thing, race prejudice has yet to be discarded on the trash heap of history. Besides,
there were countless others who made great sacrifices for justice
and tolerance, including some (of whom Dr. King is only the
most famous) who made the ultimate sacrifice. Mr. Poitier
would argue that his sacrifices were few in comparison and that
he has been blessed by a long life in which he has had love and
honors in abundance, which is all true. But his onscreen courage
and dignity (and restraint) and his off-screen determination and
dedication have all the marks of a warrior, reminding us that, as
Disraeli said, "To believe in the heroic makes heroes."

Yet, although I believe that a warrior can be an actor or an
intellectual, I would be unfaithful to my sense of the truth about
the compleat gentleman if I failed to suggest that there is, generally speaking, a requirement of physical fitness. As a rule there is.
And as a rule he will admire in other men—and, these days, in
women—what he requires of himself. This means that he will
appreciate the best soldiers and athletes probably more than he
will admire the best actors and politicians. From the ranks of
these latter groups have come some consummate gentlemen
(Ronald Reagan, for instance), and there have been plenty of
rogues among GIs and jocks. On balance it's easier to esteem soldiers and athletes because they do their jobs with less pretense.

It's a familiar criticism of professional and collegiate sports that they are little different from the gladiatorial games of the ancient coliseums; the excitement of seeing superb athletes in contests of skill certainly is similar, but the realities on modern fields and in modern arenas are vastly different from the life-and-death struggles that went on in Rome. Maimings and killings are rare today, even in ice hockey, and even more rarely are they intentional, except in ice hockey. Sport is worthy of a gentleman's admiration because it is a fair measure of prowess. Since a gentleman aspires to prowess, he naturally appreciates it in others.

The sporting life is fine, but it is not exactly the knight's life. True, the tournament evolved into little more than a game, but there was a time when it was a deadly game, literally and figuratively. Men got whacked about, bruised, and bloodied, but they learned the art of war. They became warriors, not just sportsmen, and some crucible of strength, courage, and honor is what's missing from the experiences of most modern men.[‡]

To say that a gentleman is courageous is to say that he is willing to risk his own life, safety, and comfort in the battle of good versus evil. It is not enough simply to be strong; a gentleman must also be brave enough and committed enough to put life and limb at risk. It is hard for anyone to know how he will react to danger, since we "become brave," as Aristotle put it, "by doing brave acts." Courage is a quality measured not potentially, but actually. As playwright Jean Anouilh has Thomas à Becket say, and this was the epigraph to this book's first chapter title: "Until the day of his death, no man can be sure of his courage."

[‡] It's fair to note here, I think, that many intellectual commentators—liberal and conservative—tend to overlook, and, therefore, undervalue sport as a key to understanding contemporary America. As Jacques Barzun—a truly towering intellectual figure—noted: "Whoever wants to know the heart and mind of America had better learn baseball."

Of course, courage is necessary not only in combat—combat, anyway, in the sense of man versus man; it is required of a gentleman when he faces his own fears: man against himself. C. S. Lewis wrote that courage is "not simply one of the virtues but the form of every virtue at the testing point, which means at the point of highest reality." The hardest victories are almost certainly over the self. Again, the great Aristotle: "I count him braver who overcomes his desires than him who conquers his enemies; for the hardest victory is over self."

Courage in battle often garners the recognition and praise of spectators; however, the truest kind of courage, as La Rochefoucauld put it, "is to do without witnesses what one would be capable of doing with the world looking on."

Courage is the child of commitment. If a man lacks commitment, he will not be courageous. As Viktor Frankl said: "Those who have a 'why' to live can bear with almost any 'how.'"

The accompaniment to courage is honor. Without honor, courage may be nothing more than bravado or even cruelty.

In some ways, this is the most important of the characteristics of the warrior gentleman—if not of the chivalrous man himself—because it stands not only as the culmination of his martial virtues but also as perhaps the highest of all his fine qualities.

To be honorable is to be a man of one's word—that anyway is the most familiar sense. But there is more. Honor is nobleness of mind. It is—and here is a word we use too little—*uprightness*. A chivalrous man is upright; he stands at a proper angle—straight. Things in his life are in line; his priorities are in line. He is dependable, which is not to say that he comes to the party just as the clock strikes the hour, but that you know he will be standing with you, shoulder-to-shoulder, when you need him.

In a West Point publication from the 1920s, Robert Wood wrote that an honorable man "esteems his moral health too much to lower himself willingly by any act that may seem base. He is true to himself and values honor for its highest meaning—that of an exalted tribute of respect and reverence. He shrinks from wrong-doing with his whole nature; he clings to what he knows to be right with all his strength. There can be no real success in life unless it is accompanied by this high sense of honor." It's what Thomas Jefferson called the exercise of "moral muscles."

"He has honor," Walter Lippmann wrote in *A Preface to Morals* (1913), "if he holds himself to an ideal of conduct though it is inconvenient, unprofitable, or dangerous to do so."

But hold on. We recall that the honor of our chivalrous knights circa 1100 was rather more like Mafia honor than the elevated moral stance recommended by Wood, Jefferson, and Lippmann. I am suggesting that it is an older sort of honor we must recover, one wedded to strength and courage—in other words, to prowess. Speaking about Theodore Roosevelt and the Western, or frontier, idea of the gentleman, David Castronovo says that the "gentleman was a tough guy who understood manners, the formalized nature of honorable combat—and the fine points of style and assertion." I am not calling for a tough-guy hooliganism, of course, but I am very much aware that the embrace of prowess, which involves a preparation for violence, may involve unintended consequences—the sort of penalties the twentieth century knew only too well as the fallout of other grander social experiments. Soldiers and policemen and martial artists embrace a code of honor which, properly employed, opts for force only when it is just to use it. Still, some caution is appropriate, and it is offered by UCLA professor Eugen Weber in a 1999 article ("The Ups and Downs of Honor") in the *American Scholar.*

Weber looks at the contemporary world and recalls W. B. Yeats's famous lament (in "The Second Coming") that "Things fall apart; the center cannot hold." He worries that we are in the twilight of the state's monopoly on violence and that we are returning to a more primitive sort of life, to a state that we have until now thought to be "as primitive as chastity," which is to say: "Retaliation looks more effective than reprieve. Experience teaches that if you give way, more people push you. The logic of violence is crude but simple: violent reaction against transgression deters others who might follow suit. And there is little evidence that litigation affords a better chance of justice or satisfaction than forceful direct action does."

I agree with the analysis, but not with the conclusion, which is that "aggression is reasserting itself as the better part of valor, and a new kind of honor that looks disturbingly like the old kind of honor is seeping back in." The truth is, it had better.

I can hear what is almost always thrown up as the Christian rejection of violence: *He who lives by the sword shall die by the sword.* You won't hear me dispute it. However, that sword cuts two ways. Yes, violent men invite violent deaths, but that is merely the fact. And not all men who live by violence are themselves violent men, which statement is to my mind not paradoxical. The calculus of the biblical warning is not absolute, except perhaps for those for whom the sword is absolute. Most of the soldiers who have fought for liberty and justice have ended up dying in their beds, rather like William Marshal, "full of years and honor." Those who give the "last full measure of devotion" may die by the sword, and it may be honor that has brought them to their ends. However, their blood truly does consecrate the ground upon which they have fallen, as anybody will attest who has visited (and taken the time to learn about) the battlefields and cemeteries at Gettysburg or in Normandy.

Most men are dangerous, if only because evil is never very far from winning human allegiance. When violence erupts, most folks are mostly shocked. "He always seemed like a regular person," a witness tells the *Nightly News*, and Everyman and Everywoman profess shock that violence could happen where they live. Of course the pretense of astonishment has become harder to maintain in some localities, and yet people seem always to be caught off guard. Seen sociologically, this is ludicrous. But in the realm of personal experience it is not so absurd. Most of us hide the violent potential; we hide it because we are taught that it is unacceptable, as indeed it is in most situations. The problem comes in the tension between the reality of aggression and the illusion of tranquility.

There are two kinds of men for whom violence is an integral part of character: criminals and compleat gentlemen. Some criminals and most regular folks may be unaware that the violence is pivotal, but most criminals are only too aware that their brutal side is near the surface. For a gentleman, the aggressiveness is not brutal, but he remains aware of its presence and of its usefulness. For the gentleman and the criminal alike, violence is a tool, with the difference that the former uses it for good and the latter for evil.

In any case, the restoration of a more primitive style of chivalry is not the death of civility. Our new compleat gentleman does have manners; he simply has a different response to the "unmannerly" than did the gentleman of more recent generations.

The reinstatement of the compleat gentleman's soldierly character flies in the face of most "correct" thinking since about 1970.

Henry Adams (1838–1918) once quipped that the successors to the nineteenth-century gentleman would be the alienated intellectuals, and that insignificant but overexcited bunch pretty much had its way in the twentieth century: one or another version of pacifism became the true faith of journalists and pedagogues, and, between 1993 and 2001, almost became the centerpiece of American foreign policy. Only as the last century ended and the new one began did we come to reflect warmly on the contributions of our beloved warriors, and I suspect that there was a tinge of anxiety coloring the nostalgia. The single symbolic representation of the emerging mood is Steven Spielberg's *Saving Private Ryan* (1998).

I need not review the plot of a film that was among the most celebrated in recent years (and one that stands with *Schindler's List* (1993) as a tribute to Mr. Spielberg's genius). You'll recall that the film begins and ends with shots of a flag framed against the sky. Never has the phrase "Old Glory" seemed so appropriate: the flag is faded almost to transparency, suggesting that the patriotism we are about to recall is disappearing before our eyes.

The weekend that my wife and I saw the movie happened to be the one in which Mr. and Mrs. Spielberg were playing host at their home in Southampton, New York, to then-president and Mrs. Clinton. As we drove home from the theater, I wondered aloud how a "Big Liberal" like Spielberg could make a right-wing movie. My wife looked at me as though I were nuts. (It's a look I've seen before.)

"You think *Saving Private Ryan* is a right-wing movie?"

I started to say yes—to assert that it was in spite of itself—but quickly realized I was wrong. With somebody of Spielberg's intelligence, it's important to assume he knows exactly what he's putting up on the screen.

"I guess it's a patriotic movie. And patriotism at the movies just seems conservative."

The question Americans have often asked is this: *Where do we find such men? Where do heroes come from? How do they always manage to come forward just when we need them?* The answer, of course, is that heroism awakens in cultures that dream of it. Men pray for peace, but train for war. God willing, their heroism will not need to stir, but it will arise and conquer if they have dreamed the dream.

The dream is like a flame passed from generation to generation. At first I wrote "eternal flame," but the chivalry that nurtures heroism is not eternal for the very reason that it is human. If the flame is not tended, it can extinguish. The events of September 11, 2001, seemed to have awakened the chivalric spirit; we are blowing furiously on the ember of heroism, and we have seen it light the way in Afghanistan and in Iraq. But how much illumination does it throw here at home? The flame, the ember is in men's hearts. How many American hearts are truly on fire today?

Having come to this point in time, living as we do in an ideological age, one in which much of our education—primary, secondary, and higher—fails to lay bare the darker realities of life, it may be jarring to read that combat can never be far from a compleat gentleman's mind. But whereas self-interest has always moved some men to conclude that the important battles to be fought may be adequately handled by someone else (think of the hiring of poor men by rich men to take their places in the Union army in the Civil War), it is a more recent development that so many believe that conflict itself is inherently wrong. A man cannot be a compleat gentleman if he is either a coward or a conciliator. In this latter regard it must be admitted that, of course, there is a place for conciliation (so long as it has not become an ideology), and I would not be entirely comfortable claiming that there is no such thing as a gentleman pacifist. If such a man has arrived at his swords-into-plowshares conviction through religious passion, so be it (although he had better be a saint in the making and be ready for martyrdom—ready to see all that he treasures trampled underfoot). The kind of conciliation that disqualifies is the "moral neutrality" that refuses to acknowledge actual evil. A man who is not roused to combat evil is no gentleman. Mencius, who lived some three centuries before Christ, said, "Anger at a petty offence is unworthy of a superior man, but indignation for a great cause is righteous wrath."

Politesse

This may seem an odd place to discuss courtesy, manners, or whatever we wish to call formal politeness, especially since the *courtoisie* of that earlier code of chivalry is associated with the lover more than the warrior. But our man's manners have a tinge of belligerence.

Here's a proposition that can only give some readers reason for concern: *The compleat gentleman is not always polite.* This goes with his willingness to sacrifice his body in defense of the good, and in this he is not so far removed from the knights of the Middle Ages, although our modern gentleman is bereft of any means of justifying cruelty.

But to say that he may not always be polite is not the same thing as saying that he is ever rude. The root of the word "rude" is interesting: it comes from the Latin *rudis*, originally meaning unsophisticated, which remains its primary dictionary definition today. It wasn't until the late Middle Ages that the word came to mean ill-mannered, which is to say the opposite of polite.

And what about "polite"? We think of the word today as meaning, more or less, *mannerly*. A polite person is somebody with manners; somebody who has the kindness to say "please" and "thank you." But in origin the word is closer to *polish*, with the sense that the polite person is a sort of gleaming silver teapot. From its Latin roots (*politus*, the past participle of *polire*, to smooth or to polish) through its emergence in Middle English and well into the 1700s, the word meant a thing buffed up or cleansed or even organized, although other meanings also emerged. So it always is with important words.

The *New Shorter Oxford Dictionary* explains:

2 transf. Refined, elegant, scholarly; exhibiting a refined taste; well-regulated, cultured, cultivated. L15. **b** Courteous, treating others with respect and consideration; having or displaying good manners. M18.

Once upon a time it was a man's sword that might be polite—if his squire kept it burnished; then, late in the 1400s, the knight himself might be polite if he'd been to school and was "polished" enough to be able to declaim upon the liberal arts; and finally, sometime after 1750 or so, a man might be thought gentlemanly, to a degree at least, simply for doffing his cap to a lady.

I am generally in favor of politeness because I believe with Henry Hazlitt (1894–1993) that "manners are minor morals. Manners are to morals as the final sand papering, rubbing, and polishing on a fine piece of furniture are to the selection of the wood, the sawing, chiseling, and fitting. They are the finishing touch." (I've seen the "manners are minor morals" quote attributed to John Dewey, C. S. Lewis, Aristotle, and others. The estimable Judith Martin, aka Miss Manners, has been pressing the phrase into American minds for many years.) Manners are good.

On the other hand, I am inclined to believe in tit-for-tat, in what Robert Axlerod (in his 1984 book *The Evolution of Cooperation*) has called the "robustness of reciprocity." A gentleman is a warrior, not a doormat, and he will cooperate with others only insofar as they cooperate with him. Cooperation begets cooperation, kindness begets kindness, but neither cooperation nor kindness is quite the appropriate response to aggression or rudeness.

It is true that chivalry, especially in the tradition of courtly love, has always been concerned with manners and style, whether in the medieval court at Poitiers or in the Renaissance court at

Urbino. It's as Russell Kirk wrote (echoing his hero, Edmund Burke): "Between the decay of manners in our time and the decline of artistic taste and faculty, there exists some close connection. From the beginning, the perfection of the arts has been bound up with the idea of religion and the idea of a gentleman."

For Dr. Kirk (1918–1994), the gentleman was not simply the traditional patron of the arts; he was their inspiration as well. He was, in his own way, a living work of art. A chivalrous man has always been recognized in part by his refinement: his fine etiquette, his spiffy clothes, and his elevated ideas. But all these were, and are, available to any man, which is why in literature since at least the seventeenth century, a man called a "gentleman" has often as not been a cad.

Far be it from me to call for a purge of style from the definition of the compleat gentleman. But, trust me, nobody has better manners or finer suits or more skill in debate than the devil himself. Does anyone doubt that the devil appears to be a consummate gentleman? And is there any question that he completely lacks chivalry?

I reject the devil, and I hang up on telephone marketers, often without so much as a "No thanks." I am usually genial with a bad waiter, at least until the meal is finished, because there is no benefit either to him or to me in a confrontation (although I have called for a manager more than once to ask that someone else be assigned to my table). It is important always to extend courtesy as a first action in any encounter. If that courtesy is reciprocated, further courtesies will flourish. If, however, proper decorum is greeted with an affront to civility, then the gentleman must consider that his next action may have to be retaliation. Honor demands it. Mercy will come quickly to the cad who repents, but he will be in no doubt that the gentleman will treat every instance of incivility in the same way.

Professor Axelrod's book details the reasons why the tit-for-tat strategy outperforms all others in a computer game called Prisoner's Dilemma. The scheme's success, he writes, is "due to being nice, provocable, forgiving, and clear." A further amplification provides an ideal description of the compleat gentleman: "Its niceness means that it is never the first to defect [fail to cooperate], and this property prevents it from getting into unnecessary trouble. Its retaliation discourages the other side from persisting whenever defection is tried. Its forgiveness helps to restore mutual cooperation. And its clarity makes its behavioral pattern easy to recognize; it is easy to perceive that the best way of dealing with tit-for-tat is to cooperate with it."

If I may be allowed a short digression into international politics, the best "constitutional" structure in the macrocosm is simply an extension of the well-ordered microcosm, which is to say of the compleat gentleman. And I emphasize that this gentleman is sweetness and light to his friends, acidity and fire to his enemies. He may be slow to anger, but he will be awesome in action when he strikes. Having purged his righteous anger, he will then be quick to forgive. It is a historical miracle that among America's (and Canada's and France's and Britain's) closest allies today are those countries who were once our greatest enemies: Germany, Italy, and Japan, the earlier Axis of Evil. Their friendship is directly proportional to Allied generosity.

As the war against terrorism fans out to affect the nations that harbor the enemies of liberty, and as our power justly crushes those enemies, we must remember that punitive postwar policies will be counterproductive. Victory will not come soon, but when it does come it must be accompanied by gentlemanly compassion. As George W. Bush said during his 2000 campaign for the presidency: "If we are an arrogant nation, they'll resent us. If we're a humble nation, but strong, they'll respect us."

The Lover

Times have changed.

In the resonance of the feminist racket, it is worth wondering how gentlemen have thought of women throughout American history. By one view—the radical feminist view—the answer is, poorly. Andrea Dworkin quotes with approbation the words of Virginia Woolf: "I detest the masculine point of view. I am bored by his heroism, virtue, and honour. I think the best these men can do is not to talk about themselves anymore."

I might agree with Ms. Woolf about that last part, but I am skeptical about the rest. Ms. Dworkin—this is from her book *Pornography: Men Possessing Women* (1991)—amplifies what she believes Woolf meant and presents a classic statement of modern feminist analysis. Adult men, she writes, "treat women, and often girls, and sometimes other males, as objects. Adult men are convinced and sincere in their perception of adult women in particular as objects. This perception of women transcends categories of sexual orientation, political philosophy, nationality, class, race, and so forth. How does it happen that the male child whose sense of life is so vivid that he imparts humanity to sun and stone changes into the adult male who cannot grant or even imagine the common humanity of women?"

This is a very grand statement that also happens to be fictitious. I will not question Ms. Dworkin's sincerity, but I sense that she lives in a world of self-justification, listening only to voices crying oppression, never hearing the women who cry freedom.

Begin with the fact that we all objectify the substance of perception. Dworkin takes a simple word such as "objects" and makes it into a pejorative. The trap for gullible men is to believe that what all men and women do—which is simply to see the objects in a field of perception—is evil. All Ms. Dworkin is really griping about—and with some justice—is the *injustice* of certain forms of discrimination. But that is a far cry from the existential claim that men cannot even imagine the "common humanity of women."

More than a century and a half earlier, Alexis de Tocqueville wrote (in *Democracy in America*) that he found that American men considered American women to be superior. He acknowledges what any objective man, French or American, would have to have admitted in the 1830s: women's roles in life were sharply restricted, as logically were men's. No judgment of history can deny it. Evolving history has changed it. But does that mean that history itself, at least prior to our post-feminist age, is a spectacle of sexual oppression? Here is Tocqueville's view, and there never was a more perspicacious observer of America and Americans:

It has often been remarked that in Europe a certain degree of contempt lurks even in the flattery which men lavish upon women; although a European frequently affects to be the slave of woman, it may be seen that he never sincerely thinks her his equal. In the United States men seldom compliment women, but they daily show how much they esteem them. They constantly display an entire confidence in the understanding of a wife and a profound respect for her freedom; they have decided that her mind is just as fitted as that of a man to discover the plain truth, and her heart as firm to embrace it; and they have never sought to place her virtue, any more than his, under the shelter of prejudice, ignorance, and fear.

It is only too true that battles remain to be fought for the full access of women to the panoply of roles in society, but this does not mean that American women are now, or ever were, oppressed. Tocqueville concludes: "As for myself, I do not hesitate to avow that although the women of the United States are confined within the narrow circle of domestic life, and their situation is in some respects one of extreme dependence, I have nowhere seen woman occupying a loftier position; and if I were asked . . . to what the singular prosperity and growing strength of [the American] people ought mainly to be attributed, I should reply: To the superiority of their women."

Naturally, the positivist wing of feminism will find Tocqueville's judgment risible, but that is because their ideology forces them to entertain only those facts that confirm their prejudices. In a lecture to the American Enterprise Institute in 1997 ("Is Manliness a Virtue?"),[§] political scientist Harvey Mansfield drew a distinction between the new model of the "sensitive male" and the old "manly man." The appeal of the new guy is that by definition his sensitivity is "to things women feel strongly about." On the other hand, "[t]he traditional manly male is protective of women, but when it comes to sensitivity, he is a sorry flop. He does not observe women and he does not listen to them: for all the love that he may profess, he does not take women seriously. His gallantry, women may suspect, is protection not for women but for himself, because it keeps women safely inferior to him, agents of his success unable to share the benefits of his reputation and recognition."

These were the thoughts of Professor Mansfield, preliminary to a work in progress, and we may hope that the quote is out of context with a more apposite final judgment. Of course, when anybody speaks about tradition or history, he is necessarily

---

[§] The article was expanded and published as a book, *Manliness*, in 2006. I recommend it.

manipulating some small part of those immensities. To say that men have been selfish is to state a view and a reality unchanged since Genesis. But to suggest that truly gallant men fail the sensitivity test is to turn chivalry into a social movement. Are most men pigs? Maybe. But the compleat gentleman is not most men, and most men will never be compleat gentlemen—or even particularly manly.

But it seems to me that this is all much ado about nothing. The complicated social and political machinations regarding the status of women notwithstanding, the stance of the chivalrous man is simplicity itself. He simply gives a woman what she desires. I do not believe that this is any sort of new insight, although the extension of the principle into all those political and social arenas may be. But it should not matter to a gentleman who a woman is or what she looks like or what she believes or even whether she gives a damn what he thinks. He is complaisant, but not because he is a doormat. He gives the woman— lover or stranger—what she wants because every aspect of the chivalric code ordains equality: his *loyauté* does, his largesse does, his *courtoisie* does, his franchise does, and even his *prouesse* does. It may be that the heart of chivalry is finally nothing more complicated than friendship coupled with courage. Whether or not a gentleman has a strong arm—which, in my experience, most women admire—he must have a strong heart. If she is at risk, he will defend her, even if there's not a chance in a thousand he can save her. He would rather die than be dishonored, and the ultimate dishonor is the failure of civility and justice.

He is a lover of women, but he also loves his country, his state, and his community—this especially. It is his "little platoon," as Burke called it: family, friends, and neighbors. Love and civility require no political philosophy; neither does sexuality.

A man—a chivalrous gentleman—need know nothing else

about how to be a proper lover than is revealed in the story of Sir Gawain and the "loathly lady." We cannot know what sort of lover Gawain became to Ragnelle; in any case, the lovers are a fiction, a symbol of marriage, then and now. But the answer both Gawain and his liege lord got from their "loathly lady" is the key that unlocks the mysteries of marriage, and here "marriage" may stand for all relations between men and women.

Recall that the conundrum put to King Arthur was more or less the famous Freudian interrogatory: *"Was will das Weib?"* ("What does a woman want?") Ragnelle's answer, which Freud apparently could not accept and which many men have failed to embrace, was: *To have her own way.*

I'm struck by how an answer that seems superficially glib and even petty is actually magisterial. In the early 1970s, Norman Mailer proclaimed himself "The Prisoner of Sex," by which he meant that, while he was willing to acknowledge certain feminist claims, he was unable to surrender his belief in fundamental male dominance. Ever since, there has been confusion about what people like to call "sex roles." But that perplexity and the debate about it mostly exist in academia. Nearly everyone else has at least begun to adapt to the push-pull between powerful women and powerful men.

From the mid-seventies through the early nineties, academic feminism was a dominant force in college life, and its style of neo-Marxist analysis was all the rage among faculty and students in most departments. But this period of—to use a favorite word of the avant-garde—hegemony appears to be over, marginalized by the progress of less ideologically inclined women and by the demonstrated failures, analytical and practical, of Marxism and its epigones.

I live in a community—and who these days does not?—in which most women have paying jobs, inside or outside the

home. At the gym where I exercise, most of my training part-
ners are women, even though I'm not a member of some trendy
spa but of the "conservative"—and formerly all-male—New
York Athletic Club. At the dojo where I have studied karate,
more than a third of the black belts were women, mostly very
young women. Like many men, I have a very successful wife,
and our two sons—each in his own way a pretty macho character—understand without ideological hectoring that upon first encounter men and women alike deserve the benefit of an
assumption in favor of spiritual and intellectual equality.

After that, equality tends to diminish, and it is then that
chivalry asserts itself. What does a woman want most? To have her
own way. This is the key to both conjugal joy and social harmony.

That's a pretty big claim, and I must explain it. Simply stated:
chivalry demands that a man respect a woman's wishes. Needless
to say, this does not mean that a compleat gentleman is his lady's
lackey. It means rather that he respects her, listens to her, and
does all that he can to give her what she desires. This is true in
terms of her existential ambitions, and it is equally—if not especially—true of her physical needs.

We are past the time at which any event in history—social
or personal—is likely to drive the feminist genie back into a sexist bottle. I speculated—also in chapter five—about the future
role of women in the armed forces, but however that plays out
(especially in regard to combat), it is obvious that women's roles
will only increase. I can imagine no force on Earth—short perhaps of some great fundamentalist revolution (which, in the
United States, would have to trample the Constitution)—that
would prevent women from rising to more or less equal status
with men in every aspect of civil life. For the gentleman, I believe, this can only be thought of as a good thing, since it so
clearly represents the fulfillment of Dame Ragnelle's answer.

Also, in the bedroom, a woman must have her own way. Rest assured, dear reader, that I am not now going to lapse into a discussion of sexual technique. I wouldn't under any circumstances; as it happens, such a discussion is quite unnecessary. All a man needs to do is respect his wife's wishes—to give her what she wants. She, of course, bears a considerable responsibility too: she must know what she wants and be able to say what that is. The lover—in the classic sense of the word—is simply a gentleman who gives a woman what she wants. It follows that she will then return the favor. It may fly in the face of conventional wisdom to say so, but the next best thing a gentleman brings into bed is his restraint. The best thing is his love, but self-control, a leisurely attention to his wife's wishes—these are a close second.

I have not just pronounced that chivalry is synonymous with non-ideological feminism. A gentleman takes a woman on her own terms, yet in doing so he puts the lie to ideological drivel about oppression. History settles general questions concerning the capabilities of women, but only shared, personal experience can judge for any man what any woman wants. There are deeply religious women for whom fulfillment means subservience to their husbands. There are sexually willful women for whom fulfillment means subservience to their lovers. But for most men and women fulfillment is manifest in some measure of equity.

Nonetheless, it is an enduring tenet of chivalry that a gentleman defends the oppressed. It may be that, in terms of physicality, most men are stronger than most women, and that this imbalance amounts to oppression in the sense that a woman is subjugated by her relative weakness. In such a condition, a gentleman's role is clear. In the reverse, which is not so rare these days, the chivalrous man simply stands shoulder-to-shoulder with a warrior woman.

We may come in the not-so-distant future to a point in time at which the biological differences between the sexes will be equalized, at least in terms of physical strength. (Only science fiction writers can begin to conjure the implications of manipulating the human genome, but it is far from impossible that the interface of technology and politics may attempt to create a third sex.) I don't happen to believe that our organic differences are in any immediate danger of obsolescence, but I'm willing to keep an open mind. As I've already said, the physical "inferiority" of women is, relative to past generations, in rapid retreat, and in functional (although not in absolute) terms the differences between men and women are all but meaningless now. That said, I remain unable to—nor do I wish to—escape the conviction that combat remains an all-male responsibility, an activity suited naturally to the one sex but not to the other. This is a case in which tradition is in service to reality. Freud's much-maligned quip that "biology is destiny" is largely false, but not completely false. Every bit of experience I've had and the preponderance of knowledge I've gained tell me that combat—ground combat, anyway—is man's work and that chivalry is a male mission.

The Monk

Because the previous chapter dealt with the compleat gentleman's resemblance to the monk, I will only briefly re-emphasize a few key points here. There are certain interior qualities a chivalrous man ought to have, chief among them reserve—in the sense of the ability to be decorous and taciturn—and erudition, which is the quality of possessing knowledge that is tested and ready.

Of reserve or restraint, decorum and taciturnity, I need say little, since the next and final chapter of this book is all about "The Art of *Sprezzatura*."

Of erudition there is much to be said.

A man is not made chivalrous by reason of an extensive

education. A college degree and advanced academic achieve-ment are as often impediments to chivalry as they are induce-ments to it. The chattering classes, by which I mean pundits and professors, are as cowardly a bunch as any in American so-ciety. I'll assert that without citing supporting evidence—since the fact seems self-evident—and jump to consideration of why this is so. Why are news commentators and university lecturers such a lot of weasels?

The answer is that they are ideologues. In his magisterial 1985 work *Alien Powers: The Pure Theory of Ideology*, author Kenneth Minogue summarizes the ideological elite's point of view: "The great discovery of ideology has been that modern European civi-lization, beneath its cleverly contrived appearances, is the most sys-tematically oppressive despotism the world has ever known. All history, indeed, is a record of oppression, but it is only in modern time that oppression has begun to hide itself behind a façade of freedom." Thus the ideologist sees chivalry, the warrior, the lover, and the monk as exemplifying the mystifications of oppression.

What is often unclear in ideological analysis is a vision of a functional future—of what sort of society would emerge if the various structures of oppression were outlawed. The ideologi-cal project is criticism and revolution, not compassion and re-form. The analyses of ideologues are brutally reductive, insisting, for instance, that a rapist is the agent of all men, per-forming a work of terror necessary for women to believe in and accept male dominance. This is the modern equivalent of phrenology or alchemy.

That such notions are held by the best-educated people is amazing, given their idiocy. It begs the question of what sort of learning is appropriate for the chivalrous man. The answer is "just" education, *just* in the sense of true and appropriate. Wisdom, which ought to be the end of an education, is justice in learning.

There is no point in trying to shelter oneself from the ideological storm. One can learn as much from a Marxist professor as from any other kind, even if the insights a chivalrous man takes away are not those the teacher intended. As Camille Paglia has said: "Education has become a prisoner of contemporaneity." She goes on to note the restorative: "It is the past, not the dizzy present, that is the best door to the future."

To be properly educated, one must reject contemporary pedagogical enthusiasms. But it is nearly impossible to avoid them and learning must go on in a kind of radical commitment to wisdom. As Allan Bloom stated in *The Closing of the American Mind* (1987): "Education in our times must try to find whatever there is in students that might yearn for completion, and to reconstruct the learning that would enable them autonomously to seek that completion."

This is akin to the Talmudic wisdom that giving a starving man a fish is not nearly as compassionate as teaching him how to fish. Education is the empowerment of the mind to continuously seek the true and the beautiful, regardless of ideological distractions.

A gentleman is contemplative, which is to say that he never ceases to refine his grasp of reality. It is tempting to state the principle differently and say that a gentleman is refined. Trouble is, I can't shake free of the sense that *refinement*—a perfectly decent word—is associated with dilettantism, which itself is not as bad a thing as we make it out to be. But unlike the ideologues, a compleat gentleman will embrace the imperfection of his knowledge. And that is refinement. We encounter again the gentleman's urbanity. His education shows him how the current crop of ideologues resembles erstwhile heretics. They are like the Orwellian demagogues who shriek that freedom is slavery, except that their claim is that rigidity is openness. The campus, which was once a place of excitement, is now a slough of despond.

We may be living, in fact, in a time not unlike that which

preceded the decline of Grecian glory in the several centuries just prior to the birth of Christ. Although in all such declines there are numerous causes, one principal element of malaise in ancient Greece was the ascendancy of Epicureanism (known in its day as The Garden), which was atheism with a pretty face. Indeed it was atheism with the heady coloring of hedonism: the good is what gives pleasure; evil is what gives pain. To give the Epicureans their due, they were neither crass materialists nor obsessive voluptuaries. They were sensible enough to recognize the prudence of simplicity: the simpler the pleasure, the more abundant. But they disdained civic involvement. They turned on, they tuned in, they dropped out. Our contemporary intelligentsia is very much a cadre of Epicureans.

In contrast, the Stoics believed that good is what is virtuous, and evil is what is sinful, the latter concept being defined as that which is out of conformity with natural law as good is in harmony with it. The Stoics dwelt rather a lot on their particular version of "physics" (which, by the way, is garnering new attention among Internet technologists) because their ethics depended so greatly upon the discernment of nature. While natural law, having a divinely ethical source, has as its first principle *do good, avoid evil*, there is obviously much in life that, although considered fundamentally "indifferent" by the Stoics, is "preferred" beyond the basic axiom. Health, wealth, and honor are preferred; sickness, poverty, and shame are "dispreferred." But, much as in Rudyard Kipling's poem "If . . ." that concludes this book, it is actually irrelevant to the Stoic's happiness what life gives him. Never before or since has there been a philosophy so rooted in inner liberty. Thus Baruch Spinoza, the seventeenth-century Dutch philosopher who was very much influenced by Stoicism, could write: "Peace is not the lack of war, but an inner virtue which has its source in the courage of the soul."

Much of Stoic philosophy and of chivalrous living derives from the effort to live in accordance with nature. David N. Sedley describes Stoic physics this way in *The Cambridge Dictionary of Philosophy* (1999): "All human lives are predetermined by the providentially designed, all-embracing causal nexus of fate; yet being the principal cause of their actions, the good and the bad alike are responsible for them: determinism and morality are fully compatible."

The Stoics were certain of what common sense tells us about reality: there are things and people in the world that we are capable of perceiving more or less accurately. Thus Stoicism remains an antidote to the fantasies of contemporary academicians who claim that there is no objective meaning in any test or act or man.

Prior to his conversion, St. Paul was something of a Stoic Jew, and he was able to make the transit to Christianity in part because Stoicism was an ideal bridge between Judaism and the new faith. Although Paul's teaching is suffused with the spirit of Christ, he employs the means and, to some extent, the ends of Stoicism in his presentation. Above all, the Christian-Stoic gentleman strives to live without illusion. For Paul, the life lived without illusion is the saint's life, and that is not the way of the compleat gentleman.

The example of Cicero is important because it makes clear why a gentleman is different from a saint. In many of the great man's orations—some given in court cases where the charges ranged from corruption to murder—Cicero shows himself a true warrior, using the tools of legal combat in whatever way necessary for victory. A saint might plead his case strictly according to law and morality, but Cicero does not. In a case of bribery—of a jury no less—Cicero knows that though his client was technically guilty, bribery was required under the corrupt system, and that justice requires a messy adaptation to worldly, not heavenly, reality.

In so many ways, Stoicism provides a framework for the gentleman's philosophy of life. It may be objected that such an ancient philosophy is redundant, given the structure available in the major religions. But despite religious claims, perhaps especially of Christianity, a gentleman per se is not defined by his religion. The status of "gentleman" in no way denies the claims of religion, and the gentleman may very well—certainly will, if he is religious—recognize the higher claim of faith upon his soul; however, his gentlemanliness is a nexus of secular attributes. Indeed, this whole business will not be grasped properly unless gentlemanliness is understood to be one tool among others of a man's *life craft*.

I shrink from such a term, *life craft*, because I have no wish to coin novel nomenclature. But the distinction needs to be made between cosmology and theology, which we could call *soul craft*, and the practicality which is life craft.

Cardinal Newman saw this and reacted against it, his subtle sarcasm usually taken for approbation. The cardinal would not like what I have written, since I seem to confirm his fear that the compleat gentleman, a fellow, as he put it, of "a cultivated intellect, a delicate taste, a candid, equitable, dispassionate mind, a noble and courteous bearing in the conduct of life," is likely, with all these virtues, nonetheless to be someone who fails to put God at the center. But for all its historical association with religion, chivalry is meant for the battlefield and not for the sanctuary. But this is where the gentleman rediscovers his medieval roots—in his willingness to die for his faith as surely as for his family and community.

But before we come to the brink, to death, we need to cool down a bit and consider that the embrace of honor amounts to the same thing as the embrace of Christ—even if the former is not as true as the latter. Now Newman might consent.

His view of a university, as he said, was compatible with the goal of educating gentlemen—at least a certain sort of gentleman. Still, as he knew, it would be asinine to suggest that a man's efforts to increase his knowledge necessarily make him a better man. After all, universities are overflowing with creeps. Education, like the conversation around a gentleman's dinner table, must be about morality or be worthless. No matter what a compleat gentleman believes, no matter whether he is Paul or Cicero, he must live in such a way that his life is true to nature, that he achieves a balance between the realities of good and evil, which balance is justice. Chivalry is always on the side of the good—that is the irreducible quality of chivalrous justice—but it recognizes evil. That recognition is almost a diplomatic arrangement. Although he is evil's implacable enemy, the compleat gentleman is acquainted with evil; because he knows it, he is able to fight it. He does not feverishly shun evil as the self-righteously, and falsely, virtuous might.

What, after all, is virtue? In derivation it is from the Latin *virtus*, meaning "manly power," which was in turn derived from the Greek notions of strength in battle. In religious parlance, there are natural and supernatural virtues, and the qualities of a compleat gentleman are primarily of the natural variety. The end of Man's aspirations ought to be happiness, but a special kind of happiness. It does not result from sating impulses, but from the achievement of—in the words of Robin Campbell (in the introduction to his 1969 translation of Seneca's *Letters from a Stoic*)—the ideal "called *aretê* in Greek and in Latin *virtus*—from which the English word 'virtue' is so unsatisfactory a translation. This, the *summum bonum* . . . [has] four qualities: wisdom (or moral insight); courage; self-control; and justice (or upright dealing)." According to some, the Stoics set the bar unrealistically high.

Perhaps. But we're currently living through an era in which expectations are far too low.

The compleat gentleman's rectitude does not prohibit him from having a sense of humor. His Stoic sense of life and his urbane education ought to give him wit. To say that a compleat gentleman has "wit" is to say that he has a ready sense of humor (often manifest as a "wicked wit") and that he "has his wits about him." In both senses of the word, wit is the consequence of a balanced moral and intellectual training.

The origins of the word *wit* are fascinating. In its most primitive meaning, it was simply *consciousness*. But it came early on to stand for right reason, for the ready sagacity acquired by learning. Eventually this little word took on the sense of mental quickness or intuitiveness, and only later did it become firmly associated with (as the *Shorter Oxford* says) "the apt, clever, unexpected, or (now esp.) humorous expression of thought." Of all the refinements that may result from a "classical" education, none is more desirable than wit.

This concern with the ancient meanings of words is in keeping with a belief that the explication of gentlemanly character must be undertaken in continuity with its antecedents. We've seen how some important terms have evolved—words such as "gentle" and "polite"—and while we may certainly employ these terms with knowledge only of their contemporary senses, still we miss a lot when we lose touch with their derivations.

As definitions go, although it is not from my beloved *Shorter Oxford Dictionary*, I rather like the one that appeared some time ago in an editorial in the *Salisbury Review*: "A gentleman is not a person with feminine gender and masculine sex. He was through and through a man. But he was gentle—in all the senses of that lucent word. He was not belligerent, but courageous; not possessive, but protective; not aggressive to other men, but bold, even-tempered, and ready to agree on terms. He was animated by a sense of honor—which meant taking responsibility for his actions, and shielding those who depended on him. And his most important attribute was loyalty, which implied that he would not deny his obligations merely because he was in a position to do so." This brings us very near the end.

Reasonable and Determined Men

In the preceding pages we've had occasion to consider many words important to our topic and to reflect upon the ways their origins affect our understanding today. Some of these derivations may seem unimportant, even if they are interesting, as in the case of "gentle." That once the term meant to "elevate to a high estate" cannot alter the sense we have now, which is simply "not violent, severe, or boisterous." I'm saying that the fact that the origins of a word may carry primary meanings hidden to those who employ the term today does not necessarily mean that the word is currently being misused. In fact, the more and the longer a word has been used in a variant sense, the more clearly its fundamental meaning may be said to have changed. These changes may not always be for the better, but they are facts requiring some caution in their correction. Caution, but not timidity.

I raise this because I am convinced that a definition of the compleat gentleman requires a return to fairly ancient notions of honor and prowess. The gentleman of the twenty-first century is more "civilized" than the knight of the twelfth century, but he has—or he'd better have—a more martial spirit than most of his contemporaries, and in that he is more like the knight. The gentleman of the twenty-first century is more straightforward than the courtier of the sixteenth century, yet he exercises more restraint than his contemporaries; this, his *sprezzatura*, bonds him to that courtier. The gentleman of the twenty-first century is more democratic than his nineteenth-century predecessors, but he does not surrender to the enthusiasms of popular culture; this makes him more like his great-grandfathers. He is, finally, a man we have not seen so often or valued so much for these many centuries: he is a man of honor.

Although there can be no official honor code of the compleat gentleman, per se, there are some official (and unofficial) codes that do exist and are meant to inculcate gentlemanly virtues in young men. They are the rules of behavior required by the armed forces, the aim of which is to govern "officers and gentlemen." Some are very terse such as the Honor Code of the United States Air Force Academy: "We will not lie, steal, or cheat, nor tolerate among us anyone who does. Furthermore, I resolve to do my duty and to live honorably, so help me God." Or the even more terse Honor Code at West Point: "A cadet will not lie, cheat, steal, or tolerate those who do."

Others are more detailed such as, for instance, the Honor Treatise of the Brigade of Midshipmen of the United States Naval Academy:

> As a Brigade we cherish the diverse backgrounds and talents of every midshipman yet recognize the common thread that unites us: the trust and confidence of the American people. They have appointed us to defend our country by developing our minds, our bodies, and most especially, our moral character.
>
> It is our responsibility to develop a selfless sense of duty that demands excellence both of ourselves and of those with whom we serve. We must honor our loyalties

without compromising our ultimate obligation to the truth. Our leadership must set a standard that reflects loyalty to our goals and the courage to stand accountable for all our actions, both those that lead to success and those that end in failure. We will never settle for achieving merely what is expected of us but will strive for a standard of excellence that reflects the dedication and courage of those who have gone before us. When we attain our goal, we will raise our expectations; when we fall short, we will rise up and try again. In essence, we espouse leadership by example, a leadership that will inspire others to follow wherever we may lead.

Countless challenges and trials lie before us. We believe that those with the strongest moral foundation will be the leaders who best reflect the legacy of the Naval Academy. This is our call as midshipmen: it is a mission we proudly accept.

In every case, cadets and servicemen find such codes to be a burden, at least initially. Especially nettling is the "non-toleration" policy, which amounts to a mandate to rat out one's mates. As a recent white paper issued by the Center for the Professional Military Ethic puts it: "Today, cadets continue to find non-toleration to be an uncomfortable issue—some have trouble with the critical notion that members of a profession must choose loyalty to the profession over loyalty to friends." But to be an officer and a gentleman is above all a moral duty, and this is true no matter how often soldiers fail to uphold the standard set.

A true gentleman—a chivalrous man—is just a bit more savage than most people imagine. The refinements associated with the word *gentleman*—such things as adroit banter, superb manners,

elegant clothes,** and the ability to make a decent dry martini—
are wonderful qualities in a man, but any cad may master them.
This is the dark side of the Castiglione heritage. Our gentleman
manqué moves smooth as a snake through life, simply begging
you to call him a gent. He's irresistible—until you get to know
him. Then, unless he is also chivalrous, you find he's actually re-
pellant. His fine speech comes from news summaries and other
conversations, not from scholarship and experience. His manners
are mere legalism and don't spring from a true consideration of
others. The suit he's wearing may come from the finest tailor, but
he came to the tailor because the tailor is trendy. And that martini—well, let's just say it offers him no pleasure at all unless it
brings him praise from you. If you don't tell him how absolutely
fabulous he is, he'll have too many martinis and show himself an
ugly drunk. You realize that he'll crack under stress and have no
true honor or courage—that given a chance—and he'll get it—
he'll gossip about you the second you leave the room. The man
has not a shred of true *sprezzatura*.

To hell with him. There are men who lack education but care
deeply about ideas; men who haven't a clue which is the correct
fork but are almost instinctively kind; men whose clothes are off-
the-rack but always carefully chosen and lovingly cared for; men
who prefer beer. This sort of man doesn't draw attention to himself; he can hold his liquor and his temper, and when the chips are
down he can subdue the drunken, loudmouthed cad—with his

** On the matter of dress: we've taken casual to new lows. I love baseball and
enjoy visits to Yankee Stadium—except I don't much like seeing the crowd,
so many of whom are in T-shirts and shorts, and some of whom apparently do
not own mirrors. Although a part of me loves seeing the black-and-white
photos of the stadium before 1960, in which all the men are in jackets and ties
(and many are wearing hats), I do think we are right to dress casually for the
ballpark. But casual shouldn't be sloppy.

words or with his fists. As the scoundrel flees to save his own scales, our hero rushes into the burning building to save others. The first fellow, breathless with fright, is only too happy to grant an interview to *Eyewitness News*. The chivalrous man goes quietly about his business. Indeed, he shuns publicity believing that virtue is its own reward; it does not depend upon recognition for fulfillment.

Many times I've been in situations in which I've stood with gentlemen and observed with a mixture of sadness and repugnance another man furiously attempting to make himself the center of some small universe: a cocktail party, a business meeting, a press conference, a date with a lovely girl. Once in such a situation a pal said to me: "Time heals all heels." I took the point then, and I take it now, but I'm not really buying it, because most cads are beyond reform.

A chivalrous man, on the other hand, a true gentleman, is in a constant state of reform. But this doesn't mean that he lacks self-knowledge. As Cardinal Newman somewhere says, *To live is to change; to enter the kingdom of heaven is to have changed often*. Or, as the great Chesterton put it, reform implies form: "It implies that we are trying to shape the world in a particular image; to make it something that we see already in our minds. Evolution is a metaphor for mere automatic unrolling. Progress is a metaphor for merely walking along a road—very likely the wrong road. But reform is a metaphor for reasonable and determined men: it means that we see a certain thing out of shape and we mean to put it into shape." And we know what shape.

What shape ought a man to be in, anyway? Newman, who probably would not have wanted to be called a gentleman, was lean and ascetic. Chesterton, who was portly and jovial, never was comfortable with being called a gentleman either. Yet both would have been pleased to be called chivalrous, and both certainly saw chivalry as the fulfillment of manhood.

In the end, chivalry demands a certain view of death. In this the aspects of the gentlemanly character—the warrior, the monk, and the lover—are one. The warrior faces death squarely because it is his duty; the monk because it is his destiny; the lover because it is his desire. In this last sense, the lover desires death because his life is given for the sake of his beloved. It is no exaggeration to say that on that fateful September 11 many men died as warriors, some as monks, and a few as lovers. Of the valor of police and firefighters we need not speak, because our gratitude has put their sacrifice beyond words. However they may have lived, they died as warriors.

I think of the story of Father Mychal Judge, a Franciscan chaplain of the of New York City Fire Department, whom Mayor Giuliani quickly passed by on the sidewalk on September 11—"Pray for us, Mychal!" the mayor shouted; "I always do!" the priest shouted back—as Judge was running into one of the Trade Center buildings in order to give last rites to a fallen firefighter, with whom he was later crushed to death when debris came down. He died as a monk ought to die, in service to his calling. Never mind that he was gay and alcoholic, or that he was not the Catholic hierarchy's idea of the perfect priest. When it mattered, he faced death as a friend.

Death, a friend? Yes. The killers are our enemies, but not death.

I think, too, of the stories of men such as Tom Burnett, Todd Beamer, and Jeremy Glick, passengers aboard United Airlines Flight 93. Burnett and Glick, big men with muscular views of life, each spoke to their wives, expressed love for them, and then stormed the terrorist hijackers. So did Beamer. He made a call that in a roundabout way put him in touch with Lisa Jefferson, a United customer service agent, and it was Ms. Jefferson who heard Mr. Beamer say to the other men: "Are you ready, guys? Let's roll." That last phrase, *Let's roll*, has come to symbolize American commitment to the long anti-terrorist war ahead. It is even the title of a song (complete with the sound of cell phones) by Neil Young, not previously known for militancy. As Mr. Young writes:

No one has the answer,
But one thing is true:
You've gotta turn on evil
When it's coming after you.
You gotta face it down,
And, when it tries to hide,
You gotta go in after it
And never be denied.

Beamer, Burnett, and Glick thought of their wives (Lisa, Deena, and Lyzbeth, respectively) and of their families; each no doubt knew he was about to die, but each clearly knew as well that his sacrifice was an act of love. As the first sentence of a *New York Times* article about Flight 93, written just two days after the attacks, stated: "They told the people they loved that they would die fighting."

Was there ever a better summary of chivalry?

It must seem to the reader that just about any event, statement, or individual is liable to provoke me into a quotation from G. K. Chesterton. It's true, and I'm far from being a Chesterton scholar. Of the honor and courage of the chivalrous man called into terminal defense of the true and the beautiful, Chesterton says this in *Orthodoxy*:

Courage is almost a contradiction in terms. It means a strong desire to live taking the form of a readiness to die. "He that will lose his life, the same shall save it," is not a piece of mysticism for saints and heroes. It is a piece of everyday advice for sailors or mountaineers. It might be printed in an Alpine guide or a drill book. This paradox is the whole principle of courage, even of quite earthly or quite brutal courage. A man cut off by the sea may save his life if he will risk it on the precipice.

He can only get away from death by continually stepping within an inch of it. A soldier surrounded by enemies, if he is to cut his way out, needs to combine a strong desire for living with a strange carelessness about dying. He must not merely cling to life, for then he will be a coward, and will not escape. He must not merely wait for death, for then he will be a suicide, and will not escape. He must seek his life in a spirit of furious indifference to it; he must desire life like water and yet drink death like wine.

It is not necessary to make a decision about eternal life in order to face death with courage, although it helps. ("All argument is against it," Dr. Johnson said, "but belief is for it.") It is enough to know that the best of life, the true and the beautiful, is preserved in some measure by one's death. As Chesterton anticipates, this principle separates the freedom fighters on board Flight 93 from the suicidal terrorists who hijacked it. "For 'tis not in mere death that men die most," Elizabeth Barrett Browning wrote. The terrorist was dead before he got on the plane.

Muriel Spark thought through the burden of living with the reality of death and concluded in *Memento Mori* (1959): "If I had my life over again I should form the habit of nightly composing myself to thoughts of death. I would practise, as it were, the remembrance of death. There is no other practice that so intensifies life. Death, when it approaches, ought not to take one by surprise. It should be part of the full expectancy of life. Without an ever-present sense of death life is insipid. You might as well live on the whites of eggs."

I will acknowledge another of Dr. Johnson's sage observations that it does not "matter how a man dies, but how he lives," especially given that death itself takes us so quickly. But it is not the actual moment of transition from living to dead that ought to matter. What matters is the ability to live honorably no matter what happens. Elisabeth Kübler-Ross, who studied death and the fear of death as extensively as anyone, has concluded: "Those who have been immersed in the tragedy of massive death during wartime, and who have faced it squarely, never allowing their senses and feelings to become numbed and indifferent, have emerged from their experiences with growth and humanness greater than that achieved through almost any other means." Perhaps this in some measure applies to many Americans in the wake of 9/11.

We may hope that men will take up the burden of chivalry today. It matters only a little what the truth about former knights and gentlemen is. They may have had feet of clay, but they aspired to the chivalrous attributes: fidelity, prowess, generosity, courtesy, and honor. I've suggested that the quality unifying them all is justice. The best men, chivalrous or not, as warriors, lovers, and monks have always been just men. Of all the chivalrous attributes, honor is the greatest, because it brings the burden of justice into every moment of a man's life.

CHAPTER EIGHT

The Art of *Sprezzatura*

Thou maintainest whether touching religion, state, or vanity; for if thou err in the first, thou shalt be accounted profane; if in the second, dangerous; if in the third, indiscreet and foolish.

–SIR WALTER RALEIGH, "PRIVATE QUARRELS TO BE AVOIDED" (1632)

T his chapter being last is by way of being a summary, and if "honor" is properly the one word that epitomizes the character of a gentleman, then "*sprezzatura*" is the last word about the gentleman's "conduct of life." (A fine phrase, that "conduct of life"; it's the Library of Congress subject heading for all the gentlemanly handbooks written between about 1500 and 1900.)

Sprezzatura, you'll recall, was the coinage of Count Baldassare Castiglione, man of the Renaissance. He was born in Castatico, Italy (near Mantua), in 1478. He was a nobleman classically educated to be at home in royal and papal courts, and from his early twenties until his death at the age of fifty he served the high and the mighty, including Popes Leo X and Clement VII and Holy Roman Emperor Charles V, who considered him the perfect gentleman. He was a good friend of the painter Raffello Santi, better known as Raphael, with whom he collaborated on a plan to preserve Roman antiquities.

Castiglione wrote *Il Cortegiano*, or, as it became known in English, *The Courtier* (or, more completely, *The Book of the Courtier*), between 1513 and 1518, although it was not published until 1528. His book has freshness even today; in his own time it was revolutionary. Yet even Castiglione's novel takes on manliness owed much to Greek and Roman antecedents, to Aristotle and Cicero especially. The ideal courtier was to have Aristotelian *aretê*, which is to say "excellence." An *aristos* (from whence "aristocrat") was a man educated in the best ideas and tempered by training to possess the best impulses. He was, to borrow a phrase from Jacob Burckhardt—of *The Civilization of the Renaissance* in Italy (1818–1897)—engaged in "self-fashioning." For Aristotle—and for men of the Renaissance such as Castiglione and even Shakespeare—the standard for self-fashioning is the "golden mean," the center between extremes. As Peter Burke explains it: "Courage is defined as the mean between rashness and cowardice, liberality as the mean between extravagance and parsimony, and so on." From Cicero he, Castiglione that is, took the concept of *neglentia diligens* ("studied negligence"), an obvious precursor to *sprezzatura*. Like all writers of this period, he respected Ovid's famous observation, "*Ars est celare artem.*" *The purpose of art is to conceal itself.*

Catiglione's own definition of *sprezzatura* appeared as follows, translated into Elizabethan English by Sir Thomas Hoby:

Not to crake and boast of his actes and good qualities. To shon Affectation or curiosity above al thing in al things. To do his feates with a slight, as though they were rather naturally in him, then learned with studye: and use a

Reckelesness to cover art, without minding greatly what
he hath in hand, to a mans seeminge.

Ever since these words were published, Castiglione's motives
(and those who embraced his counsel) have been suspect. To
many he seems to be advocating "art," which to some extent he
obviously is, and by art his critics mean pretense or dishonesty.
Castiglione's courtier has come down to us as a superficial fellow
content to fake it if he can—so long as the deception is shrewd.

Gordon Bull nicely summarizes the truth about *sprezzatura* in
the introduction to his translation of *The Courtier.* "The great virtues
it proposes for a gentleman are discretion and decorum, nonchalance and gracefulness." Yet he, too, sides with those who believe
Castiglione's book "conceals the most shameless opportunism
under the cloak of a tiresome refinement." Professor Bull expressed
this opinion in 1967. One wonders if the decline of discretion and
decorum, nonchalance and gracefulness in the intervening decades
might have led him to second thoughts today. Even if the sum of
Castiglione's thoughts on the gentleman's calling cannot stand
today as a perfect manual for modern men, it is wrong, I believe, to
accuse Castiglione of encouraging "shameless opportunism."

Because, you see, no one is born a gentleman, and this implies that becoming one is a matter of education. Castiglione's
"art" is really the practice of the principles that when finally in-
ternalized—"digested," you might say—create the man whose
urbanity, wit, athleticism, and restraint are second nature, in his
sinews. Unlike most "masters of the universe," though, he won't
crow about it because implicit in *sprezzatura* is not only this ef-
fortless elegance but also a strenuous self-control. Confucius—
about whom I'll write more in a moment—said that "although
the gentleman may not have attained goodness, he acts in such a
way so that he might become good."

Creating a Self

There are two ways to look at a fellow's *sprezzatura*. On the one hand, it means *discretion*, or, more grandly, *prudence*; on the other hand it means *restraint*, which may even be *concealment*. The first is a rare and marvelous quality these days, one that folks may admire when they encounter it. Still, we live in a culture that is simply aghast at taciturnity. We may appreciate the few men and women who actually exhibit restraint in some situations (especially when anger is suppressed), but we distrust anyone we suspect of not being "open."

Perhaps this is a legacy of the much-maligned decade of the 1960s: of Leary and LSD, of hippies and hemp, of "do your own thing," and "let it all hang out." One of that decade's prophets of libertinism, Henry Miller, once whined: "Why are we so full of restraint? Why do we not give in all directions? Is it fear of losing ourselves? Until we do lose ourselves there is no hope of finding ourselves." This is the modern worldview as plainly stated as we may hope to have it. Miller's final sentence has an attractive, almost mystical allure: to find the "self" we must first lose the "self." It's alluring, but ridiculous. The self can be neither lost nor found; it isn't some sort of psychic unicorn, mysterious and magical. The "self" is a creative process, perhaps *the* creative process. And the development of character—and even the enjoyment of sex, which was Miller's obsession—depends as much upon cunning as upon spontaneity. Of course, there's some truth in Miller's conviction that in the surrender to sexual passion we learn something important. The trouble is that, among men, sex without restraint usually amounts to premature ejaculation.

Even if most of us have learned that an abstraction such as

"lose ourselves" is mere literary hogwash, many of us still cultivate lifestyles characterized by a lack of tact. We live in the Age
of Premature Ejaculation, a dreadful period of spontaneous, ill-
considered, naked spouting-off.

To me, this proclivity for displays of openness is appalling.
Consider, for instance, that in the New York metropolitan area,
where I live, we have come to expect the kind of aggressive
journalism that sends television reporters to interview a mother
within minutes after her son has been murdered in a drive-by
shooting. It has become commonplace, but I cannot accustom
myself to the spectacle. I'm dismayed whenever anybody bares
bereavement to strangers.

Or consider how the Internet has exposed the way
voyeurism can make fools of millions and make millions for
fools, or how so-called "reality" TV has fulfilled the Warholian
prophecy about fame.

Consider, too, that one year after the death of John F.
Kennedy Jr. and his wife and sister-in-law, the media were once
again exploiting the nation's obsession with celebrity and
confirming the observation of Blaise Pascal—made more than
three hundred years ago—that the "charm of fame is so great that
we like every object to which it is attached, even death."

We seem unwilling and unable to leave one another alone,
and apparently most of us do not wish to be left alone. When
asked, we tell, boldly asserting that we have nothing to hide, ev-
idently believing that there really is nothing about which to feel
shame, or—if we are embarrassed—that surrender to fleeting
media attention is better than silent suffering, if not actually a
kind of redemption made through expiation. When President
Bill Clinton decided, initially, not to tell the truth about his sexual liaison with a White House intern—on the advice of his chief
pollster—predictions were that his later confession would cost

him his job, which in his impeachment trial it nearly did. But in the end his popularity was not only undiminished, it was actually magnified, demonstrating the way in which celebrity, which is to say exposure, insulates against risk.

It's a trend that is likely to continue. The current libertarian legal climate, which, it must be said, has much to recommend it, will continue to erode the line between public and private acts, just as the Internet continues to obliterate it. No doubt we will retain a vestigial appreciation of privacy, but there's no stopping the process leading to—just for instance—the emergence of pornographic content as a part of basic coaxial-cable and satellite-TV services. We are just about at a point where we cannot protect our children from exposure to inappropriate viewing material, even if we wish to.

To be a compleat gentleman in the midst of this pageant of candor is more than ever to exist in a state of alienation. Either you feel like Cotton Mather, seeing witches everywhere, or like H. L. Mencken, laughing at all the ninnies. Better to laugh, of course. Sometimes when I break for lunch, I'll turn on the office television and watch a few minutes of *Jerry Springer*, which certainly provides risible evidence of the extent to which some Americans adore exposing themselves— figuratively and literally. It's bad enough (not to say astonishing) that "My Lover Doesn't Know I'm a Transsexual," but why break the news to him on national television? The lady who'd do that is no gentleman.*

---

* Whenever I have shamelessly quoted myself to this effect on radio programs, I've gotten laughs from the host. But one man stopped me and said: "Wait a minute. Don't you get into arguments with people? Don't you chastise the dopes who say stupid things? I do. I get right up in their faces." My reply was that I sometimes argue but usually don't. "Why," I asked him, "should I care if the dopes know what's on my mind?"

Openness vs. Discretion

It's hard not to be sucked into this eddy of tastelessness, if only because of its ubiquity. As Chesterton, witty, prescient Chesterton, said: "It is always simple to fall; there are an infinity of angles at which one falls, only one at which one stands." And being "upright," as folks used to put it, is ever more difficult, and to most it probably seems silly.

For many, the notion of being upright is downright offensive since they infer that the man standing straight stands in judgment. Not to be "open" to every "lifestyle" and every "preference" is to be unjust. Of course, many who profess "openness" are in fact themselves hostile to those who refuse to acknowledge the equality of all opinions and behaviors. This is akin to the sophomoric insight that there are no absolutes except the statement "there are no absolutes." This is what has turned some of the politically correct bluestockings on college campuses into latter-day versions of Czarist or Jacobin secret police.

But I must guard against the temptation to adorn the restrained gentleman in well-cut, conservative clothes. He is not necessarily a conservative, especially not in terms of his politics. That being said, it remains the case, I think, that "liberals" believe it right and even necessary to tolerate more bizarre behavior than do "conservatives" and are less quick to condemn the unrefined and the obscene. But it's one thing to defend the rights of the boor and the pornographer, quite another to dignify discourtesy and obscenity as valid "choices." The gravest of dangers lurks here, even if the day-to-day "tolerance" and "openness" of liberals are merely annoying and not particularly harmful, even if—to be fair—we all owe a great debt to liberality. (Indeed, I've met just one contemporary conservative who was not actually a classical liberal, that is, a believer in individual liberty, free markets, and republican democracy. This European gentleman—and he was a gentleman—pined for the return to Austria of the Habsburg monarchy and an attendant stratification in society along pre-Enlightenment class lines.)[†]

In this context, the gentleman's restraint will make him seem to many both dyspeptic and dishonest. *This fellow is hiding something! He's one man in private and another in public! What's up with that?* What's it supposed to mean if (as probably he *never* would) he raises a hand to the objection and says, "It's just my *sprezzatura*"?

A man who has *sprezzatura* is a man content to keep his own counsel. He not only does not need to have his motives understood, he prefers that they not be understood. His actions, including his carefully chosen words, speak for him. It is not necessary for others—save his intimates—to know more.

It's a little like the scene in *The Godfather* when Don Corleone takes aside his oldest son and admonishes him never to let anyone outside the family know what he is thinking. Or, as Cervantes has Sancho Panza put it (in one of his "catalogues of musty proverbs"): "A closed mouth catches no flies." Another 1960s icon, the singer Joni Mitchell, a woman well known for her naked candor, still had the good sense to admit to the *London Independent*, "[t]here are things to confess that enrich the world and things that need not be said."

Although it is not specifically a reason for embracing circumspection, it so happens that a discrete gentleman amasses, over time, a tremendous edge in the affairs of this world. He hears

---

[†] I no longer describe myself as a conservative. I'm a Roman Catholic classical liberal.

things that others do not, simply because people of all sorts confide in him, knowing that he will not betray their trust. The knowledge of the human heart that the compleat gentleman thus develops can be a burden, but it is also something of a liberation. It may call upon every bit of his strength to restrain himself from saying or doing more than he ought with knowledge gained from friendship, but there it is.

Years ago, an unfortunate incident (an instance of a betrayal of trust—more than this I won't say) taught me a valuable lesson—that almost everyone has someone else to whom he will tell your secret. It's folly to begin with to share a confidence with another on the condition that the secret is "just between the two of us." It may be that it is necessary to impress upon a true friend that what is said ought not be shared with others (since not all intimacies are necessarily sensitive, it's common courtesy to say which ones are), but it is a violation of the terms of a true friendship to thus burden a pal with a tasty tidbit and then to instruct him in the ethics of intimacy. If he doesn't already know, you've got no business confiding in him.

And I should add this: a young man or young woman who wakes up naked next to a stranger may well have spent the night sleeping with an enemy. The whole point of restraint—and the etiquette supporting it—is to give us a chance to negotiate slowly and carefully the difference between being strangers and becoming friends. Not every man or woman we'll meet will become a friend; there are some who ought to be our enemies—they don't need to know that, but the fact remains.

It is very hard to keep this in mind these days, since most people address us by our first names immediately upon meeting, and I've managed to offend many people over the last few years simply by refusing to do so—as if using Mr. or Miss were like a slap in the face.

The Ruler's Son

I've lived in a part of seven decades now, and in my life I've known fewer than six individuals who could dependably keep a secret. Intimate knowledge tends to burn inside, tries to escape the brain in telegraphic outbursts, like the "dish" in the headlines of supermarket tabloids. It's the sensibility expressed by Louisa May Alcott a century ago:

> A little kingdom I possess,
> Where thoughts and feelings dwell;
> And very hard the task I find
> Of governing it well.

°Of course there is more to *sprezzatura* than just restraint. There is that quality people refer to when a man is called suave. Cary Grant was usually a gentleman in his film roles because he seemed able to do difficult things with ease and because he seemed a "man of the world," not only suave but urbane as well. One could not imagine Cary Grant saying anything inappropriate, and it was inconceivable that he would blurt out an intimacy, perhaps not even to an intimate friend. He knew the difference between a true friend, a friend, an acquaintance, and a stranger. But to a very great extent we may think of a compleat gentleman as a man who—whatever other virtues he may possess—is known (if indeed we are capable of seeing and appreciating these qualities) by his discretion and his restraint.

Restraint may seem the least of the gentlemanly virtues, although it is the most recognizably Stoic. The ability to pause before acting and then to act sensibly is manifest prudence, which is the first among the cardinal virtues. But here again it may be objected that a gentleman's restraint, being a quality of *sprezzatura*, is nothing more than ostentation, albeit of a subtle variety. The objection may be finally answered only in the person of a gentleman.

Most gentlemen today are as Matthew Arnold described his friends at Oxford: believers in "lost causes and forsaken beliefs." Here Arnold is joined in comradeship with T. S. Eliot who, although he usually mocked Arnold, was also a believer in lost causes, in the necessity of holding fast to the permanent things the modern world no longer values. In the end, to be a gentleman is to hold Stoically, quietly to the conviction that he not be seen doing his "gentleman thing." Silence really is golden.

For heaven's sake, men, just shut up!

In a *New York Times* article a few years back, sportswriter Harvey Araton was pleased to note that for once a pro athlete had refused to rise to the bait of another jock's taunts. Of Derek Jeter's decision not to respond to derogatory remarks made about him by his "friend" Alex Rodriguez,[‡] Araton wrote: "In the context of budding controversy, this solid contact with the increasingly elusive concept of restraint was the equivalent of a two-out, ninth-inning hit with the tying run on second." For those who don't follow baseball: *a winner.*

This is where Clark Kent steps in. In all of American popular culture, Superman is our strongest hero. He is also the most restrained. True, Kent's *sprezzatura* conceals more than any other gentleman's. But then the art (and depth) of *sprezzatura* is defined by a man's power: the stronger and wiser he is, the gentler his manner and the more circumspect his speech; the more, in other words, his true self is hidden.

Kent is a fiction, but an interesting one, both in terms of his

---

[‡] This was before A-Rod joined the Yankees.

enduring appeal and his history, by which I mean the real story of his invention. His first appearance in comic-book form was in 1938. His creators, illustrator Joe Shuster and writer Jerry Siegel, were Jewish teenagers living in Cleveland, Ohio, and the Man of Steel actually began as an illustrated rendering of Nietzsche's *Übermensch*, complete with will-to-power villainy. But this was Siegel's first, unpublished version. By the time DC Comics introduced *Superman in Action Comics #1*, he'd become a good guy with a nerdy alter ego—rather like his creators, apparently—who got his name from two of the era's movie stars: Clark Gable and Kent Taylor. (Taylor was not a big star, although he did appear in some notable films, including *I'm No Angel* (1933), with Mae West and Cary Grant, and *Death Takes a Holiday* (1934), with Fredric March and Evelyn Venable. He starred in the early 1950s' TV series *Boston Blackie* and ended his career appearing in ghastly horror flicks.) The original model for the look of Superman was another actor, Douglas Fairbanks Sr., whose classic arms-akimbo, feet-apart stance (think of 1924's *Thief of Bagdad* or *The Black Pirate* from 1926) became the most common motif on Action Comics covers. For Clark Kent's appearance and demeanor, the boys thought of silent-film comedian Harold Lloyd.

Although Superman was born in an alien world (the planet Krypton) and was raised by gentle Kansas Protestants (Jonathan and Martha Kent), there was a strong sense of Jewishness about him. His real name is Kal-El, a clearly theophorous name; the word "El" comes from a root word meaning "god" or "of God" in Hebrew. Kal-El in the cornfield is rather like Moses in the bulrushes, Martha Kent being equivalent to Pharaoh's daughter. If this seems a stretch, consider that Joseph Goebbles, Hitler's propagandist, once railed against Superman's "Semitism" in a cabinet meeting, probably spurred on by a scathing attack on Siegel that appeared in the SS newspaper, *Das Schwarze Korps*, in which he was referred to as "intellectually and physically circumcised." Of course, there was also the 1944 cover that showed a grimly triumphant Superman holding Hitler and Goebbles by their collars: Hitler in one hand, Tojo in the other. Goebbles couldn't have liked that.

Contemporary scholars enjoy bashing Superman almost as much as the Nazis did. Umberto Eco sees him as a "conservative" hero, a defender of the status quo (a common misunderstanding of social and political conservatism) and fundamentally a capitalist lackey, since he only attacks criminals and never—as American liberals would put it—the "underlying causes" of crime. That he exemplifies "truth, justice, and the American Way," that he is a *chivalrous* hero, makes him as much a figure of fun as the character of Benjamin Guggenheim in *Titanic*.

Perhaps Bruce Wayne is more exemplary than Clark Kent, since, as Batman, the Dark Knight, he lacks superhuman powers. He's simply a martial artist with a powerful sense of right and wrong and sufficient learning and wealth to fill his basement with myriad crime-fighting gear. But, like Kent, he has to shut up about it. When these guys meet their Lois Lanes or Vickie Vales, they *never* say, "Hi, I'm Clark [or Bruce]," but [whispering]— "I'm really Superman [Batman]." Some of the most important things about a man are the things he keeps from most people all the time and from those closest to him until the time is right.

This also applies to a gentleman's views about politics and religion and everything else under the sun. It may be tempting when hearing a topic discussed—and recalling Jonathan Swift's quip that it is "useless to attempt to reason a man out of a thing he was never reasoned into"—to say to the idiot defending the militia movement or touting economic redistribution that he is an ignoramus. This is tempting, but why ought this knucklehead know what's in your heart?

Is it insincerity thus to withhold one's true thoughts? If so, why object? It is among the more familiar aspects of living that when knowledge is first acquired—especially moral knowledge—it is necessarily raw, which is to say that it is in a form that is so undeveloped as not to be the thing itself. For instance, the first political notions of teenagers are as self-righteous as they are self-contradictory, and only the tempering of many years of experience and study will transform these airy opinions into solid convictions. In a similar vein, when we teach manners to our children they often object—at least the bright ones do—to rules the meaning of which neither they nor their parents can quite explain. Yet over time these minor morals take on inestimable value. It doesn't matter if the form as practiced often disguises some insincerity. The practice of courtesy, even when artificial, will likely lead to a very concrete civility. When at the end of a war two former combatants embrace, it is not because they have come suddenly to love their enemies. It is because gestures of hope are preferable to expressions of hostility.

So if a gentleman practices *sprezzatura*, it is so he can get it right. The cult of spontaneous sincerity has it that it is better for a man to behave like a creep until he's really a gentleman, until he has genuinely and completely digested civility. But that's both silly and depressing.

A gentleman may be vain, but he will maintain a hold on his vanity in order not to be, as Walter Raleigh put it in the epigraph that begins this chapter, "indiscrete and foolish." There is almost a tradition of foppishness among gentlemen, since their love of the true and the beautiful often extends to dress; however, the sort of vanity that worries over such details as cuffed trousers and silk pocket squares is fundamentally harmless and may even be beneficial, virtuous. (Why shouldn't a man look his best? Why shouldn't he give attention to traditional details of elegance and quality?) But the rule of fine tailors ought always to govern a man's style—that when a customer leaves the tailor's shop and meets a friend on the street, the friend ought to compliment the man, not his clothes: "How are you, Reggie? You're looking well. Have you lost weight?"

But if Reggie's chum can't stop talking about the suit, the tailor has failed, because his handiwork is drawing too much attention to itself and not enough to the man. In the same way, a man's behavior should never draw attention to himself. Well, obviously there are times when a man, standing upright, can't help but be in the center of things, but the point is that recognition ought to be without appeal to the gentleman.

The hardest thing of all in some situations may be silence—the ability to keep quiet when one knows the answer to a question one hasn't been asked. But, as Spinoza said, all things excellent are as difficult as they are rare.

Wisdom East and West

I find it deeply pleasing to note that Confucius, who taught a half millennium before Christ, defined the gentleman along lines remarkably similar to those we've discussed in this book. Of course, he did not use the word "gentleman," and scholars dispute that this is the best translation. But the term he did use, *chun-tzu,* has a history startlingly like that of "gentleman." Literally, *chun-tzu* is "ruler's son" and was originally applied only to the virtuous aristocrat. But Confucius did with *chun-tzu* what the Europeans more than a thousand years later were to do with *gentleman*: he made the term classless.

"A gentleman," Confucius said, "is distressed by his own lack of capacity; he is never distressed at the failure of others to recognize his merits." He will be "slow in word but diligent in action."

Indeed, he is "ashamed to let his words outrun his deeds." And he remains "unperturbed when not appreciated by others."

Note how the Confucian virtues are like those of the European knight. The *chun-tzu* possesses five essential qualities: integrity, righteousness, loyalty, altruism, and goodness. Missing from this list are prowess, the notable characteristic of the knight; and restraint, the signature quality of the gentleman. But the master's extensive commentary on the proper "conduct of life" amplifies the similarities between the Asian and European models. The martial arts, where prowess and restraint are paramount, are inconceivable—in China, anyway—without the Confucian model.

I have encountered conservative Christians, mostly fundamentalist Protestants, who view the martial arts with suspicion and even revulsion. When in karate class the student sits in meditative posture and then bows to his teacher, he is engaged, so these critics say, in idolatry. I've even heard it asserted that the *chi* (or *ch'i* or *ki*) force that the martial artist calls upon when delivering a hand strike or a kick is a "power" that may only be conjured through Satan. But no Christian gentleman can plausibly assert such nonsense. The bow is no different than a soldier's salute to a superior officer, and the *chi*, which means blood in Japanese, is no different than "heart," as when we say, "Put your heart into it," or when we say, "I felt my blood rise." A Christian gentleman needs to be enough of a "man of the world" that he doesn't feel contempt in encounters with different cultures.

Confucius said, "The true gentleman is conciliatory but not accommodating. The lesser man is accommodating but not conciliatory." Chesterton once quipped: "Bigotry is an incapacity to conceive seriously the alternative to a proposition." Or, as Cole Porter put it: *Live and let live.*

For a people who, it seems to me, are in fact no more forthright than any previous American generation, we make rather a lot of noise about hypocrisy and dishonesty—both our own and history's. We ought to condemn lying—although as the case of Bill Clinton shows, we often don't—but we ought not to confuse honesty with impulsiveness, prudence with naked candor. It's true that the art of *sprezzatura* involves a degree of cunning, but the same may be said for social order at every level. Writ large, morality exists in part to endorse goodness and in part to restrain evil; writ small, morals are the manners we employ to repress the impulse for base behavior and to provide others with status in the kingdom of ourselves. And, if you like, these restraints and repressions are false, like fine clothes that we can barely afford and that are uncomfortable to wear. They are pretensions that in a democracy reveal a sordid affection for aristocracy.

Or so one hears.

In fact, these little artificialities are as important to a cohesive culture as the loftiest ideals or most humane laws.

Of course I know that for Christian readers no calling can be higher than the call to faith in Christ, and this is true for this author as well. But the calling of the compleat gentleman remains a high calling, conflicting in no way with that higher calling. If we are to "render unto Caesar that which is Caesar's and unto God that which is God's," religion shows us the way to the latter. I hope this book shines some small light on an approach to the former.

· · ·

So this is the compleat gentleman. He is a fellow you may not recognize at first, such is the mask of *sprezzatura*. He is the descendant of the medieval knight and the Victorian gentleman;

he is very much like them, except that he has a newer and more realistic view of women. He is a conservative liberal, a man educated in tradition but not bound by it. If he is very different from other men, it is by virtue of his commitment to honor and his devotion to restraint.

He is like a warrior, because he knows that there are things worth fighting for, and will fight. He is a lover, because he allows his wife and family to liberate him from the tyranny of his ego. He is like a monk, because he employs learning to unlock the mysteries of the human heart. He is possessed of that co-mingling of restraint and detachment that is *sprezzatura* and that we can as easily call *cool*.

In closing, although I will be accused of resurrecting the "gods of the copybook," I present what I consider the best short summary ever written of the compleat gentleman's profession. Let the critics wail. "Right is right, even if nobody does it," Mr. Chesterton once wrote, "wrong is wrong, even if everybody is wrong about it." I close with "If . . ." by the great Victorian, neo-Stoic Rudyard Kipling (1835–1936). My most sincere apologies to the critic Edmund Wilson, who called it the "Polonius precept." He couldn't have been more wrong.

If . . .

If you can keep your head when all about you
Are losing theirs and blaming it on you;
If you can trust yourself when all men doubt you,
But make allowance for their doubting too;
If you can wait and not be tired by waiting,
Or, being lied about, don't deal in lies,
Or, being hated, don't give way to hating,

And yet don't look too good, nor talk too wise;

If you can dream—and not make dreams your master;
If you can think—and not make thoughts your aim;
If you can meet with triumph and disaster
And treat those two impostors just the same;
If you can bear to hear the truth you've spoken
Twisted by knaves to make a trap for fools,
Or watch the things you gave your life to broken,
And stoop and build 'em up with worn-out tools;

If you can make one heap of all your winnings
And risk it on one turn of pitch-and-toss,
And lose, and start again at your beginnings
And never breathe a word about your loss;
If you can force your heart and nerve and sinew
To serve your turn long after they are gone,
And so hold on when there is nothing in you
Except the Will which says to them: "Hold on";

If you can talk with crowds and keep your virtue,
Or walk with kings—nor lose the common touch;
If neither foes nor loving friends can hurt you;
If all men count with you, but none too much;
If you can fill the unforgiving minute
With sixty seconds' worth of distance run—
Yours is the Earth and everything that's in it,
And—which is more—you'll be a Man my son!

ACKNOWLEDGMENTS

My education in the martial arts has been always rewarding, occasionally painful, and never boring. For their expert instruction in karate and in life, I want to thank Shihan James Chillemi, Sensei Robert Chillemi, and the staff of the New York Goju Karate Association, including especially Eva Cheung and Eric Cheung, Steve Caprara and Anthony Palumbo, Eric Radoman and Brian Fitzgerald. I would be remiss if I were to fail to tip my hat to one very special second-degree black belt, my older son Sensei Robert Miner.

I am grateful to Mitchell Muncy, my original editor, and Thomas Spence, this book's original publisher, for their encouragement, advice, and patience.

Since I met her, I have never done anything the best part of which does not owe much to Sydny Weinberg Miner, my wife and inspiration. I owe much to my younger son, Jon, not least for his generosity in loaning me the rubber skull he keeps in his room. It sat atop the computer monitor in my office as I studied, thought, and read about medieval life.

I also want to acknowledge five men who have inspired and encouraged me over the years—many years: Douglas E. Hoover, Bill Jamieson, Roland Millar, Don Russell, Tom Smith, and Peter Zuidema. Thanks, gents.

Finally, I am most grateful to Richard Vigilante, whose confidence in this book led to this new edition. Richard is truly a Renaissance Man.

SELECTED BIBLIOGRAPHY

*The dates given for each book are for the edition used,
which is often not the original year of publication.*

– A –

Ackerman, Diane. *A Natural History of Love*. New York: Random House, 1994.

Adams, Henry. *Mont-Saint-Michel and Chartres*. Princeton: Princeton University Press, 1981.

Anderson, Digby, ed. *Gentility Recalled: Mere Manners and the Making of Social Order*. London: London Social Affairs Unit, 1996.

Aresty, Esther B. *The Best Behavior*. New York: Simon & Schuster, 1970.

– B –

Babbitt, Irving. *Character and Culture*. New Brunswick: Transaction Publishers, 1995.

Barber, Richard. *Henry Plantagenet*. New York: Roy, 1964.

_____. *The Reign of Chivalry*. New York: St. Martin's Press, 1980.

Barber, Malcolm. *The New Knighthood: A History of the Order of the Temple*. New York: Cambridge University, 1995.

Beard, Geoffrey W. *The Compleat Gentleman: Five Centuries of Aristocratic Life*. New York: Rizzoli, 1993.

Begley, Ronald B. "Too Diffident to Define: The Gentleman in Newman's Idea of a University." *Faith & Reason* (Winter 1993).

Bergengren, Ralph. *The Perfect Gentleman*. Boston: Atlantic Monthly Press, 1919.

Biel, Steven. *Down with the Old Canoe: A Cultural History of the Titanic Disaster*. New York: Norton, 1996.

Bloom, Allan. *Closing of the American Mind*. New York: Simon & Schuster, 1987.

Boethius, Ancius. *The Consolation of Philosophy*. New York: Penguin, 1969.

Bogin, Meg. *The Women Troubadours*. New York: Norton, 1980.

Brander, Michael. *The Victorian Gentleman*. London: Gordon Cremonesi, 1975.

Brauer, George C., Jr. *The Education of the Gentleman: Theories of Gentlemanly Education in England, 1660–1775*. New York: Bookman Associates, 1959.

Brennan, Joseph Gerard. *Foundations of Moral Obligation*. California: Presidio, 1992.

Briggs, Asa. *The Age of Improvement, 1783–1867*. New York: McKay, 1959.

Brooks, Polly Schoyer. *Queen Eleanor*. Boston: Houghton Mifflin, 1983.

Bryson, Anna. *From Courtesy to Civility: Changing Codes of Conduct in Early Modern England*. New York: Oxford, 1998.

Bulfinch, Thomas. *Age of Chivalry*. Philadelphia: McKay, 1900.

Bumke, Joachim. *Courtly Culture: Literature & Society in the High Middle Ages*. Berkeley: University of California, 1991.

Burke, Edmund. *Select Works of Edmund Burke,* vol, 2. Indianapolis: Liberty Fund, 1999.

Burke, Peter. *The Fortunes of the Courtier*. University Park: Penn State University Press, 1996.

Buruma, Ian. *Anglomania*. New York: Vintage, 1998.

Butler, Daniel Allen. *Unsinkable: The Full Story of* RMS *Titanic*. Mechanicsburg: Stackpole, 1998.

– C –

Cady, Edwin Harrison. *The Gentleman in America*. Syracuse: Syracuse University, 1949.

Cantor, Norman F. *Inventing the Middle Ages: The Lives, Works, and Ideas of the Great Medievalists of the Twentieth Century*. New York: Morrow, 1991.

_____. *Medieval Lives: Eight Charismatic Men and Women of the Middle Ages*. New York: HarperCollins, 1994.

Capellanus, Andreas. *The Art of Courtly Love*. New York: Columbia University, 1990.

Carson, Gerald. *The Polite Americans*. New York: Morrow, 1966.

Carter, Stephen L. *Civility: Manners, Morals, and the Etiquette of Democracy* New York: Basic, 1998.

Castiglione, Baldassare. *The Courtier*. Translated by George Bull. New York: Penguin, 1967.

Castronovo, David. *The American Gentleman: Social Prestige and the Modern Literary Mind*. New York: Continuum, 1991.

_____. *The English Gentleman: Images and Ideas in Literature and Society* New York: Frederick Ungar, 1987.

Cervantes, Miguel de. *Don Quixote*. New York: Everyman's Library, 1991.

Chesterton, G. K. *Orthodoxy*. New York: Image, 1959.

Chrétien de Troyes. *Arthurian Romances*. Rutland: Everyman, 1993.

Cicero, Marcus Tullius. *Letters of a Roman Gentleman*. Boston: Houghton Mifflin, 1926.

_____. *Selected Works*. New York: Penguin, 1960.

Coulton, G. G. *Medieval Panorama*. New York: Cambridge, 1938.

Cox, Stephen. *Titanic: Hard Choices, Dangerous Decisions*. Chicago: Open Court, 1999.

Crothers, Samuel McChord. "The Evolution of the Gentleman." *Atlantic Monthly*" (May 1898).

– D –

Dahmus, Joseph. *Seven Medieval Queens*. Garden City: Doubleday, 1971.

Dawson, Christopher. *Religion and the Rise of Western Culture*. New York: Image, 1991.

Dorsett, Lyle W, ed. *The Essential C. S. Lewis*. New York: Collier, 1988.

Drake, Durant. *Problems of Conduct*. Boston: Houghton Mifflin, 1935.

Duby, Georges. *The Chivalrous Society*. Berkeley: University of California, 1977.

_____. *Love and Marriage in the Middle Ages*. Chicago: University of Chicago, 1994.

_____. *The Three Orders: Feudal Society Imagined*. Chicago: University of Chicago, 1978.

_____. *William Marshal: Flower of Chivalry*. New York: Pantheon, 1985.

Dysinger, Luke, O.S.B., trans. *The Rule of Saint Benedict*. Trabuco Canyon: Source Books, 1996.

– E –

Edelstein, Ludwig. *The Meaning of Stoicism*. Cambridge: Harvard, 1966.

Elias, Norbert. *The Civilizing Process*. New York: Urizen, 1978.

Eliot, T. S. *Christianity and Culture*. New York: Harcourt, Brace, Jovanovich, 1939.

Epictetus. *The Discourses, The Handbook, Fragments*. North Clarendon: Everyman/Tuttle, 1995.

Erasmus. *Praise of Folly*. New York: Penguin, 1971.

– F –

Fadiman, Clifton, ed. *The Treasury of the Encyclopaedia Britannica*. New York: Viking, 1992.

Foss, Michael. *Chivalry*. New York: McKay, 1975.

– G–

Gabriel, Richard A. *To Serve with Honor: A Treatise on Military Ethics and the Way of the Soldier.* Westport: Greenwood, 1982.

Gautier, Léon. *Chivalry: The Everyday Life of the Medieval Knight.* New York: Crescent, 1989.

Gies, Frances. *The Knight in History.* New York: Harper & Row, 1984.

_____ and Joseph Gies. *Life in a Medieval Village.* New York: Harper & Row, 1990.

Gilder, George. *Men and Marriage.* Gretna: Pelican, 1986.

Gilson, Etienne. *Heloise and Abelard.* Ann Arbor: University of Michigan, 1960.

_____. *The Spirit of Mediaeval Philosophy.* Notre Dame: Notre Dame Press, 1991.

Girouard, Mark. *The Return to Camelot: Chivalry and the English Gentleman* New Haven: Yale University, 1981.

Goodrich, Norma Lorre. *The Holy Grail.* New York: HarperCollins, 1992.

– H –

Hallam, Elizabeth, ed. *The Plantagenet Chronicles.* New York: Widenfeld & Nicholson, 1986.

Heer, Friedrich. *The Medieval World: Europe 1100–1350.* New York: Welcome Rain, 1998.

Henry William, A., III. *In Defense of Elitism.* New York: Doubleday, 1994.

Himmelfarb, Gertrude. *Marriage and Morals Among the Victorians.* New York: Knopf, 1986.

_____. *Victorian Minds.* New York: Knopf, 1968.

Hollister, C. Warren. *Medieval Europe: A Short History.* New York: McGraw-Hill, 1990.

Howarth, Stephen. *The Knights Templar.* New York: 1982.

– J –

Jaeger, C. Stephen. *The Origins of Courtliness: Civilizing Trends and the Formation of Courtly Ideals, 939–1210.* Philadelphia: University of Pennsylvania, 1985.

_____. *Ennobling Love: In Search of a Lost Sensibility.* Philadelphia: University of Pennsylvania, 1999.

Janowitz, Morris. *The Professional Soldier.* New York: Free Press, 1971.

– K –

Kass, Leon. "The End of Courtship." *The Public Interest* (January 1997).

Keen, Maurice. *Chivalry*. New Haven: Yale University, 1984.

———. *The Penguin History of Medieval Europe*. New York: Penguin, 1991.

Kelly, Amy. *Eleanor of Aquitaine and the Four Kings*. Cambridge: Harvard University, 1950.

Kelso, Ruth. *The Doctrine of the English Gentleman in the Sixteenth Century* Urbana: University of Illinois, 1926.

Kersten, Katherine. "A Conservative Feminist Manifesto." *Policy Review,* no. 56 (Spring 1991).

King, Stephen. *The Girl Who Loved Tom Gordon*. New York: Scribner, 1999.

Kirk, Russell. *America's British Culture*. New Brunswick: Transaction, 1994.

———. *The Conservative Mind*. Washington, DC: Regnery, 1978.

———. *The Intemperate Professor and Other Cultural Splenetics*. Baton Rouge: Louisiana University, 1965.

———. *The Roots of American Order*. Washington, DC: Regnery, 1991.

Kreeft, Peter. *Back to Virtue*. San Francisco: Ignatius, 1992.

———, ed. A *Summa of the Summa*. San Francisco: Ignatius, 1990.

– L –

Lacroix, Paul. *Military and Religious Life in the Middle Ages and the Renaissance* New York: Frederick Ungar, 1964.

Lacy, Norris J., Geoffrey Ashe, and Debra N. Mancoff. *The Arthurian Handbook*. New York: Garland, 1997.

Lanier, Sidney. *The Boy's Froissart*. New York: Scribner's, 1919.

Laski, Harold. *The Danger of Being a Gentleman and Other Essays*. New York: Viking, 1940.

Laslett, Peter. *The World We Have Lost: England Before the Industrial Age*. New York: Scribner, 1984.

Lawlor, John, ed. *Patterns of Love and Courtesy: Essays in Honor of C. S. Lewis*. Evanston: Northwestern University, 1966.

Leggett, Trevor. *Ideal Gentlemanship*. Tokyo: New Currents, 1990.

Lehman, David. *Signs of the Times: Deconstruction and the Fall of Paul de Man*. New York: Poseidon, 1991.

Lerner, Ralph, and Mushin Mahdi, eds. *Medieval Political Philosophy*. Ithaca: Cornell University, 1963.

Letwin, Shirley Robin. *The Gentleman in Trollope: Individuality and Moral Conduct*. Cambridge: Harvard University, 1982.

Levi, Peter. *The Frontiers of Paradise: A Study of Monks and Monasteries*. New York: Weidenfeld & Nicolson, 1987.

Lewis, C. S. *The Allegory of Love: A Study in Medieval Tradition*. London: Oxford University, 1938.

Loomis, Roger Sherman. *The Development of Arthurian Romance*. London: Hutchinson, 1963.

Lorris, Guillaume de, and Jean de Meun. *The Romance of the Rose*. Translated by Frances Horgan. New York: Oxford, 1994.

Loyn, H. R., ed. *The Middle Ages: A Concise Encyclopedia*. New York: Thames & Hudson, 1989.

– M –

MacDonald, Heather. "Why the Boy Scouts Work." *City Journal* (Winter 2000).

MacKendrick, Paul. *The Philosophical Books of Cicero*. New York: St. Martin's, 1989.

Manchester, William. *A World Lit Only by Fire: The Medieval Mind and the Renaissance*. Boston: Little, Brown, 1992.

Mansfield, Harvey C. "Is Manliness a Virtue?" Bradley Lecture Series. American Enterprise Institute (October 14, 1997).

Mason, Philip. *The English Gentleman: The Rise and Fall of an Ideal*. New York: Morrow, 1982.

Matthews, John. *The Grail: Quest for the Eternal*. New York: Thames and Hudson, 1981.

McDonald, Forrest. *Novus Ordo Seclorum: The Intellectual Origins of the Constitution*. Lawrence: University Press of Kansas, 1985.

Meade, Marion. *Eleanor of Aquitaine*. New York: Hawthorn, 1977.

Merton, Thomas. *A Thomas Merton Reader*. Edited by Thomas P. McDonnell. New York: Image, 1974.

Minogue, Kenneth. *Alien Powers: The Pure Theory of Ideology*. New York: St. Martin's, 1985.

Moncrieff, A. R. Hope. *Romance & Legend of Chivalry*. London: Senate, 1994.

Morris, Colin. *The Discovery of the Individual, 1050–1200*. Toronto: University of Toronto, 1987.

Motto, Anna Lydia. *Seneca*. New York: Twayne, 1973.

Murray, Gilbert. *Stoic, Christian and Humanist*. Boston: Beacon, 1940.

Musashi, Miyamoto. *The Book of Five Rings*. New York: Barnes & Noble, 1993.

– N –

Newman, Francis X., ed. *The Meaning of Courtly Love*. Albany: State University of New York, 1968.

Newsome, David. *The Victorian World Picture*. New Brunswick: Rutgers University, 1997.

Nicolson, Harold. *Good Behaviour*. New York: Doubleday, 1956.

– O –

Osterweis, Rollin. *Romanticism and Nationalism in the Old South*. New Haven: Yale, 1949.

– P –

Painter, Sidney. *French Chivalry*. Ithaca: Cornell University, 1940.

Parkes, Henry Bamford. *The Divine Order: Western Culture in the Middle Ages and the Renaissance*. New York: Knopf, 1969.

Peacham, Henry. *The Compleat Gentleman and Other Works*. Ithaca: Cornell University, 1962.

Perry, George, and Nicholas Mason, eds. *The Victorians: A World Built to Last*. New York: Viking, 1974.

Persons, Stow. *The Decline of American Gentility*. New York: Columbia University, 1973.

Pieper, Josef. *The Four Cardinal Virtues: Prudence, Justice, Fortitude, Temperance*. New York; Harcourt, Brace & World, 1965.

Poitier, Sidney. *The Measure of A Man*. San Francisco: Harper, 2000.

Prestage, Edgar, ed. *Chivalry*. New York: Knopf, 1928.

– R –

Read, Piers Paul. *The Templars*. New York: Da Capo, 2001.

Ringer, William Andrew, Jr. "Sidney, Sir Philip." (www.britannica.com).

Rist, John M., ed. *Stoics*. Berkeley: University of California, 1978.

Robinson, Edwin Arlington. *Collected Poems*. New York: Macmillan, 1942.

Roeder, Ralph. *Man of the Renaissance*. New York: Viking, 1933.

Ross, James Bruce, and Mary Martin McLaughlin, eds. *The Portable Medieval Reader*. New York: Penguin, 1949.

Rougemont, Denis de. *Love Declared: Essays on the Myths of Love*. New York: Pantheon, 1963.

_____. *Love in the Western World*. New York: Pantheon, 1940.

Rudorff, Raymond. *Knights and the Age of Chivalry*. New York: Viking, 1974.

– S –

Seneca, Lucius Annaeus. *Letters from a Stoic*. Edited by Robin Campbell. New York: Penguin, 1969.

Senior, Michael, ed. *Sir Thomas Malory's Tales of King Arthur*. New York: Schocken, 1981.

Sennett, Richard. *The Fall of Public Man*. New York: Knopf, 1977.

Seward, Desmond. *The Monks of War: The Military Religious Orders*. London: Methuen, 1972.

Shakespeare, William. *The Complete Works*. Edited by Stanley Wells and Gary Taylor. Clarendon: Oxford, 1986.

Strachey, Lytton. *Eminent Victorians*. New York: Harcourt, Brace, 1969.

– T –

Tierney, Brian, and Sidney Painter. *Western Europe in the Middle Ages, 300–1457*. New York: Knopf, 1970/1983.

Tocqueville, Alexis de. *Democracy in America*. Translated and edited by Harvey Mansfield. Chicago: University of Chicago, 2000.

Toner, James H. *True Faith and Allegiance: The Burden of Military Ethics*. Lexington: University of Kentucky, 1995.

– W –

Weber, Eugen. "The Ups and Downs of Honor." *The American Scholar* (Winter 1999).

Weir, Alison. *Eleanor of Aquitaine: A Life*. New York: Ballantine, 1999.

Weston, Jessie L. *From Ritual to Romance*. Princeton: Princeton University, 1993.

Wiley, William Leon. *Gentleman of Renaissance France*. Cambridge: Harvard University, 1954.

Wilson, James Q. *The Moral Sense*. New York: Free Press, 1993.

_____. *On Character*. Washington, DC: American Enterprise Institute, 1991.

Wood, Charles. *The Age of Chivalry: Manners and Morals, 1000–1450*. New York: Universe, 1970.

Wright, Sylvia. *The Age of Chivalry: English Society, 1200–1400*. New York: Warwick, 1988.

Wyatt-Brown, Bertram. *Southern Honor: Ethics and Behavior in the Old South*. New York: Oxford University, 1982.

– Y –

Yao, Xinzhong. *An Introduction to Confucianism*. New York: Cambridge, 2000.

INDEX